西安交通大学本科"十三五"规划教材

欧洲文化渊源教程（第2版）

Sources of European Culture (Second Edition)

主编 刘 浩 黄 奕
编审 陈向京
编者 蔡 宁 邱 鹄 卢燕华

西安交通大学出版社

图书在版编目（CIP）数据

欧洲文化渊源教程：英文／刘浩，黄奕主编．—2版．—西安：西安交通大学出版社，2020.3(2025.2重印)
ISBN 978-7-5693-1359-8

Ⅰ.①欧… Ⅱ.①刘…②黄… Ⅲ.①文化史—欧洲—汉、英 Ⅳ.①K500.3

中国版本图书馆CIP数据核字（2019）第220539号

书　　名	欧洲文化渊源教程（第2版）
主　　编	刘　浩　黄　奕
责任编辑	牛瑞鑫　李　蕊
出版发行	西安交通大学出版社 （西安市兴庆南路1号　邮政编码710048）
网　　址	http://www.xjtupress.com
电　　话	（029）82668357　82667874（市场营销中心） （029）82668315（总编办）
传　　真	（029）82668280
印　　刷	西安五星印刷有限公司
开　　本	787mm×1092mm　1/16　印张　15.25　字数　380千字
版次印次	2020年3月第2版　2025年2月第3次印刷
书　　号	ISBN 978-7-5693-1359-8
定　　价	48.00元

如发现印装质量问题，请与本社市场营销中心联系。

订购热线：（029）82665248　（029）82665249
投稿热线：（029）82665371

版权所有　侵权必究

Foreword to the Second Edition
再版说明

　　文化是语言赖以存在的基础，它不但对语言的形成有着巨大的影响，也对语言的恰当使用起着规范作用。因此，要学好、用好一门外语，了解这门外语的文化背景便成为不可或缺的一部分。

　　《欧洲文化渊源教程（第2版）》编写组，结合多年的教学实践经验，在本教程前一版的基础上，对全书的主体内容进行了修订。经过本次修订，本教程在增长学生的文化知识、提升学生的语言技能、培养学生的文化思辨能力等方面，实现了有机融合。

　　关于本次修订的具体工作，特作以下说明：

　　1. 结合每单元的主题，我们在前一版的Further Development版块和Further Reading版块之间，增加了Cultural Exploration版块，并在其中设计了有关中西文化对比的讨论话题。新增的版块能使学生在了解西方文化根源的同时，与中国文化产生对比，从而更深入地理解和热爱中国文化，更深入地理解和拥护中国价值观，并且以自信开放的心态观察和学习西方文化，有利于培养学生的文化思辨能力。

　　2. 根据各单元的不同主题，我们替换了部分内容，使各单元的主题更为突出。

　　3. 我们改进了部分练习的形式，同时将Speaking版块和Writing版块的练习设计得更加凝练，使教学目标更突出，教学操作更方便。

　　4. 对前一版中出现的个别语言表达不妥和单词拼写失误等问题，我们在本次修订时统一进行了修改。

　　本次修订得到了"西安交通大学'十三五'规划教材第二批建设项目"以及"大学英语拓展课程三维目标一体化构建与实践研究"（2018年西安交通大学本科教学改革研究基础课专项）的支持，特此致谢。

本书编写组
2020年元月

Foreword 前言

编写依据

本教材是西安交通大学本科"十二五"规划教材,同时也得到了校重点教改项目"CBI理念下文化类大学英语拓展课程研究性学习任务的设计与实践研究"的支持。本教材是以《大学英语课程教学要求》中的一般要求和较高要求为目标、以内容依托、以输出驱动的教学理念为依据编写而成的大学英语拓展课教材。本教材以欧洲文明两大基石——希腊神话故事与圣经故事——为载体、以兴趣培养为导向,在了解欧洲文明渊源的同时,培养和提高学生的语言技能和文化素养。

希腊神话与圣经对欧洲乃至整个西方的宗教、哲学、风俗习惯、自然科学、文学艺术都产生了全面而深刻的影响。接触西方文化,必然会遇到源自希腊神话的典故;阅读西方文学经典,必然会读到源自圣经故事的内容。我们虽不必"言必称希腊",但若对希腊神话和圣经故事有所了解,则有助于我们克服东西方文化差异所造成的跨文化交际障碍。本教材选取了希腊神话和圣经中的一些经典故事,在每个单元中,这些故事既可分开阅读学习,也可与该单元其他故事一起构成本单元的文化主题。

作为大学英语教育的一个重要环节,拓展课在满足学生兴趣爱好、拓展学生文化视野的同时,还应担负培养学生语言技能的重任。鉴于此,本教材不仅能为学生传递文化知识、提升语言技能,还能使学生在掌握文化知识和语言技能的前提下,提高自己对文化现象进行思考和表达自己观点的能力。

教材特色

1. 本教材面向非英语专业本科生英语学习和大学英语教学的需要,以英语为主编写,语言难度适中。

2. 本教材内容选材融合了欧洲文明的两大基石,以其中的精彩故事为引导,以提高学生的语言能力和思辨能力为培养目标,辅以文化讨论和艺术欣赏,内容生动全面。

3. 相比其他文化类大学英语课程教材,本教材突出了对学生语言技能(即听、说、读、写)的训练与培养,使语言技能学习与内容学习相辅相成。

4. 本教材语言输入的形式多样,既有阅读又有视听,能够切实提高学生用英语读和听的能力。同时，各单元也围绕学习目标，设计了说和写的输出训练。

5. 本教材以大学英语六级词汇为选词范围，设计了适量的核心词汇训练。

6. 本教材附录中列出了重要人名和地名的读音及解释，便于教师课堂讲授，以及学生在学习时检索。

教材构成

本教材共七个单元，每个单元有一个文化主题。第一至第四单元的主题以希腊神话为主，第五至第七单元的主题以圣经故事为主。每个单元由以下部分组成：

1. Pre-information 通过听力练习的形式，介绍本单元基本的背景知识和涉及的文化典故；

2. Stories 以视听和阅读的形式呈现本单元的主要故事；

3. Vocabulary Focus 选取六级词汇及与本单元内容密切相关的词汇设计练习，学生可通过练习进一步掌握这些词汇；

4. Vocabulary Development 学生在掌握核心词汇的基础上，拓展词汇的学习方式和内容；

5. Speaking 提供语言知识和故事素材，重点培养学生复述故事、对比文化以及表达自我观点的能力；

6. Writing 重点培养学生对文化内容作小结的能力，并加深学生用书面形式来表达其对文化现象的理解；

7. Further Development 引导学生对文化内容进行深入思考；

8. Further Reading 为学生补充2篇或3篇与本单元主题相关的其他故事，加大语言输入量，进一步丰富本单元的文化主题。

本教材的视频部分仅供教学使用，不可用于其他商业用途。教材的视听材料请登录http://202.117.216.249:8002（用户名：guest，密码：guest）进入"欧洲文化渊源"课程网站的"课本材料"页面下载。教材的听力材料还可登录http://www.xjtupress.com，进入"读者服务"下载。

本教材是在西安交通大学《欧洲文化渊源》讲义（胶印版）的基础上进行大幅修改之后完成的。本教材的出版得到了西安交通大学外国语学院及大学英语教学中心历届领导的大力支持，同时也凝聚了《欧洲文化渊源》课程组历届任课教师的心血。

此外，本教材在编写的过程中，我们参考了许多国内外的图书资料和网站文章，在此向原作者一并表示衷心感谢！

编写本书乃全新的尝试与追求，虽经反复讨论和精心编写，但难免挂一漏万，甚至疏虞失慎。对本教材中可能出现的疏漏之处，还望使用者不吝赐教。

编者
2014年元月

Contents
目录

UNIT 1 Creation in Greek Myth	/1
Pre-infortmation	/2
Stories	/3
Vocabulary Focus	/11
Vocabulary Development	/13
Speaking	/15
Writing	/16
Further Developing	/21
Cultural Exploration	/23
Further Reading	/24

UNIT 2 Olympian Gods	/27
Pre-infortmation	/28
Stories	/30
Vocabulary Focus	/42
Vocabulary Development	/44
Speaking	/46
Writing	/48
Further Developing	/50
Cultural Exploration	/52
Further Reading	/53

UNIT 3 Stories in Homers' Epic	/55
Pre-infortmation	/56
Stories	/58
Vocabulary Focus	/66
Vocabulary Development	/68
Speaking	/70
Writing	/73
Further Developing	/79
Cultural Exploration	/81
Further Reading	/82

UNIT 4 Greek Heroes and Other Legends	/85
Pre-infortmation	/86
Stories	/88
Vocabulary Focus	/100
Vocabulary Development	/102
Speaking	/104
Writing	/107
Fruther Developing	/109
Cultural Exploration	/112
Further Reading	/114

UNIT 5 Creation and Pioneers in the Bible	/117
Pre-infortmation	/118
Stories	/119
Vocabulary Focus	/130
Vocabulary Development	/132
Speaking	/134
Writing	/135
Further Developing	/137
Cultural Exploration	/139
Further Reading	/140

UNIT 6 Exodus and Jewish Kingdoms	/143
Pre-infortmation	/144
Stories	/145
Vocabulary Focus	/155
Vocabulary Development	/158
Speaking	/159
Writing	/160
Further Developing	/162
Cultural Exploration	/164
Further Reading	/165

UNIT 7 Life Stories of Jesus	/169
Pre-infortmation	/170
Stories	/171
Vocabulary Focus	/183
Vocabulary Development	/185
Speaking	/187
Writing	/191
Further Developing	/195
Cultural Exploration	/197
Further Reading	/198

Appendix Ⅰ Proper Terms	/202

Appendix Ⅱ Keys to the Exercises	/214

Appendix Ⅲ Map of the Book	/232

Bibliography	/236

UNIT 1

Creation in Greek Myths

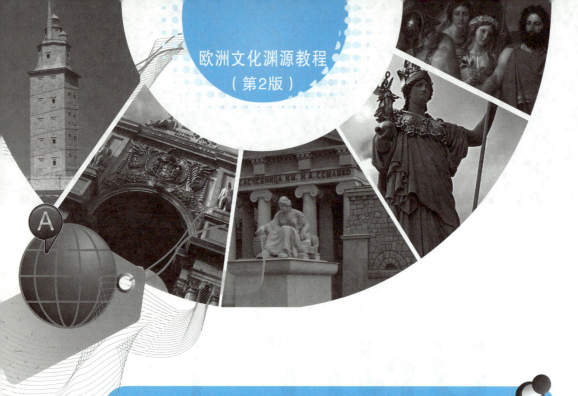

欧洲文化渊源教程
（第2版）

In this unit, you are going to
- identify, the chief primeval gods;
- explain the kinship of the chief gods;
- retell the stories in Creation myths;
- write a narrative summary;
- expand vocabulary through word formation of root.

 Pre-information

I. Listen to the passage on *Creation Myth* and fill in the blanks with the words you hear.

Like all mythologies of the past, the Greek Mythology started with the Creation myth, the story that explains the _____1_____ of life and of all things. This story is in essence an attempt to _____2_____ life's mysteries, to impose _____3_____ in the universe and explain where we came from to define the place of individuals, races and all people in the universe.

The most detailed _____4_____ of early classical Creation myths comes to us from *Theogony*, a poem _____5_____ by Hesiod, a Greek poet _____6_____.

UNIT 1

It is worthwhile to note that in Hesiod's narration about the Creation myth, from Uranus to Cronus, and then from Cronus to Zeus, the power was _____7_____ by the successor, who was challenging his predecessor's reign through _____8_____.

II. Listen to the sentences and fill in the blanks with the words you hear. Then work out the meaning of each sentence with a partner.

1. The e-tail titan prospered by continuing to offer low prices and superb _____ in hard times.

2. Plato describes a series of worldwide floods culminating in the deluge of Deucalion, dated by Greek historians to _____, about 10,000 B.C.

3. Prometheus himself knew that some day he should be _____, and his knowledge made him strong to endure.

4. When my first child was born in 1994, e-mail seemed to me some kind of Promethean gift perfectly designed to help me _____ to work at home.

5. Scientific inventions can _____; on the other hand, they sometimes might open Pandora's Box.

6. Many publishing executives like to argue that the _____ could usher in a golden age of reading, in which many more people will be exposed to digital texts.

Stories

Story One

I. Match the major characters in the story with the proper information after your first reading.

1. Chaos   a. the goddess of the Earth
2. Tartarus   b. the deepest region in the Underworld

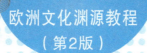

 3. Uranus   c. the beginning of the universe
 4. Gaea   d. the god of the heavens
 5. Cronus   e. the youngest Titan who dethroned his father

II. Fill in the blanks with the missing information after your second reading.

1. It was _____ that made it possible to produce offspring.

2. Gaea alone gave birth to _____, who became her husband later.

3. Uranus was a bad father and he imprisoned his children, _____ and Hecatoncheires, in their mother's womb.

4. The _____ were the offspring of Gaea and Uranus. They were spared from imprisonment, and became the first gods and goddesses.

Creation of the Universe

  In the beginning there was only Chaos, the *void* or a formless confusion. Then out of Chaos appeared Nyx (Night) and Erebus (Darkness). All else was empty, silent, endless and dark. Then also from Chaos, Eros (Love), Gaea (Earth) and Tartarus (the deepest region in the Underworld) came into being. It was Eros that made it possible to produce offspring.

  Then Erebus slept with his sister Nyx, who gave birth to Ether (heavenly light) and Day (earthly light). Then Nyx alone produced Doom, Fate, Death, Sleep, Nemesis and others.

  Meanwhile Gaea alone gave birth to Uranus, the heavens. Uranus grew as huge as Gaea and enveloped her. Uranus became the ruler of the universe after marrying his mother Gaea. Together they produced the three Cyclopes, the three Hecatoncheires, and twelve Titans. The Cyclopes were giants, with a single huge eye in their foreheads. The Hecatoncheires were also monstrous in size and strength, each having one hundred hands and fifty heads.

  However, Uranus was a bad father and husband. He hated his ugly children and imprisoned the six *gigantic* creatures by pushing them into the hidden places of the earth, Gaea's womb.

  The Titans were also his offspring, but they were smaller in size and fairer in looks. Unlike their ugly brothers they weren't imprisoned, and became the first gods and goddesses.

Imprisoning the six *gigantic* creatures within her body caused Gaea a great deal of pain. She was *furious* at the treatment of her earlier sons, and plotted against Uranus. She made a stone *sickle* and tried to get her children to attack Uranus. All were too afraid except the youngest Titan, Cronus.

Gaea and Cronus set up an *ambush* of Uranus as he lay with Gaea at night. Cronus grabbed his father and castrated him with the stone *sickle*, throwing the severed genitals into the sea. The fate of Uranus was not clear. But as he departed, he *prophesied* that Cronus would in turn be overthrown by his own son. (331 words)

I. Answer the following questions briefly after your first reading.

1. Who were the parents of Zeus?
2. How did Zeus free his siblings?

II. Decide whether the following statements are TRUE or FALSE after your second reading.

_____ 1. Gaea was angry with Cronus because Cronus swallowed his children when they were born.

_____ 2. Rhea gave a stone to Cronus who swallowed it and assumed that he swallowed his sixth child.

_____ 3. Zeus spent his early life on Crete before he came back to his parents.

_____ 4. Styx, Prometheus and Epimetheus were among Zeus' allies in the battle against the Titans.

_____ 5. Atlas, who had fought against Zeus, was punished with his fellow Titans in Tartarus.

Rule of the Titans and Rise of the Olympians

Cronus succeeded his father as the ruler of the universe, and became the leader of the Titans. He shared the world with his brothers and sisters, and married his sister Rhea. Under his rule the Titans had many offspring. He ruled for many ages.

The whole purpose that Gaea instructed Cronus and the Titans to *revolt* against Uranus' rule was to release her other sons from Tartarus. Cronus, however, did not release his brothers, the Hecatoncheires and the Cyclopes, from Tartarus. This made Gaea very angry with her son. Gaea, as Uranus had done, *prophesied* that Cronus would in turn be overthrown by his own son.

To avoid this fate, Cronus swallowed each of his children as they were born. Rhea was angry at the treatment of her children and plotted against Cronus. When it came time to give birth to her sixth child, Rhea hid herself, and then she left the child to be raised by nymphs. To *conceal* her act, she wrapped a stone in swaddling cloth and passed it off as the baby to Cronus, who swallowed it.

This child was Zeus, and he grew into a handsome youth on Crete. Zeus consulted Metis, the Titan goddess of *prudence*, good counsel, wisdom and craftiness, on how to defeat Cronus. She prepared a *potion* for Cronus, designed to make him *vomit* up the other children.

Rhea convinced Cronus to accept his son, and Zeus was allowed to return to Mount Olympus as Cronus' cupbearer. This gave Zeus the opportunity to *slip* Cronus the specially prepared drink. This worked as planned and the other five children were *vomited* up. Being gods they were unharmed. They were thankful to Zeus and made him their leader.

War broke out between the Titans against the younger gods known as the Olympians, led by Zeus. Cronus and other Titans fought to retain their power. Atlas became their leader in battle and it seemed that for some time they would win and put the young gods down.

Zeus and his brothers required aids, since they were outnumbered. Of all the sons of Uranus and Gaea, Oceanus had chosen to remain neutral. Styx, the eldest daughter of Oceanus and Tethys, was the first to change side.

UNIT 1

Prometheus and Epimetheus, the sons of Titan Iapetus, joined Zeus as well because Prometheus knew that Zeus and his brothers would eventually win.

Zeus also went down to Tartarus and freed the Cyclopes and the Hecatoncheires. He returned to battle with his new allies. The Cyclopes provided Zeus with lightning bolts for weapons. The Hecatoncheires he set in *ambush* were armed with boulders. With the time right, Zeus retreated, drawing the Titans into the Hecatoncheires' *ambush*. The Hecatoncheires rained down hundreds of boulders with such a fury that the Titans thought the mountains were falling on them. They broke and ran, giving Zeus victory.

Zeus *exiled* the Titans who had fought against him into Tartarus — except for Atlas, who was singled out for the special punishment of holding the world on his shoulders.

Zeus became the supreme ruler of the universe. The younger gods were called Olympians because they made their dwellings on Mount Olympus or in the sky above it. (532 words)

 **Story Three**

Watch the video clip on *Cronus* and fill in the blanks with the words you hear.

1. In the myth, Zeus doesn't start out as the king of the gods. He rises from obscurity to challenge his father for control of the universe, and that won't be easy. His father is Cronus. He is King of the Titans, _____.

2. The Titans are an older order of Greek gods. They're pretty rough around the edges. They're not too bright. They're also _____.

3. As leader of the Titans, Cronus is expected to produce offspring. So he mates with _____, his sister and fellow Titan Rhea.

4. Incest shows up quite a bit in mythology. Among the gods, there's really nobody else at the beginning for them to have sex with, so they _____.

5. There's an old-time aristocratic idea that says that no one else is _____ except only our family, and the Greek gods definitely seem to ascribe to this kind of a principle.

Story Four

I. Answer the following questions briefly after your first reading.

1. Who were involved in the task of creating man? What did they do in the task?

2. Why was Zeus angry at Prometheus and decided to punish him?

II. Fill in the blanks with the missing information after your second reading.

1. Since Epimetheus had given all the good qualities out and there were none left for man, Prometheus decided to make man superior by _____.

2. Prometheus was bound to a rock on _____, where he was tormented day and night by _____ tearing at his liver.

3. Prometheus was freed at last for _____ agreed to die for him, and _____ killed the eagle and unbound him.

Creation of Man and Prometheus' Gift

Prometheus (meaning Forethought) and Epimetheus (meaning Afterthought) were spared imprisonment in Tartarus because they had not fought with their fellow Titans against the Olympians. They were given the task of creating man. Prometheus shaped man out of mud, and Athena breathed life into his clay figure.

Prometheus had assigned Epimetheus the task of giving the creatures of the earth various qualities, such as *swiftness*, cunning, strength, fur, wings. Unfortunately, by the time he got to man Epimetheus had given all the good qualities out and there were none left for man. So Prometheus decided to make man superior. He made man stand upright as the gods did and gave them fire.

Prometheus was an extremely intelligent and wise god, who was gifted with foresight. He failed to persuade his father Iapetus and his elder brother Atlas not to resist against Zeus. Both Iapetus and Atlas were punished for opposing the Olympians.

Prometheus was the guardian of mankind, often trying to aid them. Prometheus loved man more than the Olympians, who had banished most of his family to Tartarus. So when Zeus *decreed* that man must present a portion of each animal they sacrificed to the gods, Prometheus decided to trick Zeus, making sure that man received the best part. He created two piles, one with the bones wrapped in juicy fat, the other with the choicest meat hidden in the hide. He then asked Zeus to pick one pile, and that would be his future offering. Zeus picked the bones. Since he had given his word, Zeus had to accept that as his share for future sacrifices.

In his anger over the trick, Zeus took fire away from man. Seeing man freezing and unable to cook without fire, Prometheus took pity on man and *defied* Zeus. He went up to the heaven, lit a torch from the sun, and brought this heavenly gift of fire back to man.

Zeus was enraged that man again had fire. He decided to punish Prometheus for *defying* him.

Zeus was angry at Prometheus for three things: tricking him on sacrifices, stealing fire for man, and refusing to tell Zeus which of Zeus' children would dethrone him. Zeus had his servants, Force and Violence, seized Prometheus, took him to the Caucasus Mountains, and chained him to a rock with unbreakable chains. Here Prometheus was tormented day and night by a giant eagle tearing at his liver.

Zeus gave Prometheus two ways out of this torment. He could tell Zeus who the mother of the child that would dethrone him was. Or he could meet two conditions: First, an immortal must volunteer to die for him. Second, a mortal must kill the eagle and unchain him. Eventually, Chiron, the Centaur, agreed to die for Prometheus, and Heracles killed the eagle and unbound him many years later. (470 words)

Story Five

▶ Listen to the story of *Five Ages of Man* and fill in the blanks with the words you hear.

According to another story, man existed on earth while the Titan Cronus ruled. The ***successive*** ages of mankind were the Golden Age, the Silver Age, the Bronze Age, the Heroic Age and the Iron Age.

The Golden Age was an age when Cronus was in power. It was an age of perfection, _____1_____, in which truth and justice ***prevailed***, not through force or power, but through man's natural goodness. _____2_____, because the earth freely gave its wealth and riches without labor. Weapons did not exist, because peace was in the hearts of men. It was always spring—the only season—and men were always young. Death, when it came, was a pleasant sleep, and men were transformed into good spirits to guard and guide men on earth.

Despite its name, the Silver Age was an age of _____3_____. Zeus introduced the seasons of the year, which meant the _____4_____ of summer heat and winter cold. Houses, not necessary in the Golden Age, _____5_____, and labor became necessary because nature no longer gave its treasures for the asking. In the Silver Age men were strong and powerful, but they refused to worship the gods. When they died, they lived under the earth as spirits but without ***immortality***.

In the Bronze Age all things were made of bronze. It was a period of _____6_____, in which strong men—stronger than those in the Silver Age—destroyed each other. In this era, when men died, they stayed dead.

The Heroic Age was an age of demi-gods and heroes. Superior to both the Silver and the Bronze Ages, it was the period of _____7_____, associated with great wars like the Trojan War.

The Iron Age was the last and the worst age. It was not merely a period of struggle and hard labor, but of toil and misery. Mean and selfish purposes ***dominated*** men. Crime, deceit, _____8_____ were common. During this age might makes right. The world was red with blood. (350 words)

UNIT 1

 Vocabulary Focus

▶ I. Match the words from *Stories* part with their corresponding definitions.

1. void
2. gigantic
3. ambush
4. sickle
5. revolt
6. potion
7. slip
8. exile
9. conceal
10. vomit
11. decree
12. prevail

a. a sudden attack on someone by people who have been hiding and waiting for them
b. expel from home or country by authority
c. prevent from being seen or discovered
d. an empty area or space
e. throw food or drink up from one's stomach through the mouth
f. an edge tool for cutting grass or crops
g. command or decide with authority
h. be widespread; appear as the more important or frequent feature
i. exceedingly large or extensive
j. rebel against constituted authority
k. insert quickly or quietly; pass on stealthily
l. a medicinal or magical or poisonous drink

▶ II. Use the words from *Exercise I* to complete the sentences.

1. Never expecting a(n) _____ on the road, he had a narrow escape.

2. The little mermaid lifted the bottle and drank the magic _____ which would turn her into a human for three days.

3. Some experts say that mostly motivations for extramarital affairs differ by gender, with men searching for more sex or attention, and women looking to fill an emotional _____.

4. Some animals have the extraordinary ability to _____ themselves from predators by adjusting their skin to take on the colors,

11

shapes and patterns of their local environment.

5. After a short rest, he took the _____ and went back to reap wheat.

6. Making resolution on New Year's Day is a custom that still _____.

7. The region you live in makes a(n) _____ difference in how you will live.

8. Teenagers often _____ against parental disciplines.

9. The UN Security Council has _____ that the general election must be held by May.

10. She looked round before pulling out a small package and _____ it to the man sitting next to her.

11. The taste of blood in her throat made her want to _____.

12. The authority's attempting to imprison, _____ or execute an important character runs the risk of a civil war.

III. Choose the italicized words from *Stories* part to complete the table.

Verb	Noun	Adjective	Noun (Person)	Antonym
	fury	1_____		
2_____	prophecy		prophet	
	3_____	prudent		imprudent
	4_____	swift		
5_____	defiance	defiant		
succeed	succession	6_____	successor	
	7_____	immortal	immortal	mortal
8_____	domination	dominant	dominator	

IV. Use the words in the table from *Exercise III* to complete the sentences.

1. We will not tolerate any violence on the streets of Liverpool and have taken _____ and robust action in response.

2. He developed an overwhelming desire to exert power — to _____, control and possess another person.

3. Fortune-tellers had to be inventive because the art of _____ was a risky business.

4. Among the great books of mankind are the _____ writings by the Greek philosopher Plato.

5. There was a dispute about the rightful _____ to the throne.

6. He flew into a _____ and said that the whole thing was disgusting.

7. Despite opposition, Norway continues to _____ the whaling ban: 2010's kill quota is the highest in 25 years.

8. It might be more _____ to get a second opinion before going ahead.

Vocabulary Development
Word Roots

A word **root** is the most basic form of a word that is able to convey a particular meaning. Many words are made up of a root (or base word) and a prefix. Some words also have a suffix. The basic part of any word is the root; you can add to it a prefix at the beginning and/or a suffix at the end to change the meaning. For example, with the word "prehistoric", the prefix is "pre-" meaning "before", the base word is "history" meaning "recorded events and knowledge", and the suffix is "-ic" meaning "relating to the science of". By learning the common roots and prefixes (and a few suffixes) you will be able to discern the meaning of many new words almost immediately.

Study the following roots and the words made from them:

Root	Meaning	Example
cycl	circle, ring	bicycle — a vehicle with two wheels cycle — a sequence that is repeated cyclone — a storm with circling winds
geo	earth, soil, global	geography — study of the earth's surface geology — study of the structure of the earth geometry — study of the properties and relationships of lines, angles, curves, and shapes
chron(o)	time	chronic — lasting for a long time chronological — arranging events in time order synchronize — happening at the same time
mus	relating to art or entertainment	music — the sounds produced by singers or musical instruments museum — a building for collecting and displaying objects having scientific or historical or artistic value amuse — to make someone laugh or smile
hect(o)	hundred	hectare — a unit for measuring area, equal to 10,000 square meters hectometer — 100 meters
pan	all, any, everyone	panacea — a cure for all diseases or problems panorama — an all-around view pantheism — the worship of all gods pandemic — affecting all, or a disease that affects people over a very large area or the whole world

Now complete the sentences with a suitable word from above.

1. The seasons of the year — spring, summer, autumn, and winter — make a _____.

2. We know, from a recent World Bank estimate, that the global economic costs of the next influenza _____ could reach $3 trillion.

3. He ended the dance with an improvised shimmy shake which wasn't planned but _____ the crowd and judges.

4. They found that average fertilizer use — around 600 kilograms per _____ — can be cut by 30 to 60 percent, with farmers retaining the same production.

5. The children were asked to arrange the stories in _____ order.

6. The triangle is an important structural shape in _____ and construction.

7. We have ample reason to conclude that _____ anger is bad for our health.

8. Climb up the hill, and you can see the _____ of the town.

Speaking
Retelling a Story (1)

Basically, retelling is an oral activity in which readers restate the main ideas or events of the text. Retelling provides an opportunity for readers to process what they have read by organizing and explaining it to others in their own words.

Retelling supports good reading because students must engage in repeated readings of the text, which supports fluency. The student's retelling confirms his/her reading of the text and reveals the extent of his/her comprehension. Research also indicates that retelling increases both the quantity and quality of what is comprehended.

Tips for retelling:

1. Begin by specifically stating in a few words what you are retelling;

2. Tell when and where the event takes place, and name the person(s) involved;

3. Tell the main points of the event and some important details;

4. Make sense to listeners by

   a. following the original structure;

   b. using sequence or transitional words, like *first*, *then* and *at the same time*.

Now read the following story and retell it.

Pandora's Box

After humans received the stolen gift of fire from Prometheus, Zeus was angry and decided to inflict a terrible punishment on man to compensate for the benefits they had been given.

Zeus had Hephaestus create a mortal of stunning beauty. The gods gave the mortal many gifts: Aphrodite gave her desire and heartbreak, and all the aching sorrow of love a woman could bring to man. Athena gave her wisdom. Apollo taught her how to play various musical instruments, and Muses taught her how to sing. Hermes gave the mortal a deceptive heart and a lying tongue. Hera gave her curiosity. This creation, the first woman, was named Pandora which means "all-gifted". A final gift presented to her by Zeus was a box which Pandora was forbidden to open. Then Zeus sent Pandora down to Epimetheus who was staying amongst the men.

Prometheus had foreseen that Zeus would retaliate and warned his brother Epimetheus not to accept gifts from Zeus, but Pandora's beauty was so great that Epimetheus allowed her to stay and married her.

For a while they were very happy, but Pandora's curiosity about the contents of the box grew day by day. Knowing that she wasn't allowed to open it tormented her. Eventually, Pandora's curiosity became so great that she could stand it no longer. She opened the box and out flew all of evils, sorrows, plagues, and misfortunes. In horror, Pandora quickly closed the lid, but it was too late. However, the bottom of the box held one good thing—hope. This was the only thing that provided comfort for mankind in their suffering. (268 words)

Writing Narrative Summary

A summary is a shortened version of an original text, stating the main ideas and important details of the text with the same text structure and order of the original. Studies have shown that summarizing can enhance readers' understanding of the text.

The general model of a narrative text, or a story, is that a story consists of a series of related events, called the plot, through which characters move to solve a central problem or conflict. The story takes place in a specific time and place, called the setting, and conveys an underlying message or comment on life, the theme.

Tips for Writing a Narrative Summary
1. Read and understand
Read the story and make sure you know it well. Use a dictionary or

context clues to figure out the meaning of any important words that you don't know.

2. Reread and take notes

Rereading should be active reading. Underline topic sentences and key facts. Write down the important events as they occur in the story. Label areas that you want to refer to as you write your summary. Also label areas that should be avoided because the details—though they may be interesting—are too specific. Identify areas that you do not understand and try to clarify those points.

3. Write an introduction

State the title and author of the story. Briefly describe the setting, characters, and conflict.

4. Write the body paragraphs

Retell the story in your own words. Describe the most important events from the story including the climax and resolution. And once you are actually putting pen to paper (or fingers to keys), remember these tips:

1) Be concise: a summary should not be equal in length to the original text;

2) Add some transitional words (then, however, also, moreover) that help with the overall structure and flow of the summary;

3) If you must use the words of the author, cite them;

4) Don't put your own opinions, ideas, or interpretations into the summary. The purpose of writing a summary is to accurately represent what the author wanted to say, not to provide a critique.

5. Write a conclusion

Explain the theme (underlying meaning of the story). What comments does the author intend to tell? This part is not always required.

6. Revise and proofread

Reread your summary and make certain that you have accurately represented the author's ideas and key points. Make sure that your text does not contain your own commentary on the piece. Check your spelling, grammar, and punctuation before you hand it in.

The Hare and the Tortoise
(Original Story)

One day a hare was bragging of his running speed and laughing at the tortoise for being so slow. "You never can get anywhere with those short legs of yours. Look at my long legs! They're so swift that no one would dare race me."

All the animals of field and forest were tired of hearing the hare brag. At last the tortoise said, "If we were to run a race, I'm sure I would beat you."

The hare, looking on the event as a great joke, readily agreed.

All the animals gathered to watch the race. At the signal the hare leaped forward in a great bound and soon left the plodding tortoise far behind him on the dusty road. Having reached the halfway point, and the day being warm, the hare decided to stop for a while.

"Hum-m, I've as good as won this race already," the hare thought, "There's really no reason to hurry." So, as the sun was very warm, he decided to rest a bit under a shady tree. "I'll come in ahead of that tortoise, anyhow," he told himself.

Soon he was sound asleep, and the little rest stretched into a good long nap.

The tortoise meanwhile plodded on without rest toward the finish line. When the hare woke up, he was surprised to find that the tortoise was nowhere in sight. Off he went at full speed, but when he reached the finish line, he found that the tortoise was already there, waiting for his arrival. (253 words)

(Adapted from *Aesop's Fables*)

The Hare and the Tortoise
(Summary)

In the story *The Hare and the Tortoise* from *Aesop's Fables*, the hare was beaten by the tortoise in a race because he took a nap during the race.

In the beginning, the hare laughed at the tortoise for his slowness, but the tortoise surprised the hare by challenging him to a race. The hare thought he could easily win, and he took a nap during the race. Finally, the tortoise won the race because he didn't give up while the hare was sleeping.

The message from the story is that perseverance wins the race. (95 words)

Now write a narrative summary of Deucalion's Flood by finishing the following steps.

Step 1. Read the story and identify the key elements of the story, such as the characters, the settings, and the important events.

Step 2. Rewrite the information conveyed by conversations if it is important.

Step 3. Start your summary by stating the title of the story, and briefly describing the main characters and events.

Step 4. Follow the original order, delete unimportant details, and retell the story in your own words. If it is necessary to use the author's words, cite them.

Step 5. Organize your ideas by using some transitional words to make them clear.

Step 6. After finishing your writing, check and make certain that you have clearly retold the story and accurately represented the author's ideas. Make sure that your own commentary is not included in your writing.

Deucalion's Flood

The Greek poets say that the first men lived in happiness and innocence for many years. That was the Golden Age. After it came the Silver Age, when men were not quite so happy or so good. The Brazen Age followed, with everything growing worse and worse. Then came the Iron Age, and wickedness and wrong were everywhere. Nobody was happy; love was dead; cruelty, murder, robbery, and war filled the whole world.

Zeus, King of the heaven, called a meeting of the gods. They went to his palace, and he told them the wickedness of mankind.

"The sins of men rise up like a black cloud," he said. "There are not songs of praise, only cries of the unhappy. No smoke of sacrifice ascends, but the smell of burning homes comes up and spreads itself through the heaven. Men hate one another and do not love the gods. I will destroy this wicked race, and bring a better people upon the earth."

At first he thought he would send lightning and burn up all; then he considered that water might serve him better. He sent out the stormy winds, and the sky grew black with heavy clouds from which rain poured down. He called on his brother Poseidon to unchain the ocean, and soon its waters rolled high over the shores. The rivers rose, the ground rocked with earthquakes. Temples and homes fell, valleys filled with water, beasts and men were swept away. Villages vanished, cities were seen no more; only the mountains appeared, and on their tops and sides animals and human beings were gathered trembling. The wolf stood by the lamb but did not harm it, the lion crowded close against the deer, and both were alike afraid. Men did not strike each other; they lifted up their hands in prayer to the gods. Women did not look into mirrors; they looked to the heaven for pity and help.

The waters rose higher. The animals were gone, so were all the men who did not have boats. The waves were high and fierce. The boats were dashed against the rocks and sank.

Only one mountain stood out of the water. That was Parnassus. Only one boat floated on the sea, and in it were a man and his wife, Deucalion and Pyrrha. They had been good when everybody else was bad, and Zeus had taken care of them through the storm and the flood.

The flood lasted nine days and nights. When the winds fell, the rain stopped, and the boat rested on the mountain side. Deucalion and Pyrrha had survived the flood since they were pious couple. They stepped out of the boat and stood upon the ground.

However, Deucalion and Pyrrha were lonely, being the only survivors. They found a ruined temple, knelt down and prayed to the goddess Themis. A strange but solemn voice answered, "Cover your heads. Loosen your girdles. Go down the mountain, and, as you go down, cast your mother's bones behind you."

At first they were outraged by such suggestion, until Deucalion correctly interpreted that the stones on the ground were the bones of mother earth (Gaea).

They covered their heads and loosened their belts, and went down the mountain. As they went, they stooped and picked up stones and threw them back over their shoulders. Presently they heard a sound of running feet and of voices. They looked back. Young men were following Deucalion, holding out their hands to him and calling him "Bab-ba!" Young girls were running hard after Pyrrha, trying to catch her dress, and murmuring "Mam-ma!"

The old couple went down into the valley, throwing stones behind them. By the time they reached it, they had a large family of grown-up children, whom they taught to build houses, to plow the ground, to plant vines, to weave and sew, and to talk the Greek language. So the world was peopled again, and all the Greeks look back to Deucalion and his wife as their great ancestors. (671 words)

Further Development

I. Fill in the blanks with the proper forms of the words from the box.

> depict   represent   mortal   subject   alter   determine

The Fates

The Fates, also known as Moirae or Moerae, were the three Greek goddesses of Destiny and Fate. They controlled the thread of life of every ____1____ from birth to death. Even the gods feared them.

In Greek mythology, the three goddesses, Clotho, Lachesis, and Atropos, were often ____2____ as three very old women spinning the threads of human destiny all the time. They were believed to decree the events in one's life. The Greeks believed that Clotho spun the thread that ____3____ a person's life, Lachesis decided the extent (or length) of it, and Atropos was the one who cut it at the ____4____ span of time. The threads could be cut, or cross paths, or be twisted in several directions. All the good and evil that would happen to one was woven into his destiny and couldn't be ____5____.

The Fates, born in the beginning of time, were among the oldest deities. They were the daughters of primeval night deity Nyx, though some claim that Zeus and Themis were their parents. The Fates controlled the destinies of all. Even the gods were ____6____ to their decisions.

II. Discuss the following questions after finishing the above exercise.

1. What stories do you know about destiny in Greek and Chinese myths?

2. What is your opinion about destiny in ancient and modern society?

III. Watch the video clip on *Great Flood* and fill in the blanks with the words you hear.

1. There are many, many examples in Greek history of Zeus destroying _____ because he felt that they had overreached themselves, that they had blasphemed the gods, that they had become too proud to be allowed to live any longer.

2. When natural catastrophes occurred in the real world, the Greeks believed that they were sent by Zeus to punish evil men. Often _____ to explain what had made the supreme god so angry.

3. Nine days and nights pass. The rain is relentless and the earth slowly drowns. The waters _____ of Mount Parnassus, which stands over 8,000 feet high.

4. All these stories go back to a natural catastrophe that affected the _____ of peoples living in the eastern parts of the Mediterranean Sea.

5. In the past decade, scientists have uncovered some stunning clues that prove it did. Research has shown that as the last Ice Age ended about 7,000 years ago, runoff from melting glaciers surged into the Black Sea basin, _____ nearly 170,000 square miles of dry land.

IV. Discuss the following questions based on your watching in *Exercise III*.

1. What stories do you know about Great Flood in different cultures?
2. How did ancient people interpret such natural disasters?
3. What implications can scientists and researchers get in mythological stories?

Cultural Exploration

Read the following interpretations of *Great Flood* in Greek myths and finish the tasks.

Excerpt 1

A flood myth or deluge myth is a narrative in which a great flood, usually sent by a deity or deities, destroys civilization, often in an act of divine retribution. Parallels are often drawn between the flood waters of these myths and the primeval waters found in certain creation myths, as the flood waters are described as a measure for the cleansing of humanity, in preparation for rebirth. Most flood myths also contain a culture hero, who "represents the human craving for life".

(https://en.wikipedia.org/wiki/Flood_myth)

Excerpt 2

Without a doubt the significant rise of the oceans — a worldwide disaster that at the end of the last Ice Age erased millions of square miles of dry land around the planet—must have been the doomsday event that every culture to this day inadvertently is talking about. More particularly, it was the abrupt rise of the oceans around 8000 B.C. which ultimately led to the flooding of the Mediterranean first, and finally to the flooding of the Black Sea. The rise of the oceans was that single, long-lasting event which drastically reshaped the coastlines of our planet and the one which simultaneously affected every coastal civilization around the world at the time.

(https://www.ancient-origins.net/human-origins-science-religions/evidence-great-flood-real-or-myth-part-i-005340)

Task 1. Search Gun-Yu flood myth in China on line, and decide whether the definition of a flood myth (shown in Excerpt 1) can well explain the Chinese flood myth. If you can see some typical features of Chinese flood myth, please form your own definition of a Chinese flood myth.

Task 2. The sea level rise (shown in Excerpt 2) is one of the interpretations of the realistic basis of Great Flood myths in prehistoric era. What hypotheses of the formation of Chinese flood myths can you make?

Task 3. What cultural differences can you conclude after you have compared the Great Flood stories in Greek myths and Chinese myths?

Typhon

Typhon or Typhoeus, was a monster of the primitive world. He was described sometimes as a destructive hurricane, and sometimes as a monstrous giant.

Typhon was described as a gigantic winged monster that was part man and part beast. Typhon was also taller than the tallest mountain. He was a terribly horrifying sight and was deadly since flame would *gush* (涌出) from his mouth. He was the father of many monstrous offspring, such as Cerberus, Hydra, Nemean Lion, Sphinx, and the Caucasian Eagle.

When Zeus and the Olympians defeated the Titans, they were faced with an even mightier foe, Typhon, the new offspring Gaea had conceived from her brother Tartarus to revenge her giant children.

When Typhon came and attacked the heavens, the Olympians fled from Olympus. They transformed themselves into various animals to escape from the monster, and hid out in Egypt. Only Zeus dared to confront Typhon. He hurled his deadly thunderbolt, and as the monster drew closer, he attacked Typhon with the sickle, which was said to be the same one that Cronus had used against his father Uranus.

However, Zeus was over-confident, and was trapped by Typhon. With Zeus' sickle, Typhon managed to cut the *sinews* (肌腱) of Zeus' hands. He had the god imprisoned in the cave and left a monster to keep an eye on his prisoner. Without his sinews, Zeus was helpless and could not wield the thunderbolt.

Hermes and Pan volunteered to go and rescue Zeus. They found the cave and saw Typhon wasn't in. So Pan let out one of his wild echoing *panic-inducing* (引起惊恐的) cries. The watch-keeper panicked, ran up a wall and clung to a dark corner. Hermes rushed in and hurriedly replaced Zeus's sinews back. After Zeus was restored of his sinews, he regained the use of the thunderbolt.

Zeus wielded his mighty thunderbolt against Typhon, pursuing the monster to Sicily. Zeus defeated Typhon, and buried the monster under Mount Etna or the entire island of Sicily. The *volcanic eruptions* (火山喷发) of Mount Etna were the result of Typhon's *spewing* (喷) out his fire.

The Greek word "typhon", through variation, finally became "typhoon" in English. (376 words)

Answer the following questions briefly.

1. Why did Gaea give birth to Typhon to attack the young gods?
2. What was the end of Typhon?

Chinese Myths of Creation

Pangu — Creation of the World

In the beginning, the universe was a black egg where the heavens and the earth were mixed together, and in this egg was contained Pangu. After 18 thousand years Pangu woke from a long sleep. He felt *suffocated* (窒息), so he took up a broad ax and wielded it with all his might to crack open the egg. The light, clear part of it floated up and formed the heavens. The cold, *turbid* (浑浊的) matter stayed below to form the earth. Pangu stood in the middle, his head touching the sky, his feet planted on the earth. The heavens and the earth began to grow at a rate of ten feet per day, and Pangu grew along with them. After another 18 thousand years, the sky was higher, the earth thicker, and Pangu stood between them like a pillar 90 thousand *li* in height so that they would never join again.

When Pangu died, his breath became the wind and clouds, his voice the rolling thunder, and his eyes the sun and the moon. His body and limbs turned to five big mountains and his blood formed the roaring water. His veins became far-stretching roads and his muscles fertile land. The innumerable stars in the sky came from his hair and beard, and flowers and trees from his skin and the fine hairs on his body. His *marrow* (骨髓) turned to *jade* (玉) and pearls. His sweat flowed like the good rain and sweet dew that nurtured all things on earth.

Nüwa — Creation of Man

Nüwa, the goddess in Chinese myths, was the original ancestor of the Chinese nation. According to legend, Nuwa was also the younger sister of Emperor Fuxi. Nuwa loved peace and delighted in making things.

It was said that there were no men when the sky and the earth were separated. It was Nuwa who made men by moulding yellow clay, and gave them life and the ability to bear children: this is how humanity was created. One version said that the work of Nuwa was so *taxing* (累人的) that her strength was not equal to it. So she dipped a rope into the mud and then lifted it. The mud that dripped from the rope also became men. Those made by moulding yellow clay were rich and noble, while those made by lifting the rope were poor and low. (415 words)

Answer the following questions briefly.

1. According to Chinese myths, how did the universe become the one we have now?

2. According to Chinese myths, how were men created?

3. From the story of Pangu and Nüwa, what virtue can be seen from Chinese gods?

UNIT 2
Olympian Gods

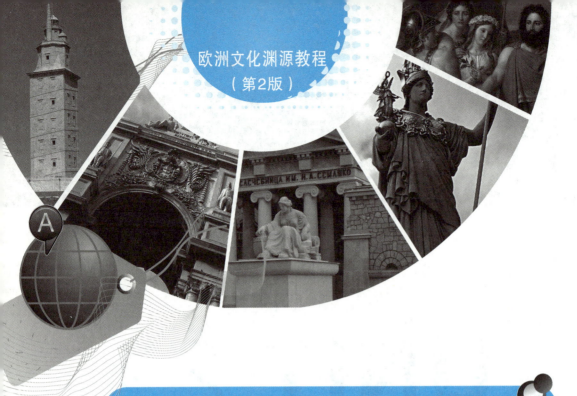

欧洲文化渊源教程
(第2版)

In this unit, you are going to
◎ identify the chief Olympian gods;
◎ explain the kinship of the chief gods;
◎ retell the stories about Olympian gods;
◎ write a paragraph summary;
◎ expand vocabulary through word formation of affixes.

 Pre-information

▶I. Listen to the following passage on *Olympian Gods* and fill in the blanks with the words you hear.

The ancient Greeks believed in gods. They thought the gods were very much like human beings. They had both ___1___ powers and ___2___ weaknesses. The gods would fight with each other, fall in love, ___3___ on one another, get angry or ___4___, and steal from each other. The Greeks ___5___ stories about all the things the gods did. These stories called myths were ___6___ through generations.

28

The Greeks believed that Mount Olympus, the highest mountain in Greece, was the home of the gods. The Greeks worshipped twelve major gods and goddesses, who were known as the Olympian gods, or simply the Olympians, for their place of _____7_____.

The gods together presided over _____8_____ of human life. They made their presence known to people through signs, such as the sound of thunder. The Greeks built temples to shelter the gods and worship them.

II. Listen to the sentences and fill in the blanks with the words you hear. Then work out the meaning of each sentence with a partner.

1. She was very sad when she _____ her brother from his slide down to Hades through alcoholism.

2. Peter who was chosen _____ boy in the senior class is quite an Adonis.

3. Some of the women-executives are usually _____ their position of being a Diana.

4. The appointment letter was _____ to me on a pleasant morning by a helmeted Hermes on a bike.

5. Some boys are as shy as Daphne. When they meet girls, they _____.

6. The committee's chairman _____ NASA of resting on its laurels after making it to the moon.

Stories

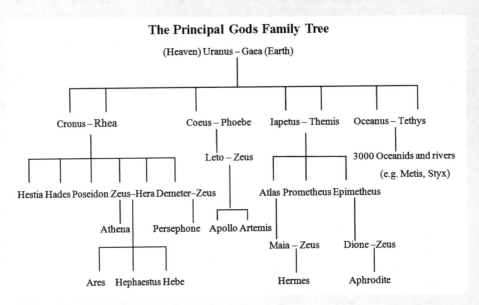

Story One

Read the story and figure out the characters described below.

_____ 1. He was the god of the waters, earthquakes and horses, and the brother of Zeus.

_____ 2. She was the sister and wife of Zeus, and the goddess of marriage.

_____ 3. She was a daughter of Zeus, and the goddess of wisdom, reason, handicrafts and defense.

_____ 4. She was the goddess of love and beauty, and was born from the sea foam.

_____ 5. She was the virgin goddess of the hunt and the moon, and the twin sister of Apollo.

_____ 6. He was the god of fire and forge, and the husband of Aphrodite.

_____ 7. She was the goddess of grain, harvest, agriculture and fertility, and was intimately associated with the seasons.

_____ 8. He was a son of Zeus, and the god of wine and ecstasy. He was also the only god who had a mortal parent.

_____ 9. He was the god of light, music and healing, and was famous for his oracle at Delphi.

_____ 10. He was the messenger of the gods, and the guide for the dead to go to the underworld.

Olympians

In general, the Olympians are the gods who live on Mount Olympus, and all of them somehow are related to the supreme god Zeus. More specifically, there are twelve Olympians as the major deities of the Greek pantheon.

However, there is some variation as to which deities should be included. Hestia is often replaced by Dionysus. Hades, in general, is excluded, because he is thought to reside permanently in the underworld and never visits Mount Olympus.

1. Zeus (Jupiter)

The most powerful of all, Zeus was the god of the sky and the king of Olympus. He was the youngest child of the Titans Cronus and Rhea. Being the supreme ruler, he was represented as the god of law and justice, and this made him the spiritual leader of both gods and men. He was also known for punishing those who lied or broke *oaths*. His weapon was a thunderbolt which he *hurled* at those who displeased him. His bird was the eagle, and his tree the oak. He was married to his sister Hera, but was famous for his many affairs.

2. Poseidon (Neptune)

Poseidon, brother of Zeus, was the god of the sea, earthquakes and storms. He was second only to Zeus in power amongst the gods. The symbol of Poseidon's power was the trident, with which he could shake the earth, call forth or *subdue* storms, and *shatter* any object. He was further regarded as the creator of the horse. Hence he was also represented on horseback, or riding in a chariot drawn by two or four horses.

Poseidon had a difficult quarrelsome personality. He had a series of disputes with other gods when he tried to take over their cities. He was also not so well-disposed toward some heroes, like Odysseus.

3. Hades (Pluto)

Hades, brother of Zeus, was the god of the underworld where he ruled over the dead. He was also the god of wealth, due to the precious metals mined from the earth. His wife was Persephone whom he abducted. As he lived in the underworld rather than on Mount Olympus, he was typically not included amongst the twelve Olympians.

4. Hera (Juno)

Hera, the youngest daughter of Cronus and Rhea, was the sister and wife of Zeus. Being the supreme goddess and the queen of Olympus, Hera was the goddess of marriage and childbirth, and a protector of married women. Most stories concerning Hera have to do with her jealousy of and revenge on her husband's numerous lovers. Hera was also known for having *viciously* attacked Zeus' *illegitimate* children, like Heracles whom she *persecuted* throughout his life. Hera's sacred animals were the cow and the peacock.

5. Hestia (Vesta)

Hestia, the first child of Cronus and Rhea, the eldest sister of Zeus, was the virgin goddess of the hearth and the family. She was one of the original twelve Olympians, until she gave her throne to Dionysus when the young god came to live in Olympus. Of all the Olympians, she was the mildest, most upright and most *charitable*, but played no part in myths.

6. Demeter (Ceres)

Demeter, sister of Zeus, was the goddess of grain, harvest, agriculture and fertility in general. Demeter was intimately associated with the seasons. Her daughter Persephone was abducted by Hades to be his wife in the underworld. During the months Persephone had to spend in the underworld, Demeter *grieved* her daughter's absence and withdrew her gifts from the world, creating winter. Her daughter's return brought the spring. The word "cereal" comes from her Roman name.

7. Athena (Minerva)

Athena, daughter of Zeus and the Oceanid Metis, was the virgin goddess of wisdom, reason, handicrafts and defense. She sprang fully grown in armour from Zeus' head after he swallowed her mother. She was his father's favorite child and was allowed to use his weapons. Her sacred tree was the olive. The owl was her bird.

8. Aphrodite (Venus)

Aphrodite was the goddess of love, beauty and sexual desire. She was the daughter of Zeus and the Titaness Dione, or perhaps was born from the *aphros* ("sea foam") after Uranus was castrated by his youngest son Cronus, who then threw his father's genitals into the sea. Though married to Hephaestus, Aphrodite had many adulterous affairs, most notably with Ares, by whom she was said to become the mother of Eros, the god of love, and Harmonia, the wife of Cadmus of Thebes. The myrtle was her tree. The dove, the swan, and the sparrow were her birds. Her name gave us the word "aphrodisiac", while her Roman name, Venus, gave us the word "venereal".

9. Apollo (Apollo)

Apollo, son of Zeus and the Titaness Leto, and twin brother of Artemis, was the god of light, music, healing, archery, prophecy, manly youth and beauty. One of his important daily tasks was to harness his chariot with four horses and drive the sun across the sky. He was famous for his oracle at Delphi. His sacred tree was the laurel tree. His symbols include the sun, the lyre, and the bow and arrow.

10. Artemis (Diana)

Artemis, daughter of Zeus and the Titaness Leto, was the goddess of virginity, hunt, and the natural environment. All wild animals were sacred to her, especially the deer. Like Apollo, she hunted with silver arrows. She later became associated with the moon. She raced across the sky in her chariot driven by milk-white horses.

11. Ares (Mars)

Ares, son of Zeus and Hera, was the god of war, violence, and bloodshed. He was considered murderous and bloodstained, but also a coward. All the other gods (except Aphrodite) *despised* him. His bird was the vulture. His animal was the dog. His Roman name, Mars, gave us the word "martial".

12. Hephaestus (Vulcan)

Hephaestus, son of Hera, either by Zeus or alone, was the god of fire and the forge. He was the only god to be physically ugly, and was also lame. He was the smith and armourer of the gods, but was kind and peace-loving. He was the patron god of both smiths and weavers. His wife was

Aphrodite. His Roman name, Vulcan, gave us the word "volcano".

13. Hermes (Mercury)

Hermes, son of Zeus and the nymph Maia, was the messenger of the gods. He wore winged sandals, a winged hat, and carried a magic wand with wings at the top and intertwined with serpents. He was the cleverest and speediest of the gods. He was the god of thieves and commerce. He was also the guide for the dead to go to the underworld. He invented the lyre, the pipes, the musical scale, weights and measures, boxing and gymnastics.

14. Dionysus (Bacchus)

Dionysus, son of Zeus and the mortal Theban princess Semele, was the god of wine, *ecstasy* and fertility, and later the patron god of drama. He was the youngest Olympian, as well as the only god to have a mortal parent. His symbols include the ivy and grapes.

Dionysus had a dual nature: On one hand, bringing joy and **divine** ecstasy; on the other hand, arousing brutal and unthinking **rage**. Thus, reflecting both sides of wine's nature. Unlike other gods, Dionysus was not only outside his believers but also within them. At these times a man might be greater than himself and do work he otherwise could not. (1209 words)

▶ Listen to the story of *Birth of Athena* and fill in the blanks with the words you hear.

Birth of Athena

Metis, one of the Oceanids and the Titan goddess of prudence, good counsel, _____1_____ and craftiness, was very much the apple of Zeus' eye. Zeus chased Metis in his direct way, and lay with her. Metis was pregnant. An oracle of Gaea then _____2_____ that Metis' first child would be a girl, but her second child would be a boy that would be more powerful than Zeus, and _____3_____ him as had happened to his father and grandfather. Fearing that the son of a union with Metis would bring his destruction, Zeus took this warning to heart. When he next saw Metis, he *flattered* her and put her _____4_____. Zeus proposed a game of changing shapes. Metis forgot her _____5_____ and decided it would be fun. They changed all sorts of shapes, big and small, but when Metis changed into a fly, Zeus suddenly opened his mouth and swallowed her. Metis _____6_____ living inside Zeus' head and giving him _____7_____ from there. This was possibly the beginning of Zeus' wisdom.

Zeus probably thought that was the end of it, and for a while it was. But one day Zeus _____8_____ a severe headache. Hermes realized what needed to be done and directed Hephaestus to take an ax and _____9_____ Zeus' skull. Out of the skull sprang Athena, fully grown and in a full set of armour. From the first moment goddess Athena came into the world, she won the heart of Zeus and became his favorite child. However, she never received a mother's care. That's why she _____10_____ possessed more *masculine* than feminine attributes. Due to her manner of birth, she had dominion over all things of the intellect.

Story Three

I. Match the major characters in the story with the proper information after your first reading.

1. Aphrodite   a. one who was attracted by the beauty of the lad and refused to give him back
2. Persephone   b. one who was so beautiful that even goddesses loved him
3. Adonis   c. one who made Myrrha commit incest with her father

II. Fill in the blanks with the information after your second reading.

1. Adonis was born from _____, into which his mother was transformed by the gods.
2. Adonis chose to spend _____ of the year with Aphrodite.
3. The story of Adonis' death provides a basis for the origin of _____, which grew from Adonis' blood.

Aphrodite and Adonis

Aphrodite loved and was loved by many gods and mortals. Her favorite lover was the god of war, Ares. Among her mortal lovers, the most famous was perhaps Adonis.

Adonis was a handsome young man. There is some confusion as to his parentage and his birth. The generally accepted version is that Aphrodite punished Myrrha (or Smyrna) for failing to honour her by compelling Myrrha to commit incest with her father, the king of Cyprus. When the king discovered that his daughter was pregnant with their incestuous child, he chased her with a sword. To avoid the king's **wrath**, the gods turned the daughter into a myrrh tree. The tree later burst open, allowing Adonis to emerge.

Once the child was born, Aphrodite was so moved by his beauty that she sheltered him and **entrusted** him to Persephone, who was also taken by his beauty and refused to give him back. The dispute between the two goddesses, in one version, was settled by Zeus; in others it was settled by Calliope, one of the Muses, on Zeus' behalf. The decision was that Adonis was to spend one-third of every year with each goddess and the last third with whomever he chose. He always chose to spend two-thirds of the year with Aphrodite.

This went on till Adonis' death, when he was fatally wounded by a wild boar, said in one version, caused by Aphrodite's lover, Ares, who was jealous of Adonis. The story of Adonis provides a basis for the origin of the myrrh and the origin of the rose, which grew from each drop of Adonis' blood that fell. (271 words)

Watch the video clip on *Hades Kidnapped Persephone* and fill in the blanks with the words you hear.

1. Hades has kidnapped a young maiden named Persephone. He holds her captive _____. Hades has taken her away to his realm to be his wife forever.

2. The ancient Greeks believed Demeter was responsible for the

changing of the seasons. And that Persephone's _____.

3. She didn't know what had happened to her daughter, so she wandered the earth and in her grief at the loss of her daughter, she forgot to give fertility to the land. So plants *withered* and died, human beings _____, the earth descended into the deepest, deepest of winters.

4. Hades knew that if he could get her to eat food belonging to the underneath that she would then become _____.

5. He offers Persephone a snack of pomegranate seeds. She naively accepts and seals her fate. It is a mistake for which the entire planet will pay. She must now spend three months of every year in the underworld, one month _____. The rest of the year she can spend with her mother.

6. When Persephone is down in the underworld, Demeter doesn't give earth the fertility that it needs, and that is what the Greeks understood as winter. When Persephone returns to her mother, Demeter _____ and that's what we have as spring and summer.

Story Five

I. Answer the following questions briefly after your first reading.

1. Why did Daphne try to escape from Apollo's pursue?
2. What was Daphne transformed into?

II. Decide whether the following statements are TRUE or FALSE after your second reading.

_____ 1. Apollo desperately fell in love with Daphne because Daphne was very beautiful.

_____ 2. Eros struck Apollo's heart with his golden arrow and made him in love.

_____ 3. Apollo stopped Daphne from escaping by transforming her into a tree.

_____ 4. Laurel tree became the symbol of victory through the story of Apollo and Daphne.

Apollo and Daphne

Daphne was Apollo's first love. It was not brought about by accident, but by the malice of Eros. On one occasion Eros became angry with Apollo for mocking the power of his arrows. As a way to punish him, Eros drew from his quiver two arrows of different workmanship, one to excite love, the other to repel it. The former was of gold and sharp-pointed, the latter blunt and tipped with lead. With the leaden one he struck the nymph Daphne, the daughter of the river god Peneus, and with the golden one Apollo, through the heart. Instantly, the god was seized with love for the maiden, but Daphne hated the thought of loving.

Apollo fell desperately in love with Daphne, and longed to obtain her. He began to pursue Daphne in the woods, but as he approached, she began to run faster and faster.

Apollo asked Daphne to stop running and said he pursued her for love, but Daphne continued her flight. However, Apollo was more rapid. When her strength began to fail, and was about to be grasped, she called upon her father, "Help me, Father! Open the earth to enclose me, or change my form, which has brought me into this danger!" Scarcely had she spoken, when a stiffness seized all her limbs; her bosom began to be enclosed in a tender bark; her hair became leaves; her arms became branches; her feet stuck fast in the ground, as a root; her face became a tree-top, retaining nothing of its former self but its beauty.

Apollo stood amazed. He touched the stem, and felt the flesh tremble under the new bark. He embraced the branches, and kissed the wood. Still in love with Daphne, Apollo declared that the leaves of the laurel tree would always be green and he would always wear a wreath of laurel leaves around his head. Since then the laurel tree has become the symbol of victory in Greek culture, and Apollo has often been depicted with laurel leaves on his golden hair. (340 words)

UNIT 2

I. Decide whether the following statements are TRUE or FALSE after your first reading.

_____ 1. Semele was a beautiful goddess whom Zeus fell in love with.

_____ 2. Semele insisted that Zeus show his true form before her because she was curious about her lover.

_____ 3. Hera visited Semele in disguise and convinced her of the divine identity of her lover.

_____ 4. Dionysus was born from Zeus' head.

II. Fill in the blanks with the information after your second reading.

1. When Zeus visited Semele, he made himself _____ but felt as a divine presence.

2. When Zeus next came to her, Semele made him swear on _____ to grant her one wish.

3. Zeus appeared in his true form and Semele was instantly _____ by the sight of his glory.

4. Dionysus' birth from Zeus conferred _____ upon him.

Birth of Dionysus

Dionysus, the god of wine, was the son of Zeus and Semele. He was the only god to have a mortal parent.

Semele was a daughter of Cadmus, the first king of Thebes, and Harmonia, the daughter of Aphrodite and Ares. She was famous for her extraordinary beauty and grace. When Zeus saw the princess, he fell in love with her. Zeus came to Semele in the night, invisible, felt only as a divine presence. Soon Semele became pregnant. She was pleased to be a lover of a god, even though she did not know which one. Word soon got around and Hera quickly assumed who was responsible.

Hera went to Semele in disguise, planted seeds of doubt in Semele's mind, and convinced her that she should see her lover as he really was. When Zeus next came to her, Semele, curious, demanded of Zeus that he promise to grant her one wish. She went so far as to make him swear on the River Styx. Zeus was madly in love and agreed. She then asked him to reveal himself in all his glory as proof of his godhood.

Zeus first tried to hold back, but he had already made a sacred *oath* and had no choice. He appeared in his true form and Semele was instantly burnt to death by the sight of his glory. By that time, Dionysus was still in Semele's womb. Zeus managed to rescue the infant and stitched him into his thigh to hold him until he was ready to be born. Then he handed Dionysus to his messenger Hermes, who brought the baby to some nymphs to be raised. His birth from Zeus alone *conferred* immortality upon him. (284 words)

Story Seven

I. Match the major characters in the story with the proper information after your first reading.

1. Eros   a. one who was jealous of Psyche's beauty
2. Aphrodite   b. one who had two types of arrows to arouse or repel love
3. Psyche   c. the god of love and sexual desire
4. Zeus   d. mother of Eros
                 e. one who once lost her lover for not obeying her lover's request
                 f. one who fell in love with Psyche
                 g. one who gave consent for the couple to marry
                 h. one who became the goddess of soul

II. Decide whether the following statements are TRUE or FALSE after your second reading.

_____ 1. Eros is usually depicted as a young winged boy, with his bow and arrows at the ready to shoot.

_____ 2. Eros fell in love with Psyche because he was wounded by his arrow accidentally.

_____ 3. Eros visited Psyche every night, but made himself invisible in disguise.

_____ 4. Overcome by her curiosity, Psyche one night lit a lamp to see her lover's true identity.

Eros and Psyche

Eros (Cupid), the Greek god of love and sexual desire (*eros* means sexual desire), was the son of Aphrodite and Ares. He is often represented blindfolded because love is often blind.

Eros is usually depicted as a young winged boy, with his bow and arrows at the ready, to either shoot into the hearts of gods or mortals which would rouse them to desire. His arrows came in two types: golden with dove feathers which aroused love, or leaden arrows which had owl feathers that caused indifference. Being cruel to his victims to some extent, he was also charming and very beautiful. Being a danger to those around him, Eros would make as much ***mischief*** as he possibly could by wounding the hearts of all. But according to one legend, he himself fell in love.

The legend says that Aphrodite became jealous of the beauty of a mortal, a beautiful young woman named Psyche. In her fit of jealousy, Aphrodite asked Eros to shoot his arrow into the heart of Psyche and make her fall in love with the ugliest man on earth. He agreed to carry out his mother's wishes. But on seeing her beauty, Eros fell deeply in love with Psyche himself. He would visit her every night, but he made himself invisible by telling Psyche not to light her chamber. Psyche fell in love with Eros even though she could not see him, until one night curiosity overcame her. She concealed a lamp and while Eros slept she lit the lamp, revealing the identity of Eros. But a drop of hot oil spilt from the lamp awakening the god. Angered, Eros fled and Psyche roamed the earth trying in vain to find her lover. In the end Zeus took pity and reunited them, and he also gave his consent for them to marry. Psyche was also made immortal upon Eros' request, and became the goddess of the soul. (321 words)

Vocabulary Focus

I. Match the words from *Stories* part with their corresponding definitions.

1. oath
2. hurl
3. shatter
4. subdue
5. viciously
6. despise
7. ecstasy
8. flatter
9. masculine
10. wrath
11. entrust
12. wither

a. put down by force
b. look down upon with contempt
c. extreme anger
d. a solemn or formal promise
e. break into many pieces
f. become dry or dead
g. feeling or state of great joy or happiness
h. throw forcefully
i. wickedly, maliciously
j. associated with men and not with women
k. trust somebody to take charge of something / somebody
l. praise somebody too much or insincerely

II. Use the words from *Exercise I* to complete the sentences.

1. In the conflict, groups of angry youths _____ stones at police.

2. Don't cheat at examination, or you will be _____ by others.

3. All sport is very male-dominated and some coaches want the women cyclists to be as _____ as possible.

4. He made a tour of the room to _____ his rising anger.

5. He was the kind of person who would _____ you to your face, and then slander you behind your back.

6. The children's unruly behaviour incurred the headmaster's _____.

7. Safety glass won't _____ even if it's broken.

8. When she was abroad, she _____ her friend with the care of her house.

9. Government employees swear a(n) _____ not to reveal official secrets.

10. The flowers will _____ if you don't put them in water.

11. The two companies compete _____ for a bigger share of beverage market.

12. He was in _____ when he got the news of his daughter's birth.

III. Choose the italicized words from *Stories* part to complete the table.

Verb	Noun	Adjective	Noun (Person)	Antonym
legitimize	legitimacy	legitimate		1_____
2_____	persecution		persecutor	
	charity	3_____		
4_____	grief	grievous		
	divinity	5_____		
enrage	6_____			
7_____	conferment		conferrer	
	8_____	mischievous		

IV. Use the words in the table from *Exercise III* to complete the sentences.

1. Nazi's undisguised effort to _____ the Jews met with worldwide condemnation.

2. Their daughter died over a year ago, but they are still _____.

3. She was _____ by his arrogance and stupidity.

4. He is the _____ heir to the property.

5. Certain countries, including Switzerland, Japan and much of the European Union, do not _____ citizenship automatically to

babies born on their soil.

6. In ancient mythology, there was no impassable gulf separating the _____ from the human beings.

7. The _____ boy often causes trouble to his parents.

8. Every time you donate clothes, books or toys to a _____ shop, you are helping people.

Vocabulary Development
Prefixes and Suffixes

Prefixes and suffixes are grammatical and lingual "affixes". Prefixes are affixed before and suffixes after a base word or word stem to add information. For example, the root word "port" means "to carry or to bear". Attach the prefix "ex-", meaning "out or out of", and you have the word "export", meaning "to carry out". Attach the prefix "im-", meaning "in" or "into", and you have "import", "to carry in". Attach the prefix "trans-", meaning "across", and you have "transport", "to carry across". Now let's attach the suffix "-able", meaning "able to be", and you have "importable", "exportable", and "transportable".

Study the following prefixes and suffixes, and the words made from them:

Prefix / Suffix	Meanings	Examples
co-, col-, com-, con-	with, together, joint	coauthor — writer who collaborates with another author collaborate — to work together commemorate — to remember by gathering together contemporary — of the same time period as others, belonging to the present time
e-, ex-	out, away	eject — to throw out forcefully excavate — to dig out extract — to pull out
ig-, il-, im-, in-, ir-	not, without	illegal — not legal impossible — not possible inappropriate — not appropriate irresponsible — not responsible

UNIT 2

Prefix / Suffix	Meanings	Examples
-arian, -ant	a person who	vegetarian — a person who never eats meat or fish applicant — a person who applies for something such as a job or a college immigrant — a person who comes to live in a country from some other country
-fy	make, cause (makes the word a verb)	amplify — to increase in size, volume or significance terrify — to fill with terror simplify — to make simpler or easier
-ible, -able	able to be	audible — loud enough to be heard plausible — apparently reasonable, valid, and truthful portable — easily or conveniently transported preventable — capable of being prevented

Now complete the sentences with a suitable word from above.

1. The music was _____ with microphones.
2. A series of major celebrations will be held to _____ the 100th anniversary of the university.
3. As we all know, tobacco use is the single greatest _____ cause of death in the world today.
4. Although nutrients from animals may be of higher quality or more readily absorbed than vegetable sources, it is possible for a _____ to have a healthy diet.
5. Both ideas sound _____ and there was no way of telling in advance who was right.
6. Those who _____ sites of ancient culture or ancient tombs without permission will be punished.
7. Some scientists attribute environmental deterioration to a series of natural factors, while others place the blame solely on _____ human behaviour.
8. Some years ago, I was discussing music with two friends, one of them a distinguished _____ composer.
9. The pilot managed to _____ safely before the plane crashed in the desert.
10. Qualified ESL teachers are needed especially in schools with large

_____ populations where English is not the first language of many students.

Speaking
Retelling a Story (2)

Retell the Episodes about Zeus' lovers based on the instructions in Unit 1. Please choose to use the following transitional words and phrases to indicate time sequence in your retelling.

> then, afterward, next, subsequently, previously, first, second, at last, meanwhile, in the meantime, immediately, soon, eventually, during, later, before, after, while

Episode 1: Europa

Aside from Hera, Zeus' lovers were many and varied, sometimes his affections falling to goddesses, others to mortal women. As the supreme god, Zeus had easy access to the goddesses and mortal women and took advantage of it. Also, his power made him difficult to resist.

Europa was a Phoenician princess. One day, Zeus looked down from the heavens and saw Europa. He was immediately overwhelmed with her beauty. Again as was normal with the tales of Zeus, the supreme god decided to act upon his desires, and sought to seduce her. Zeus transformed into a glamorous white bull and presented himself to the maiden.

At first, Europa was afraid of the creature, but the bull appeared very tame, and even gently lay down at her feet. Relaxed, Europa petted the creature and then climbed onto his back to see whether he was tame enough to ride. Zeus spotted his opportunity and ran off with her, carrying her to the ocean and swimming to the island of Crete. There, he changed back to his true form. Europa then readily agreed to be his lover. Europa became the first queen of Crete and bore Zeus three sons, including Minos, a king of Crete.

The continent of Europe is named for her. (210 words)

Episode 2: Io

The story of Io is one of the best-known stories of Hera's revenge.

Zeus fell in love with Io, a beautiful princess, and seduced her. Zeus, in an attempt to avoid the rage and jealousy of Hera, his wife, transformed Io into a handsome white heifer. Hera, seeing right through it, asked for the heifer as a present. Zeus could not refuse. Hera deposited Io in the safe keeping of Argus, the watchman with a hundred eyes. Since Argus had a hundred eyes and could have some of them sleep while others were awake, he made himself a fine watchman. Desperate, Zeus sent Hermes to rescue Io. Disguised as a shepherd, Hermes had to employ all his skills as a musician and storyteller to gain Argus' confidence and lull him to sleep. Once Argus closed all his eyes, Hermes killed him. As a memorial, Hera took his hundred eyes and set them into the tail of her favorite bird, the peacock.

Though Io was eventually rescued by Hermes, that wasn't the end of the persecution. Hera sent a gadfly to sting the heifer wherever she went. Trying to escape, she wandered all over the world, and ran farther and farther away in her attempts to avoid this torment. One day she came across Prometheus, while he was bound to his rock at Caucasus. Prometheus, though he couldn't provide direct comfort, told her that, though her future would be filled with hardship and toil, she would, upon reaching Egypt and the Nile, be restored by Zeus and bore him a son. Furthermore, and perhaps more importantly, a descendant of this child would be a great hero and set him free.

Prometheus' prediction came true. During her wanderings many geographical locations were named after her, including Ionian Sea. She eventually reached the Nile where Zeus restored her to human form. She bore a son, and eleven generations later her descendant Heracles set Prometheus free. (322 words)

Episode 3: Callisto

Callisto was a beautiful nymph, and a virgin maid of Artemis. Young women who were devoted to the goddess should remain virgins, like Artemis herself. Callisto upheld the ideals faithfully. She followed Artemis in hunting regularly, and quickly became the goddess' favorite.

While Callisto spent her days and nights with Artemis' other followers, she caught the eye of Zeus. Knowing that the maiden had taken a vow of chastity, Zeus resorted to deception. He came to her disguised as Artemis, and the young huntress let down her guard. Seizing the opportunity, Zeus raped her.

Callisto became pregnant, and tried desperately to conceal her condition from the goddess. After all, she had, in a way, broken her vow to the goddess and she feared her anger. Later, however, Artemis discovered the secret and was furious. She banished the young woman, and Callisto wandered off to have her child alone.

Hera, as usual, was jealous, and decided to take her revenge. She turned the beautiful maid into a bear, though remained human in heart. The child that Callisto had by Zeus was rescued by Hermes. The child was named Arcas, meaning "bear", and he grew up to be a fine hunter.

When Arcas was out hunting as a young man, he encountered the bear. Callisto recognized the handsome youth as her son. Overjoyed, Callisto forgot her present form, and tried to come near her son to give him a hug. The bear scared Arcas, and he took aim at her with his spear. At that moment, Zeus took pity on his former victim and intervened. He placed Callisto in the sky as the constellation Ursa Major, or "great bear", and Arcas following behind as Ursa Minor, the "little bear". They are also referred to as Big Dipper and Little Dipper nowadays. (296 words)

Writing
Assignment Summary (1)
Paragraph Summary

Besides narrative summary, we make summaries of many different things, including meetings, lectures and readings. The purpose of such a summary is to give the reader a short, clear and objective picture of the original lecture or text. The summary restates only the main points of a text or a lecture without giving examples or details. These summaries may be for our own personal use or for future reference. At the university especially, the summary can form an essential part of our preparation for an exam, a class discussion, a research paper, a thesis or a dissertation. Your instructor may assign you to review or critique articles, or even to summarize some recent literature that could be useful for your research group. Hence, assignment summaries can be extremely challenging to write.

The ability to identify the key points in a paragraph and summarize it with 1—2 sentences in your own words helps to make an effective summary of a complete passage.

UNIT 2

Original Paragraph

There are times when the night sky glows with bands of color. The bands may begin as cloud shapes and then spread into a great arc across the entire sky. They may fall in folds like a curtain drawn across the heavens. The lights usually grow brighter, then suddenly dim. During this time the sky glows with pale yellow, pink, green, violet, blue, and red. These lights are called the Aurora Borealis. Some people call them the Northern Lights. Scientists have been watching them for hundreds of years. They are not quite sure what causes them. In ancient times people were afraid of the Lights. They imagined that they saw fiery dragons in the sky. Some even concluded that the heavens were on fire. (124 words)

Summary

The Aurora Borealis, or Northern Lights, are bands of color in the night sky. Ancient people were frightened by them, and even modern scientists are not sure what they are. (30 words)

Now write summaries of the following paragraphs by finishing the following steps.

Step 1. Read and mark out the key words and phrases. Pay attention to the first sentence, for it often contains the main idea of the paragraph.

Step 2. Write one or two sentences in your words, which connect properly the key words you have marked out.

Step 3. Compare your summary to the original paragraph. Your first sentence should not be exactly the same as the original one, though they may convey similar points.

Step 4. Check and avoid adding information that is not in the original paragraph, and avoid copying the paragraph.

Paragraph One

Greek mythology is a patchwork of stories, some conflicting with one another. Many have been passed down from ancient times in more than one version. The roots of this mythology reach back to two civilizations that flourished before 1100 B.C.: the Mycenaean, on the Greek mainland, and the Minoan, on the nearby island of Crete. The ancient beliefs merged with legends from Greek kingdoms and city-states and myths borrowed from other peoples to form a body of lore shared by most Greeks. (82 words)

Paragraph Two

The geography and climate of the Mediterranean region directly influenced Greek mythology. Most Greek gods and goddesses are representations of the active physical elements that made up the local landscape. The volcanoes of Lemnos, an island in the Mediterranean, and Mount Etna, on the island of Sicily, were believed to be the forges of Hephaestus, the Greek god of fire. Ancient Greeks also believed reigning gods imprisoned lesser gods underneath the volcanoes. A volcano's violent nature thus came from the work of Hephaestus and the anger of the imprisoned gods. (90 words)

Further Development

I. Fill in the blanks with the proper forms of the words from the box.

> feed   swear   lightly   boundary   summon   aid

The river Styx is the main river in the underworld in Greek mythology. There is also a Greek goddess Styx, who is the goddess of this river. She was the daughter of the Titans Oceanus and Thetis.

When Zeus ____1____ all the gods to help him fight the Titans, Styx was the first to come to Zeus' ____2____, together with her children including Nike (victory). As a reward for her help, Zeus gave Styx the honour of being the one in whose name the solemn oaths were taken. That's why she was feared by gods, because oaths ____3____ in her name or on her river could not be taken ____4____. If such a solemn oath was broken, there would be a severe punishment for the gods: For one year, they could not breathe and they could not ____5____ on nectar

and ambrosia, and they would just lie on a bed, in a kind of coma. After that, for nine more years, they could not take part in other activities of the gods, counsels or banquets.

As regards the river Styx, it was considered the _____6_____ between our world and the underworld. That's why sometimes the name Styx was used instead of "Hades".

II. Discuss the following questions after finishing *Exercise I*.

1. What stories do you know about keeping one's word in Greek myths?

2. What's your opinion on keeping one's word?

III. Watch the video clip on *Hera's Revolution* and fill in the blanks with the words you hear.

1. As Zeus' fame and power grow across ancient Greece, more and more cities and towns want to be associated with him, and they therefore claim that there was some kind of actual liaison between Zeus and some _____ that then produces the offspring that produces the local ruling families.

2. Evidence of this connection can still be found in cities throughout the Greek world. Athens, Thebes, Magnesia, Macedonia: All are named after children of Zeus. But there is one individual who isn't happy about Zeus' _____. In the myth, his wife, Hera, has had enough.

3. Zeus awakes from a nap to find himself tied down, a prisoner in his own bed. It is the _____, a conspiracy carried out by the siblings he once saved.

4. The god revolt was the greatest threat that Zeus ever faced. There was never any sense that mortals could challenge his power, but the _____ really could have defeated him.

5. But just when all seems lost, help comes in the form of an old ally: the hundred-handers. When they hear Zeus is in trouble, they _____, breaking his chains as the Olympians run for cover.

6. His wife, Hera, is sentenced to hang from the sky by golden chains.

His son Apollo and brother Poseidon are _____. They are ordered to build one of the ancient world's most iconic monuments: the massive walls of Troy.

IV. Discuss the following questions based on your watching in *Exercise III*.

1. Why was Zeus depicted as a man with a lot of children?
2. What was implied in this story about woman's status in family and society in ancient Greece?

Cultural Exploration

Read the following passage on *Anthropomorphism* and finish the tasks.

In religion and mythology, anthropomorphism is the perception of a divine being or beings in human form, or the recognition of human qualities in these beings.

Ancient mythologies frequently represented the divine as deities with human forms and qualities. They resemble human beings not only in appearance and personality; they exhibited many human behaviours that were used to explain natural phenomena, creation, and historical events. The deities fell in love, married, had children, fought battles, wielded weapons, and rode horses and chariots. They feasted on special foods, and sometimes required sacrifices of food, beverage, and sacred objects to be made by human beings. Some anthropomorphic deities represented specific human concepts, such as love, war, fertility, beauty, or the seasons. Anthropomorphic deities exhibited human qualities such as beauty, wisdom, and power, and sometimes human weaknesses such as greed, hatred, jealousy, and uncontrollable anger. Greek deities such as Zeus and Apollo often were depicted in human form exhibiting both commendable and despicable human traits.

(https://en.wikipedia.org/wiki/Anthropomorphism)

Task 1. What is your understanding of anthropomorphism? Please use some mythical figures you have known to illustrate the term.

Task 2. Greek gods are often portrayed as quite emotional. The author of the following excerpt gave her ideas on this feature. Do you agree or disagree with the author? Please give more specific information to support or reject the author's ideas.

The gods that they (some ancient writers) portray are both kind and cruel; they are in fact capricious. This to me seems more realistic, for this is what matches our experience of nature, not just the nature outside ourselves, but also our own nature, our un-chosen instinctual nature.

— *Being human when surrounded by Greek gods*, by M. J. Lee

Task 3. It is often believed that the outside surroundings may help to shape one's character. Ancient Chinese and Greeks lived in places with different geographic features, and experienced different social and economic development. Do you think the different features in nature (as *outside ourselves and also our instinctual nature* mentioned above) contribute to the differences in gods' characters between the two cultures? Please give more specific information to support your ideas.

Further Reading

The Underworld

The underworld was hidden in the earth. It was the kingdom of the dead and ruled over by Hades. The underworld was a place where the souls of humans found their resting places. For most, life in the underworld was not particularly unpleasant. It was rather like a miserable dream, full of shadows, without sunlight or hope. It was a joyless place where the dead slowly faded into nothingness.

The deepest region was called Tartarus. It was a place of punishment for the mortal who committed the worse sins or crimes. Tartarus also served as a prison for the Titans and monsters.

The underworld was surrounded by a series of rivers. Once across the rivers, a gate formed the entrance to the kingdom. Cerberus, a three-headed dog, guarded the gate, and kept the living and the dead apart. Cerberus had only allowed few of the living to pass through the gate of Hades: Heracles, Theseus, Orpheus, Aeneas and Psyche.

Upon death a soul was led by Hermes to the entrance of the underworld and the ferry to cross the river. There was a single ferry, run by Charon, to take the souls across the river. Only those who could pay the fare, with coins placed on their lips when buried, received passage. The rest were trapped between two worlds.

The souls then entered through the gate. Cerberus would allow all to enter, but none to leave. The souls then appear before a *panel*(小组) of three judges. The very good went to the Elysian Fields, the home of the blessed afterlife. Others were singled out for special treatment.

Charon, son of Erebus and Nyx, was a god in the underworld. He required the fare of a coin from each shade, to ferry the dead across. It was Greek custom to put a coin in the dead before burial. The others, who couldn't pay, would wander restlessly for over hundred years before being allowed across. Few passed Charon without proper burial.

In some exceptional cases, the livings were also allowed to cross. Psyche paid Charon to ferry her across Styx. Heracles got away from paying Charon by threatening the ferryman. Orpheus had also got a free ride because of his enchanting music. (372 words)

Answer the following questions briefly.

1. According to Greek myths, do the underworld and Tartarus mean the same?

2. Why was a proper burial of the dead an important ritual for the Greeks?

UNIT 3

Stories in Homer's Epics

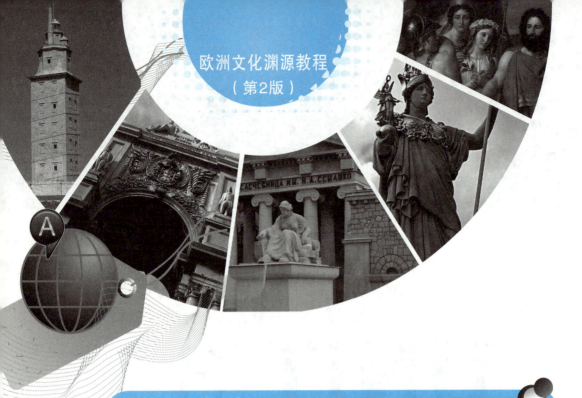

In this unit, you are going to
- identify the major characters in the Trojan war;
- explain the causes of the Trojan War;
- describe pictures pertaining to the return stories of Odysseus;
- write an assignment summary;
- expand your vocabulary through collocations.

Pre-information

I. Listen to the following passage on *Homer's Epics* and fill in the blanks with the words you hear.

Homer was probably born in the 8th century B.C. somewhere along the ____1____ of Asia Minor. He was Greek. At some point after his death he started ____2____ as blind. The two most famous epic poems ever written, the *Iliad* and the *Odyssey*, are both ____3____ to him.

The *Iliad* tells stories during the final year of the Trojan War featured with Achilles and the Trojan horse. Achilles was a very ____4____ character, and was destined to die in the war. The *Odyssey*, also set at the end of the Trojan War, is about Odysseus known as Ulysses in Roman myths. After fighting in the war, Odysseus tried to return home to his wife. When he finally passed _____5_____ mythical creatures, he returned home, punished everyone who had been against him, and was _____6_____ his family.

▶II. Listen to the sentences and fill in the blanks with the words you hear. Then work out the meaning of each sentence with a partner.

1. The black gold in the Middle East seems to be _____ discord since many countries are involved in war to fight for it.

2. He is always buying you expensive clothes. I'm afraid they are _____ for you.

3. We will need to ensure that those same technological innovations that provide advantage do not become our Achilles' _____.

4. It is not proper that people always attribute the fall of a country to _____ of Troy.

5. "No way for me to _____ Circe's wand," he shouted at his girlfriend.

6. Stop complaining! How lucky for you to marry a Penelope to share all _____ in life, which is the sweet dream for most men.

7. Honey, won't you finish this job quickly? You are not _____ a Penelope's web, are you?

8. Unlike other films of that era, *A Space Odyssey* showed _____ as a silent place, rather than as a hotbed of deafening explosions

Stories

I. Listen to the story of *Origin of the Trojan War* and fill in the blanks with the words you hear.

The Trojan War has its roots in the marriage between Peleus and Thetis, a sea-goddess. Peleus and Thetis had not invited Eris, the goddess of ***discord***, to their marriage, and the outraged goddess stormed into ____1____ and threw a golden apple onto the floor. The apple belonged to, Eris said, whoever was the fairest. Hera, Athena, and Aphrodite each reached for the apple. Zeus proclaimed that Paris would act as the judge.

Paris was the son of Priam, King of Troy. As his mother dreamed at his birth that he was bearing a fire brand, the baby was regarded as signifying ____2____. To save the kingdom from possible disaster, the parents had the helpless infant left on top of Mt. Ida to die. However, he survived his ill fate. Brought up by a herdsman, he became a strong and handsome lad.

Hermes went to Paris, and Paris agreed to ____3____. When Paris ***grazed*** his sheep on the mountain side one day, he found the three goddesses standing in front of him. Hera promised him power, Athena promised him wealth, and Aphrodite promised him ____4____ in the world. Moved by his primitive instinct, Paris chose Aphrodite, who promised him that Helen, wife of Menelaus, would be his wife. Guided by Aphrodite, Paris then went down the mountain and took part in ____5____ held in Troy. There, he was recognized by the aged King and Queen and was warmly welcomed back to their palace. Later, He went to Greece as the head of a great fleet. In Sparta, Menelaus, husband of Helen, treated Paris ____6____. However, when Menelaus left Sparta to go to a funeral, Paris abducted Helen (who perhaps went willingly) to Troy. In Troy, Helen and Paris were married. (311 words)

I. Answer the following questions briefly after your first reading.

1. Why did Thetis dip her baby in the river of Styx?
2. Who was the peddler appearing in the palace of Scyros? Why was he there?

II. Decide whether the following statements are TRUE or FALSE after your second reading.

_____ 1. Achilles determined to attack Troy and win Helen back.

_____ 2. As the heel by which the sea goddess held the baby boy was dry, it became the one mortal spot in the whole body of Achilles.

_____ 3. While most of the ladies stared at the silks and veils, Achilles eagerly grabbed the sword and joyfully played with it.

_____ 4. Zeus didn't show any sympathy for both sides in the war.

Gathering of Forces

Helen, whose parents were believed to be Zeus and the queen of Sparta, was married to Menelaus. Menelaus later succeeded to the throne of Sparta.

To *avenge* the insult of Helen being captured by Paris to Troy, Menelaus determined to attack Troy and win his wife back. He *summoned* all the kings and princes in Greece, calling them to observe their *oaths* to protect Helen and *retrieve* her from Troy.

On the Greek side, Agamemnon, brother of Menelaus and king of Mycenae, was the leader of all the Greek troops. Other famous heroes were Achilles and his close friend Patroclus, Ajax, and Odysseus. At first, Odysseus, king of Ithaca, avoided being enrolled into the war by pretending to be mad while finally joined the Creek army after being seen through by the tactful Greek prince Palamedes.

Achilles was the son of Peleus, a brave *warrior*, and Thetis, a beautiful sea goddess. Thetis loved her son very much. When Achilles was still a baby, Thetis was shocked by a prophecy that her son would die in war. To save her son, the sea goddess dipped her baby in the waters of Styx which could protect the human body from the fire and sword. But as the heel by which she held him was dry, it became the one mortal spot in the whole body of Achilles. When fighters all over Greece came together and urgently took arms against Troy, a prophet *foretold* that Achilles was sure not to return from the war. Determined to keep her son from the disaster, Thetis sent young Achilles to the court of the king of Scyros, where he worked in disguise as one of the handmaids waiting on the princess of Scyros. For a time the trick worked. Messenger after messenger came, but all left without him. One day, a peddler appeared in the palace, bringing with him a wide variety of womanish small things. There was, however, also a sword among such goods. While most of the ladies stared at the silks and veils, one of them eagerly grabbed the sword and joyfully played with it. At this moment, the peddler threw off his disguise and came out with his true identity. The *artful* Odysseus had come to fetch the hero, and he had not laboured in vain.

On the Trojan side, there were Priam who was the king of Troy, his son Hector who was the leader of the Trojans and the greatest warrior of Troy, Paris, Aeneas who was a Trojan prince and son of Aphrodite, and various allies as well.

As for the gods on Mount Olympus, except for Zeus, who remained *detached* but showed sympathy for both sides, they also took their stands. Hera, Athena, Poseidon, Thetis, and Hephaestus helped the Greeks, while Aphrodite, Apollo, Artemis and Leto were on the side of the Trojans. Ares was the one without a clear stand, who fought for both sides and merely sought fun from the war. (495 words)

I. Match the major characters in the story with the proper information after your first reading.

1. Agamemnon   a. was brought up on the Mountain Ida.
2. Achilles   b. acted as the leader of the Greek Army.

3. Hector   c. thought of the idea of the Wooden Horse.
4. Paris   d. was the leader of the Trojans.
5. Odysseus   e. was shot dead by Paris on his ankle.

II. Fill in the blanks with the missing information after your second reading.

1. Achilles' friend Patroclus was killed by Hector because the former was in _____ in the battle.

2. Agamemnon was killed by _____ when he was back to Mycenae.

3. Trojans believed that _____ was sent by Athena, and they hauled it into their capital.

4. After narrowly escaping from the war, Aeneas, one of the Trojan princes, became the founder of _____.

The Sack of the City

The Greeks took up arms to *revenge* on the *abduction* of Helen. The Trojan war broke out.

As the Greek ships gathered at the port of Aulis, no favourable wind blew up. A prophet told the commander of the *expedition*, Agamemnon, that he had upset Artemis when he killed one of her sacred stags and boasted he was a better hunter than the goddess. As punishment, Artemis becalmed the Greek fleet and only the sacrifice of his eldest daughter Iphigenia would appease the goddess into granting a fair wind to Troy. Iphigenia was placed before the goddess' altar but Artemis took her away at the last minute, putting a red deer in her place. Afterwards, favourable wind blew and the Greek ships set sail for Troy. Agamemnon's wife Clytemnestra was greatly enraged at her husband's cruelty, which led to the death of Agamemnon after the war.

The war lasted ten years, during which both sides suffered the misfortunes of war. Greek soldiers were tired at the end of the ninth-year and wanted to go back home and were on the verge of mutiny. It was because of the army of Achilles that they were forced to stay. After one battle, Agamemnon fought with Achilles over a *captive* princess, Briseis,

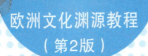

and took her away from Achilles. Enraged at the dishonour Agamemnon had inflicted upon him, Achilles refused to fight. His friend, Patroclus, borrowed his *armour* and went out to change the situation of war, but was killed by Hector, the eldest son of Priam and the leader of the Trojan army. Achilles, maddened with grief, swore to kill Hector in *revenge*. He was reconciled with Agamemnon and received Briseis back, untouched by Agamemnon. He received a new set of arms, forged by the god Hephaestus, and returned to the battlefield. He killed Hector and dragged his dead body three times around the walls of Troy. However, the gods, seeing that Achilles had killed too many of their children, decided that it was his time to die. Paris, who was guided by Apollo, shot Achilles dead with a poisoned arrow at his heel from behind. This was the only part of his body which was *vulnerable*, and Achilles died on the spot. Paris didn't live long either, for he was killed by a friend of Achilles'.

As Achilles left his *armour* to the bravest of the Greeks, there was a bitter struggle between its two worthy contestants. When the weapons were finally given to Odysseus by judge, Ajax took his own life for grief and shame.

Though the Greeks had won many important battles, they could not break down the walls of Troy. Seeking to gain entrance into Troy, clever Odysseus ordered a large wooden horse to be built. The Greeks hid many soldiers inside the wooden horse, and made believe to withdraw. Taken in by rumours that the horse had been sent by Athena, the overjoyed Trojans hauled it into their city. At night the hidden Greeks crawled out and threw the whole city into confusion. Troy was sacked.

King Priam was slain. The Queen and the princesses were all carried into slavery. Helen and Menelaus were on good terms again and disappeared in the west. Agamemnon went back to Mycenae, only to be murdered by his own wife and her lover. His son Orestes killed his mother and was pursued by the Furies. Odysseus went through untold hardships, struggling with winds and waves, before he reached his home island Ithaca to reunite with his faithful wife Penelope. Aeneas, one of the Trojan princes, after narrowly escaping death at Troy, wandered from land to land for a long time and became, in the end, the founder of the Roman race. (619 words)

UNIT 3

Story Four

I. Answer the following questions briefly after your first reading.

1. How many years did it take Odysseus to go back home?
2. Why did Odysseus tie each of his men to the bellies of the sheep?

II. Decide whether the following statements are TRUE or FALSE after your second reading.

_____ 1. The one-eyed giant on the island was the son of Hades.
_____ 2. Odysseus told the Cyclopes that his name was "Nobody".
_____ 3. Polyphemus was blinded by a sharpened tree trunk thrust by Odysseus and his men.
_____ 4. Polyphemus tried to strike Odysseus and his men with stones but failed.

Odysseus and Polyphemus

After the Trojan War, Odysseus set off for Ithaca, which turned out to be an **adventurous** journey covering a decade. During the ten years, he experienced all kinds of hardships as well as seductions, but finally he managed to arrive at his homeland and reunite with his family.

On one of the many adventures, Odysseus and his crew landed on the island of the Cyclopes after a heavy storm. Leaving his ship and some of his men on the seashore, Odysseus and his other men came to the cave of Polyphemus, one of the Cyclopes, on the island. Odysseus introduced them and asked Polyphemus for any help he could provide. Polyphemus *ridiculed* this idea and asked where Odysseus' ship was. The crafty leader lied and said it was wrecked and that they were the only survivors. The giant shut the men inside his cave, ate a few of them and talked with Odysseus, who told the Cyclops his name was "Nobody". To make Polyphemus unwary, Odysseus gave him a barrel of very strong, unwatered wine. When Polyphemus had fallen asleep Odysseus convinced the men to prepare a tree trunk, making it into a sharp weapon, which they put in the fireplace, and then thrust into

Polyphemus' only eye. Polyphemus' scream woke the other Cyclopes up, and they shouted to him what was wrong. Polyphemus then answered, "Nobody has blinded me", which made the other Cyclopes go back to bed, thinking Polyphemus had finally gone out of his wits. When Polyphemus had to let his herds *graze* in the *pasture* the following day, Odysseus tied each of his men to the bellies of the sheep, while he hanged on to the belly of a huge ram. The Cyclops passed his hands along the back of all the animals as he let them out, and detected nothing because their wool was long and thick, and he never thought that anyone would be tied up underneath their bellies. When they were free, Odysseus told his men to make haste and drive as many of the sheep and goats as they could to the ships. So they drove the sheep and goats down to the shore and hurried them into the ship, and began to row away.

After he learnt what had happened, Polyphemus was furious. He chased after Odysseus and his men, broke off huge rocks from the mountain and hurled them at Odysseus' ship with all his might. One of the rocks fell just behind the ship and almost sunk the ship under the sea, but it only sent Odysseus and his men further out of the reach of the Cyclops. Though Polyphemus hurled more rocks after Odysseus and his men, the rocks fell far behind in the sea and did Odysseus and his men no harm. Even when they had rowed a long way, they could still see Polyphemus standing on the high cliff, shaking his hands at them in rage and pain. Nevertheless, no one came to help him for all his shouting because he had told his friends that "Nobody" was doing him harm. (515 words)

Story Five

I. Match the major characters in the story with the proper information after your first reading.

1. Penelope   a. told Odysseus he was in Ithaca.
2. Athena   b. were on the verge of forcing Penelope to marry one of them.
3. Suitors   c. asked Odysseus to move the bed.
4. Telemachus   d. helped Odysseus kill those suitors.

UNIT 3

II. Fill in the blanks with the missing information after your second reading.

1. _____ had promised to make a decision whom she would marry when she had finished the death shroud of her father-in-law.

2. Odysseus was disguised as a beggar in _____.

3. Penelope showed _____ Odysseus' bow and said she would marry whoever could shoot through the holes of twelve axes in a row.

4. The bed in Penelope's bridal room was carved out of _____ twenty years ago.

Odysseus' Return and the Reunion

When Odysseus eventually was on the shore of an island, Athena came to him in the form of a young man and informed him he was in Ithaca. Odysseus made up a story about how he came to Ithaca. Athena good-naturedly told him she knew he was lying, and then revealed her identity and told him about the *suitors* in his palace. Those *suitors* were on the verge of forcing Odysseus' wife Penelope to a decision, since they discovered she had tricked them. She had promised to make a decision whom she would marry when she had finished the death shroud of her father-in-law. At night, she tore it up again, but a treacherous maid revealed this to the *suitors*.

Odysseus now went to the swineherd Eumaeus, and revealed his identity to him and Telemachus who was the son of Odysseus and Penelope. Together, they went to the palace. Odysseus was disguised as a beggar, and was beaten and *ridiculed* by the *suitors*. Only his old dog Argus recognized him and wagged its tail.

When Penelope looked after the beggar, she asked him if he had heard anything of her husband. Odysseus told her that her husband would be back very soon, but Penelope did not dare to believe him. Cleaning him, Odysseus' old nurse recognized a scar on his body, but he told her to be silent.

Penelope now put the *suitors* through a final test. She showed them Odysseus' bow and said she would marry whoever could shoot an arrow through the holes of twelve axes in a row. One after one they tried, but they couldn't even pull the string.

The beggar Odysseus asked to have a go, and under *ridicule* and laughter, he shot a perfect arrow through the twelve axes, then turned the bow against the *suitors* and started killing them with the help of Telemachus. After this, the treacherous maid was punished, and finally the palace was clear. Penelope still doubted the identity of Odysseus, and she suggested the moving of the bed in their bridal room. Odysseus responded that the bed couldn't be moved because he had carved the bed out of an olive tree trunk when they got married over twenty years ago, a secret only he would know. The couple was reunited. Odysseus then went to his old father, and they all lived happily ever after. (393 words)

Vocabulary Focus

I. Match the words from *Stories* part with their corresponding definitions.

1. vulnerable   a. a formal promise
2. pasture   b. a man who wants to marry a woman
3. retrieve   c. a field covered with grass or herbage and suitable for grazing by livestock
4. oath   d. a journey organized for a particular purpose
5. discord   e. capable of or susceptible to being wounded or hurt, as by a weapon
6. suitor   f. get or find back
7. revenge   g. protective covering made of metal and used in combat
8. graze   h. disagreement and argument between people
9. warrior   i. ask to come; gather or bring together
10. expedition   j. action taken in return for an injury or offense
11. armour   k. let feed in a field or pasture or meadow
12. summon   l. someone engaged in or experienced in warfare

II. Use the words from *Exercise I* to complete the sentences.

1. Suddenly we were _____ to the interview room.

2. We would rather there not be any _____ in our society today.

3. Regularly at daybreak, they drive their herds to the _____.

4. The attackers were said to be taking _____ on the 14-year-old, claiming he was a school bully.

5. Not long afterward a(n) _____ came who appeared to be very rich, and because the miller could find no fault with him, he promised his daughter to him.

6. He took a(n) _____ of loyalty to the government.

7. There is good grassland here for your cattle and horses to _____ on.

8. In Japan during the War of Dynasty in 1357, each _____ wore a yellow chrysanthemum as a pledge of courage.

9. He sent the United States Navy on its first foreign _____ to punish the states along the Mediterranean Sea.

10. The men were trying to _____ weapons left when the army abandoned the island.

11. The leading role in the film is costumed in medieval _____.

12. People with high blood pressure are especially _____ to diabetes.

III. Choose the italicized words from *Stories* part to complete the table.

Verb	Noun	Adjective	Noun (Person)	Antonym
	artfulness	1_____		
2_____	detachment	detached		attach
3_____	foretelling		foreteller	
abduct	4_____	abductive	abductor	
	adventure	5_____	adventurer	
6_____	ridicule	ridiculous		
7_____	avengement		avenger	
capture	capture	8_____	capturer	

67

IV. Use the words in the table from *Exercise III* to complete the sentences.

1. "This sort of thing happens, and I take it in a rather _____ way," she said.

2. He's not very _____, he says, and needs to be pushed to try new things.

3. Some politicians have realized that there are more _____ ways of subduing people than shooting or jailing them.

4. But the new movie *Captain America: The First* _____, from Marvel and Paramount, is looking like it might struggle for an audience.

5. It's not often that one can _____ future, but I think we can in this case.

6. Richard was finally released on February 4, one year and six weeks after he'd been taken _____.

7. Even with such security measures, Rena Jones probably isn't alone in her fear that someone could still _____ a baby inside a hospital.

8. It is _____ to suggest we are having a romance.

Vocabulary Development
Collocations (1)
Introduction

A collocation is two or more words that often go together, for example, gain entrance (Para. 5, Line 2) in the story three of *The Sack of the City*. Combinations like this just sound "right" to native English speakers, who use them all the time. On the other hand, other combinations may be unnatural and just sound "wrong". Look at these examples:

Natural English	Unnatural English
the fast train	the quick train
fast food	quick food
a quick shower	a fast shower
a quick meal	a fast meal

UNIT 3

When you use collocations:
- Your language will be more natural and more easily understood.
- You will have alternative and richer ways of expressing yourself.
- It is easier for our brains to remember and use language in chunks or blocks rather than as single words.

Now complete the sentences with a suitable word from the box.

> observe   hard   heavy   catch   start   strong
> terribly   gain   vitally   deep   fully   wide

1. When I went into the children's room, the boys were both fast asleep, but Oliver was _____ awake, reading the Little Prince story.
2. Tom had to work into the _____ night to earn a living.
3. I'm sure he is _____ aware of the problem.
4. It's _____ important that we finish this work by the end of the week.
5. We are _____ sorry we are late, but we missed the bus and had to wait ages for another one.
6. We carried the carton of books up to the fourth floor, and it was very _____ work.
7. Seeking to _____ entrance into Troy, clever Odysseus ordered a large wooden horse to be built.
8. I think they want to get married and _____ a family.
9. To make Polyphemus unwary, Odysseus gave him a barrel of very _____, unwatered wine.
10. He summoned all the kings and princes in Greece, calling them to _____ their oaths to protect Helen and retrieve her from Troy.
11. Odysseus and his crew landed on the island of the Cyclopes after a _____ storm.
12. The song was so beautiful that it made me _____ my breath.

Speaking
Describing a Picture

Language tips for you to describe a picture:

1. What is in the picture?

First check the title and the author of the picture. If there is not a title or author of the picture, try to figure out the central theme of the picture.

… a painting by … (author)

It's called … (title or topic)

It was painted … (year of painting)

In the picture, I can see …

There is / There are …

There isn't a / There aren't any …

2. What can you see?

In the middle of …

On the left/right …

At the top/bottom …

In the top left/right corner …

In the bottom left/right corner …

At the back …

3. Who is doing what?

1) use people's positions

　　e.g.: The women in front of the mirror are …

2) use people's clothes

　　e.g.: The woman in grey dress is fixing her hairs.

　　　　The woman who is wearing a grey dress is fixing her hairs.

3) use people's physical appearance

　　e.g.: The tall, slim man with a moustache is …

　　　　The woman with ginger hair and painted lips is …

4. If something isn't clear:

It looks like a …

It might be a …

He could be doing …

Maybe it's a …

UNIT 3

Now read the following episodes from Odysseus' journey back home and match each episode with its picture. Then describe the pictures to your partner.

a. _____

b. _____

c. _____

Episode 1: Circe

Circe was a beautiful enchantress and dwelled in luxury upon an island where one day Odysseus' sole remaining ship landed. Upon landing, Odysseus sent some of the crew members to search the island. When they came to the grant mansion of Circe, she was more than happy to welcome them into her home, and all but one, who feared trickery, did not enter. Circe prepared a delicious meal for them, adding to it a potion to cause them to forget their homeland. Once they have partaken, she struck them with her magic wand, causing them to be transformed into swine. Meanwhile, the one member of the search party who did not enter Circe's castle became alarmed when his companions did not return, so he rushed back to Odysseus to report. Odysseus immediately set off with a sword in hand for Circe's castle to try and retrieve his men. On his way there he was intercepted by the god Hermes who warned him of Circe's magic and gave Odysseus a herbal antidote to her potion. Odysseus followed Hermes' instructions, and Circe became obsessed with the man able to resist her spells and charms. Odysseus convinced her to restore his men to human form, and he and his entire crew spent a full year banqueting as Circe's pampered guests. At the end of a year, Odysseus' men forced him to leave this comfortable existence, at which point Circe gave him advice, provisions and help to see him safely on his way. (249 words)

Episode 2: Sirens

Sirens were terrible creatures with birds' bodies and ugly women's heads. They had the power of charming all by their songs so that sailors were impelled to cast themselves into the sea to destruction. Circe directed Odysseus to stop the ears of his seamen with wax so that they should not hear the strain. She also told Odysseus to have himself bound to the mast and to enjoin his people, whatever he might say or do, by no means to release him until they should have passed the Sirens' island. Odysseus obeyed these directions. As they approached the Sirens' island, the sea was calm, and over the waters came notes of music so ravishing and attractive that Odysseus struggled to get loose and, by cries and signs to his people, begged to be released; but they, obedient to his previous orders, sprang forward and bound him still faster. They held on their course, and the music grew fainter till it ceased to be heard, when with joy Odysseus gave his companions the signal to unseal their ears; and they relieved him from his bonds. It is said that one of the Sirens, Parthenope, in grief at the escape of Odysseus drowned herself. Her body was cast up on the Italian shore where now stands the city of Naples, in early times called by the Siren's name. (226 words)

Episode 3: Aeolus

Aeolus was appointed as regent or keeper of the winds by the gods. The mythical island of Aeolia was hollow inside and its numerous caves were the holding areas for the storm winds. It is said that the island floated freely and was surrounded by a wall of bronze, presumably to contain the winds, and Aeolus would release them according to the gods' requests or his own wishes.

In his struggle to make his way home to his wife, Odysseus was lost at sea. He and his crew landed on Aeolus' island. Aeolus showed them hospitality for one month and was quite sympathetic to their plight. To help them, he confined all unfavourable or adverse winds in a bag and gifted Odysseus and his men the favourable west wind, which would safely carry them home. But on board, while Odysseus was asleep, his sailors suspected him of hoarding riches in the bag and opened it out of curiosity. The strong and uncontrollable storm winds were unleashed. They melded together to form a powerful storm and took Odysseus' ship right back to Aeolus' island. On meeting Odysseus for the second time, Aeolus regarded it as a sign of the will of the gods and understood Odysseus was hated by the gods, especially Poseidon who hated him for defeating his son Polyphemus. So, Aeolus refused to help them. Instead he advised them to leave the island and never return. (237 words)

Writing
Assignment Summary (2)
A Complete Essay

Since many of the summaries you write will be woven into your own original text, it is very important to identify at least the source author, if not the title as well when you write a complete assignment summary. Most summaries will have a sentence near the beginning that contains two elements: the source and a main idea. The following is a sample summary format.

Author Tag

You need to start your summary by telling the name of the article and the author. Here are three examples of how to do that. Pay close attention to the punctuation.

In "How the Civil War Began", historian John Jones explains...

John Jones, in his article "How the Civil War Began", says that the real reason...

"How the Civil War Began" by historian John Jones, describes...

In more academic writing, writers would start in the following ways:

According to Boskin (2004), ...

Young and Song's 2004 paper on fluoridation discusses...

Bernstein (2004) states /claims/argues/maintains ...

First Sentence of Summary

Along with including the author tag, the first sentence of the summary should be the main point of the article. It should answer the question: What is this essay about?

Example:

In "How the Civil War Began" by John Jones, the author argues that the real reason for the start of the Civil War was not slavery, as many believe, but instead the clash of cultures and greed for cash.

Rest of Summary

The rest of your summary is going to give the reasons and evidence for that main statement. In other words, what is the main point the writer is trying to make and what are the supporting ideas he uses to prove the point? Does the author bring up any ideas he disagrees with? How does he refute those ideas? Remember you should always try to use your own words, except for technical terms, and make sure the summary reads smoothly by using enough transition devices and supporting details. It is not proper to give your comments in the summary as a conclusion. The comments or analysis could serve as a separate part in a thesis as required.

Limiting Children's Media Diet
(Original Article)

Parents not only refer their child's physical ailments to doctors but lately, the child's behavioral problems as well. Riding on this trend, the American Academy of Paediatrics (AAP) has recommended that doctors, during routine medical check-ups, inquire about children's use of the media. This will go a long way in helping to identify patterns that can threaten the emotional and physical health of the child.

Many times parents have received complaints from the school about their child's aggressive behavior. Often, this has been referred to the family physician rather than the behavioral psychologist. Says a doctor at the AAP, "You look at the history and then note that the child has not only been sitting in front of the TV for hours, watching violent shows but also playing aggressive computer games. At the least, this is something to start with." Says another, "The child could be modeling violent behavior and the parents are unaware of it."

Another related problem is obesity. This problem troubles many parents. After talking to the child, the doctor discovers that the child has similarly spent hours watching TV and video and not getting sufficient exercise. "It's another way where media habits can affect health," says the doctor.

The AAP recommends that two hours of quality TV or video shows a day for older children is sufficient. However, as far as toddlers below two are concerned, the AAP recommends that they should not be allowed to watch any TV. Excessive and indiscriminate media viewing can lead to other side effects and these include repeated aggression with peers or adults, poor grades, frequent nightmares, increased eating of unhealthy foods; and later, smoking, drinking and drug use.

Critics on the other hand are quick to point out that adults should cultivate an overview of parenting rather than attack one aspect: the media. At present, parents seem to be caught up with the material pursuits of life to the extent that they are unable to find sufficient time for other priorities in life. These critics say that if parents could only take stock of the situation and sort out their priorities, then there is a strong likelihood that they would spend more time with their children, supervise them, and watch over their viewing habits.

It is an undeniable fact that much lies in the hands of parents. Although the media has a responsible role to play, the home plays an overall important role in providing the right foundations in life for a child. (414 words)

Summary

In "Limiting Children's Media Diet", the author states that children's use of the media leads to their growing behavioral problems. One problem is the aggressive behavior resulting from TV programs and violent video games. The other is obesity because of lack of exercise. It is suggested in the article that two hours of quality TV and video viewing are proper for older children and none for children below two. Besides, parents should play an important role by spending more time with their children and supervising their viewing habits. (88 words)

Read the sample summary and answer the following questions:
1. Can you find the author tag?
2. Where is the general idea of this summary?
3. How many transitional words are used?
4. Are there any of the writer's comments?

Some notes on Plagiarism:
Plagiarism is best defined as a deliberate activity—as the conscious copying from the work of others. Of course, borrowing the words and phrases of the original text when writing a summary can be a useful language learning strategy. However, there is a divide between plagiarism

and quotation. The following are some approaches to writing, beginning with a plagiarizing approach and ending with an acceptable quoting technique. Where does plagiarism stop?

1) Copying a paragraph as it is from the source without any acknowledgment.

2) Copying a paragraph making only small changes, such as replacing a few verbs or adjectives with synonyms.

3) Cutting and pasting a paragraph by using the sentences of the original but leaving one or two out, or by putting one or two sentences in different order.

4) Composing a paragraph by taking short standard phrases from a number of sources and putting them together with some words of your own.

5) Paraphrasing a paragraph by rewriting with substantial changes in language and organization, amount of detail and examples.

6) Quoting a paragraph by placing it in block format with the source cited.

In fact, only the last two approaches would produce acceptable original work.

Now read the following adaptation of *Heinrich Schliemann and the Discovery of Troy* and write a summary by finishing the following steps.

Step 1. Highlight the information that you think is significant and should be included in a summary.

Step 2. Briefly explain why you think the highlighted information is important.

Step 3. Write down one-sentence summary for each section and choose the key supporting points for the topic.

Step 4. Write a complete summary of 120—150 words.

Heinrich Schliemann and the Discovery of Troy
(Adapted)

By K. Kris Hirst

According to legend, the finder of the true site of Troy was Heinrich Schliemann, adventurer, speaker of 15 languages, world traveler, and gifted amateur archaeologist. In his memoirs and books, Schliemann claimed that when he was eight, his father took him on his knee and told him the story of the Iliad, the forbidden love between Helen, wife of the King of Sparta, and Paris, son of Priam of Troy, and how their elopement resulted in a war that destroyed a civilization. That story, said Schliemann, awoke in him a hunger to search for the archaeological proof of the existence of Troy and Tiryns and Mycenae. In fact, he was so hungry that he went into business to make his fortune so he could afford the search. And after much consideration and study and investigation, on his own, he found the original site of Troy, at Hisarlik, a city in Turkey.

Ah, Romance!

The reality, according to David Traill's 1995 biography, *Schliemann of Troy: Treasure and Deceit*, is that most of this is romantic baloney. Schliemann was a brilliant, gregarious, enormously talented and extremely restless con man, who nevertheless changed the course of archaeology and focused interest in the sites and events of the Iliad and created widespread belief in their physical reality. During Schliemann's peripatetic travels around the world (he visited the Netherlands, Russia, England, France, Mexico, America, Greece, Egypt, Italy, India, Singapore, China, Japan, all before he was 45), he took trips to ancient monuments, stopped at universities to take classes and attend lectures in comparative literature and language, wrote reams of pages of diaries and travelogues, and made friends and enemies all over the world. How he afforded such traveling may be attributed to either his business acumen or his penchant for fraud; probably a bit of both.

In 1868, at the age of 46, Schliemann took up archaeology. There is no doubt that before that Schliemann had been interested in archaeology, particularly the history of the Trojan War, but it had always been subsidiary to his interest in languages and literature. But in June of 1868,

Schliemann spent three days at the excavations at Pompeii directed by the archaeologist Guiseppi Fiorelli. In July, he visited Mount Aetos, considered then the site of the palace of Odysseus, and there Schliemann dug his first excavation pit. In that pit, or perhaps purchased locally, Schliemann obtained either 5 or 20 small vases containing cremated remains. The fuzziness is a deliberate obfuscation on Schliemann's part, not the first nor the last time that Schliemann would fudge the details in his archaeological investigations.

Three Candidates for Troy

At the time Schlieman's interest was stirred by archaeology and Homer, there were three candidates for the location of Homer's Troy. The popular choice of the day was Bunarbashi (also spelled Pinarbasi) and the accompanying acropolis of Balli-Dagh; Hisarlik was favored by the ancient writers and a small minority of scholars; and Alexandrian Troas, since determined to be too recent to be Homeric Troy, was a distant third. Schliemann excavated at Bunarbashi during the summer of 1868 and visited the Troad and Hisarlik, apparently unaware of the standing of Hisarlik until, at the end of the summer he dropped in on the archaeologist Frank Calvert. Calvert, a British archaeologist, was among the decided minority among scholars; he believed that Hisarlik was the site of Homeric Troy, but had had difficulty convincing the British Museum to support his excavations. He had put trenches into Hisarlik in 1865 and found enough evidence to convince himself that he had found the correct site. Calvert recognized that Schliemann had the money and chutzpah to get the additional funding and permits to dig at Hisarlik. Calvert spilt his guts, beginning a partnership he would learn to regret.

Schliemann returned to Paris in the fall of 1868 and spent six months becoming an expert on Troy and Mycenae, writing a book of his recent travels, and writing numerous letters to Calvert, asking him where he thought the best place to dig might be, and what sort of equipment he might need to excavate at Hisarlik. In 1870 Schliemann began excavations at Hisarlik, under the permit Frank Calvert had obtained for him, and with members of Calvert's crew. But never, in any of Schliemann's writings, did he ever admit that Calvert did anything more than agree with Schliemann's theories of the location of Homer's Troy, born on that day when his father sat him on his knee. (746 words)

UNIT 3

Further Development

I. Fill in the blanks with the proper forms of the words from the box.

> lose   seduce   immortal   furious   exhaust   reluctant

In the island Ogygia, Calypso welcomed the ____1____ Greek hero, Odysseus, who was drifted for nine days in the open sea after ____2____ his ship and his army to the monsters of Italy and Sicily when coming back home from Troy.

Mythical Calypso fell for Odysseus and wanted to make him her ____3____ husband and give him the eternal youth. But Odysseus didn't accept her generosity—he was dreaming about going back to his Ithaca and his wife. Calypso was so much in love with him that despite his refusal of her offers, she kept hoping and ____4____ Odysseus. Eventually, she made him her lover.

When Poseidon was away, Athena took the opportunity to beg Zeus to help Odysseus. The god then sent Hermes to Calypso with a message to let Odysseus go. Calypso was ____5____, pointing out that male gods were allowed to take mortal lovers while female ones were not. But she could not defy Zeus, so ____6____ she agreed and informed Odysseus of the news. Later, Calypso not only helped Odysseus build the boat that would take him back to his wife and his Ithaca, but also provided enough food and wine for the long journey, and good winds. Finally, Odysseus left the island of Ogygia and was on his sailing back home again.

II. Fill in the blanks and discuss the negative and positive implications of Calypso in comparison with Penelope.

Character	Positive implication	Negative implication
Penelope	e.g.: faithful wife	/
Calypso		

III. Watch the video clip on *the City of Troy* and write down the major information by answering the following questions.

Note: The Hittites were a Bronze Age Indo-European speaking people. They established a kingdom in western Asia, comprising the majority of the territory of the present-day Turkey, in the 18th century B.C.

1. What do the tablets in the program show?
2. What was the real war based on?
3. What did the super powers fight for?

IV. Present your opinions on the Trojan War in small groups.

You believe and why	You doubt and why
e.g.: I believe there was Helen in history because she was recorded in some history books.	e.g.: I doubt the love story between Helen and Paris since it was only found in legend.

UNIT 3

Cultural Exploration

Read the following passage on *Legend and History* and finish the tasks.

The story of the Trojan War — the Bronze Age conflict between the kingdoms of Troy and Mycenaean Greece — straddles the history and mythology of ancient Greece and inspired the greatest writers of ancient times, from Homer, Herodotus and Sophocles to Virgil. Since the 19th-century rediscovery of the site of Troy in what is now western Turkey, archaeologists have uncovered increasing evidence of a kingdom that peaked and may have been destroyed around 1,180 B.C. — perhaps forming the basis for the tales recounted by Homer some 400 years later in the *Iliad* and the *Odyssey*. Legend and history seem woven together in the Trojan War.

(https://www.history.com/topics/ancient-history/trojan-war)

Task 1. Work with a partner on the definition of legend and history respectively and list the similarities and differences between them.

Task 2. Search online for one Chinese legend with some evidence and exchange your findings with a partner.

Task 3. "There are many legends about Xu Fu who sailed away from Mt. Dapeng to the east in China. However, legends cannot replace the history because history must be proved by written documents and historical relics. Legends are nothing more than made-up stories based on historical people and events and passed down orally." (Wang Taidong, 1998) Do you agree with the point in the excerpt? Please use evidence to support your ideas.

Further Reading

Passage One

Helen

Helen of Sparta was perhaps the most inspiring woman in all literature, ancient and modern. A whole war was fought over her, a war that lasted for ten years and saw one thousand ships launched. Helen was believed to be initially the chief mother-goddess worshipped through the area. Then, she was replaced by Zeus, and her role was demoted and "survived" through mythology only to the most beautiful woman of the world.

According to later version of Greek mythology, Helen was the daughter of Zeus and Leda, the wife of King Tyndareus of Sparta. Zeus seduced Leda in the guise of a swan. Their consummation, on the same night as Leda lay with her husband Tyndareus, resulted in two eggs, from which hatched Helen and her three siblings.

When it was time for Helen to marry, many Greek kings and princes came to seek her hand or sent *emissaries*（使者）to do so on their behalf. Among the contenders were Odysseus, Menestheus, Ajax the Great, Patroclus and Idomeneus, but the favourite was Menelaus who did not come in person but was represented by his brother Agamemnon. All but Odysseus brought many and rich gifts with them.

Tyndareus would accept none of the gifts, nor would he send any of the suitors away for fear of offending them and giving grounds for a quarrel. Odysseus promised to solve the problem in a satisfactory manner if Tyndareus would support him in his courting of Penelope, the daughter of Tyndareus' brother. Tyndareus readily agreed and Odysseus proposed that, before the decision was made, all the suitors should swear a most solemn oath to defend the chosen husband against whoever should quarrel with him. This *stratagem*（谋略）succeeded, and Helen and Menelaus were married. Following Tyndareus' death, Menelaus became the king of

Sparta because the only male heirs, Castor and Polydeuces, had died, and were put in the sky by Zeus as the constellation Gemini.

Some years later, Paris, a Trojan prince came to Sparta to marry Helen, whom he had been promised by Aphrodite after he had chosen her as the most beautiful of the goddesses, earning the wrath of Athena and Hera. Helen fell in love with him, as Aphrodite had promised, willingly leaving behind Menelaus to be with her new lover.

When he discovered that his wife was missing, Menelaus called upon all the other suitors to fulfill their oaths, thus beginning the Trojan War. Virtually all of Greece took part, either attacking Troy with Menelaus or defending it from them. (426 words)

Answer the following questions briefly.

1. Why wouldn't Helen's father simply send her suitors away?
2. What did Odysseus suggest to Tyndareus?
3. Why did Helen's suitors join the war?

Passage Two

Odysseus Joined the War

Odysseus was considered the cleverest hero, and not surprisingly, he was protected by Athena, goddess of wisdom. He often found solutions for important problems: He was amongst Helen's suitors, but to avoid war between them, he made them all swear to respect Helen's decision, and to protect whoever she chose. Odysseus married Helen's cousin Penelope, and they had a son, Telemachus.

It had been prophesied that Odysseus would not return for a long time if he joined the Greek army against Troy, so he decided to play crazy when Palamedes came to Ithaca to enroll him. He put on torn clothes, and tried to sow the land with salt, while ploughing the fields with a goat and an ox. Palamedes then put the baby Telemachus in front of the *plough*（犁）which made Odysseus stop, revealing his *sanity*（精神健全）.

Odysseus played an important part during the Trojan War. When Achilles was killed, he held the Trojans back while Ajax carried the dead hero back to the camp. After the burial, it was decided that Odysseus but not Ajax should get Achilles' armour, and the latter committed suicide. (195 words)

Answer the following questions briefly.

1. Among the gods and goddesses, who was always a helper to Odysseus?

2. Whose suitor had Odysseus once been?

3. What did Odysseus do when Palamedes came to recruit him to the war?

UNIT 4
Greek Heroes and Other Legends

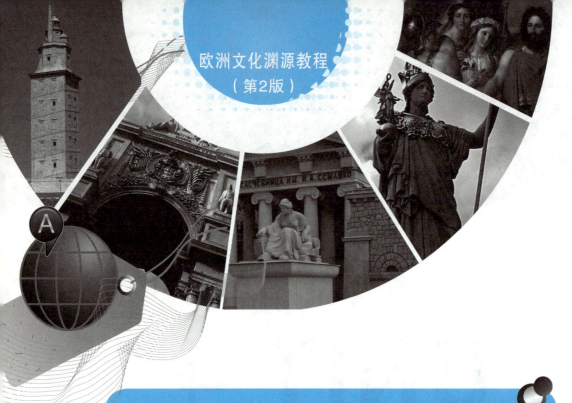

In this unit, you are going to
- identify the celebrated heroes in Greek myths;
- think critically on the well-known legends in Greek myths;
- orally compare and contrast two people;
- write a comparison and contrast essay on two people;
- expand your vocabulary through collocation.

Pre-information

I. Listen to the passage on *Greek Heroes and Other Legends* and fill in the blanks with the words you hear.

Greek myths are made up of stories not only of the gods and goddesses, but also of ____1____, who were often direct or indirect descendants of some gods or goddesses, or particular favorites of some deities, endowed with ____2____, and celebrated for their almost impossible exploits. And usually it was their destined fate to ____3____ and die an exceptionally heroic or tragic death. They all exhibited many symbolic attributes of heroism and ____4____ in fulfilling their tasks. Besides the stories of the gods and heroes, Greek myths are complemented with myriad fascinating legends on various themes: love, vanity, cunning, vengeance and punishment. Originally conceived to help early civilizations comprehend _____5_____ of an ancient world, these myths remain as compelling today as they were thousands of years ago.

II. Listen to the sentences and fill in the blanks with the words you hear. Then work out the meaning of each sentence with a partner.

1. The terrorist is the Hydra of our day popping around the globe without _____.

2. The stadium became an Augean stable after _____.

3. A Chinese market entry permit is a golden fleece for many _____.

4. Where shall we get an Ariadne's thread in _____?

5. Wherever he went, he _____ by preaching racial segregation.

6. The multimillionaire wondered, _____, if he truly had the Midas touch.

7. The young people were _____ by the Orphean singer.

8. The preparation of the _____ was a herculean task.

9. He's always buying his mother _____, and I'm beginning to wonder if he's got an Oedipus complex.

10. You have made mess of it by _____ that ambitious Phaeton.

Stories

Story One

▶ Decide whether the following statements are TRUE or FALSE after your reading.

_____ 1. Perseus was a Greek hero famous for the killing of Medusa, a nine-headed snake.

_____ 2. Perseus' father was Zeus, who impregnated Danae, Perseus' mother, in the form of a golden shower.

_____ 3. The grandfather of Perseus sent him and his mother away by locking them in a chest for fear that his throne would be taken away by Perseus.

_____ 4. Perseus was sent by Athena to bring back the head of Medusa.

_____ 5. Perseus killed Medusa with his eyes turning away so that he would not be turned to stone.

Perseus

Perseus was one of the most celebrated of the Greek heroes best known for his clever *decapitation* of Medusa, a look at whose head would turn people to stone. Perseus' mother was Danae, princess of Argos. An oracle told Danae's father that a child of Danae would kill him, so he did what he could to keep Danae from men, but he couldn't keep out Zeus in the form of a golden shower. After Danae gave birth, her father sent her and her son away, by locking them in a chest and putting it to sea. The tide washed them up on an island ruled by Polydectes.

When Perseus grew into a strong young man, Polydectes heard about Danae and tried to woo her. Polydectes thought Perseus a nuisance, so he sent Perseus on an impossible quest: to bring back the head of Medusa. Medusa was one of the three Gorgons, three snake-haired sisters whose appearance turned the beholder to stone. With the help of Athena and Hermes, Perseus obtained an invisible helm, a magical sword, and a pair of winged sandals. Athena warned him not to look directly at the Gorgon's face, but rather look at Medusa's reflection on the bronze shield which she gave him. When he finally found Medusa and her two sisters, the hero approached the sleeping Medusa invisibly, and beheaded her while watching her through the reflection of the shield, avoiding being turned to stone. When Medusa's sisters woke up and attacked him, he flew quickly away on his winged sandals.

On his way back to Greece, he spied Andromeda, an Ethiopian princess chained to the rocks as a sacrifice to a sea-monster. Perseus slew the monster, and rescued the girl, bringing her back to Greece as his bride. When Perseus came home, he found King Polydectes behaving badly, so he showed the king the very prize he had been asked to fetch, the head of Medusa. Inevitably, Polydectes was turned to stone. Perseus then travelled to his grandfather's kingdom to claim the throne. The old man fled, and was later accidentally killed by Perseus at some Games with an awry discus throw. (358 words)

▶ I. **Match the major characters in the story with the tasks in which they are involved after your first reading.**

1. Hippolyta   a. Task 11–Getting the fruit from the golden-apple tree
2. Augeas   b. Task 2–Overcoming the nine-headed snake
3. Hydra   c. Task 5–Cleaning the Augean Stables
4. Atlas   d. Task 1–Killing the Nemean lion
5. offspring of Typhon e. Task 9–Retrieving the belt of the queen of the Amazons

▶ II. **Fill in the blanks with the missing information after your second reading.**

1. Heracles was hated by _____, who sent a snake to him

when he was a baby in an attempt to _____.

2. Heracles was once invited by two women representing _____ and _____ respectively to make a choice.

3. Heracles was driven _____ by Hera, and in his madness, he killed his wife and their three children.

4. Eurystheus and _____ came up with 12 labours for Heracles to complete.

5. The Nemean lion was difficult to kill because _____.

6. Hydra was difficult to root out in that _____.

7. Heracles cleaned the Augean stables by _____.

Heracles and the Twelve Labours

Heracles, known to the Romans as Hercules, was the son of Zeus and the Mycenaean princess Alcmene, the granddaughter of Perseus. For some reason, Hera once nursed the infant by breast-feeding him. However, he drew with such force that Hera flung him down in pain, and a spurt of milk flew across the sky, forming the Milky Way.

Heracles, though bearing his name meaning "the glory of Hera", was hated and persecuted by his jealous stepmother Hera from the very start for the simple reason that he was the son of Zeus by another woman. When Heracles was around ten months old, Hera tried to destroy him by sending two terrible serpents to his cradle. Luckily, he was born with extraordinary strength and strangled both snakes, one in each hand.

Grown into a young man, Heracles was invited by two young women, representing Pleasure and Virtue respectively, to choose between the easy path of Pleasure and the rocky uphill path of Virtue. He chose the latter. Therefore, he was destined to carry out twelve labours before he became a god.

Eventually, he grew up to be a famed warrior. But then, Hera drove him temporarily insane, and he killed his wife and their three children. To expiate the crime, Heracles consulted the Oracle of Delphi. He was told to go to King Eurystheus of Mycenae and serve him for twelve years. King Eurystheus couldn't think of any tasks that might prove difficult for the mighty son of Zeus, so Hera came down from her palace on Olympus to help him. Working in joint efforts, the two came up with twelve tasks for Hera's mortal stepson to complete. These tasks are now known as the Twelve Labours of Heracles. The followings are some of his most famous tasks.

In his first task, Heracles strangled a horrible Nemean lion, which was the offspring of the terrible Typhon and whose pelt was proof against all weapons. It was then **depopulating** the area of Nemea. Heracles strangled the creature to death with his bare hands and used its **invincible** pelt as armour and its head as helmet.

The second task was to overcome the nine-headed snake known as Hydra. He attacked the snake with a sword and sickles, but no sooner was one head crushed than two or three more grew in its place. Heracles' cousin helped him out by burning the stumps of the heads after Heracles cut them off. Heracles dipped his arrows in the fatal blood after killing Hydra.

The fourth labour was to capture a wild boar that terrorized people around. It was in this adventure that Heracles somehow fatally wounded Chiron, King of the Centaurs, with one of his poisoned arrows, and the Centaur was finally made the constellation Centaur.

The fifth task of Heracles was to clean the stables of King Augeas in a single day. The stable housed thousands of cattle and had not been cleaned for many years. It spread a **pestilence** across the region. Instead of employing a shovel and a basket as Eurystheus imagined, Heracles **diverted** two rivers nearby so that they flew into the Augean stables and swept them clean. Heracles got the job done without getting dirty.

The seventh task was for Heracles to capture a Cretan savage bull. The bull was produced by the god of sea, Poseidon, but became furious later. He wrestled it to the ground despite its **scorching** flames.

The ninth labour was to retrieve the belt of the fierce Amazon warrior queen, Hippolyta. Hippolyta willingly gave her belt to Heracles, but Hera convinced the Amazons that Heracles was trying to take Hippolyta from them, so Heracles fought them off and returned with the belt.

The eleventh task was to get the fruit from the golden-apple tree, Mother Earth's wedding gift to Hera which was protected by Atlas' daughters. Heracles told Atlas that if Atlas would get the apples for him, he would carry the heavens for Atlas. When Atlas returned from his task, he didn't want to take the heavens back from Heracles. Heracles said that he needed a cushion for his shoulder, and asked if Atlas would mind taking back the heavens just long enough for him to fetch one. The Titan graciously agreed, and Heracles succeeded in tricking him into taking them back and strolled off.

In his other tasks, Heracles captured a hind with golden horns, destroyed the countless man-eating birds, subdued the four man-eating horses of Diomedes and the cattle of Geryon, and brought Cerberus, the three-headed watchdog of the underworld, to the upper world.

Eventually, after twelve years and completing the twelve tasks, Heracles was a free man. And because of his Twelve Labours, Heracles became a hero who had *transcended* human limitations through strength and patience and obtained immortality, becoming an example of steady fastness in *adversity*. After his physical death, he was accepted into the fold of the gods. He married Hebe, the goddess of Youth, and became the Porter of Heaven. (848 words)

Story Three

▶ Listen to the story of *Golden Fleece* and fill in the blanks with the words you hear.

Golden Fleece

The Golden Fleece was the treasure sought by Jason and the Argonauts. It originated in the following fashion. Phrixus and Helle were the children of King Athamas and the cloud goddess Nephele. After giving birth to the children, Nephele returned to the sky. When Athamas remarried, the children's stepmother, Ino, daughter of Cadmus, King of Thebes, ____1____ and plotted to get rid of them. She arranged to have seed corn roasted so that it ____2____. When the crop failed, messengers were sent to consult the oracle at Delphi, and Ino bribed the messengers into saying that the oracle ____3____ of Phrixus to restore fertility to the fields. The people of Greece, who feared starvation, convinced Athamas to kill Phrixus. Before Phrixus was sacrificed, however, Nephele sent a golden ram which ____4____ through the air.

Unfortunately, Helle fell into the Hellespont (which was named after her) and drowned, but Phrixus arrived safely at Colchis, where he married a daughter of King Aeetes. Phrixus sacrificed the ram to Zeus, and gave its pelt, the Golden Fleece to Aeetes. Aeetes placed the fleece in an oak tree, where it remained until _____5_____. (217 words)

I. Match the major characters in the story with the proper information after your first reading.

1. Jason   a. princess of Colchis
2. Pelias   b. king of Colchis
3. Aeetes   c. leader of the Argonauts
4. Medea   d. uncle of Jason

II. Fill in the blanks with the missing information after your second reading.

1. Jason was brought up by _____.
2. Pelias agreed to give the kingdom back to Jason if he could bring him _____.
3. The heroes who kept Jason's company in search of the Golden Fleece were known as the _____.
4. Aeetes was reluctant to give the fleece to Jason since a prophecy said he would rule as long as _____.
5. Jason slew the soldiers sprouting from the dragon's teeth after _____ and they started to attack against each other.
6. Medea killed Pelias by offering to _____.

Jason and the Golden Fleece

The story of Jason and the Golden Fleece is a classic hero's quest tale, in which the hero *embarks* on a sea voyage into an unknown world, with a great task to achieve. In the story, Jason was in search of a magical ram's fleece, which he had to find in order to reclaim his father's kingdom of

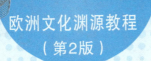

Iolcus from the usurper King Pelias.

According to legend, Jason was taken from his parents, and brought up in Thessaly by a centaur named Chiron, after his uncle, King Pelias, **usurped** the throne of Iolcus. At the age of 20, Jason set off to Iolcus and made a claim to the kingdom before King Pelias. The king replied, "If I am to give you the kingdom, first you must bring me the Fleece of the Golden Ram." Jason accepted the challenge and immediately started preparations by gathering volunteers and building the ship.

Jason's ship, the Argo, was named after its builder, Argus. Athena cut a beam from her father's oak, gave it the power of speech and prophecy, and fitted it into the ship's prow. The Argo began its journey with a crew of 50 known as the "Argonauts", who were a group of the most famous heroes, including Heracles, Orpheus, Theseus and a great many others. The Argonauts had encountered enormous obstacles before they finally reached the land of Colchis.

Once in Colchis, Jason asked King Aeetes to return the Golden Fleece. Remembering an old prophecy saying that he would rule as long as he possessed the Golden Fleece, Aeetes decided to destroy Jason. Aeetes pretended to agree to give Jason the Golden Fleece if Jason could perform a series of superhuman tasks. He had to yoke fire-breathing bulls, plough and sow a field with teeth from the dragon that used to guard the spring of Ares but was killed by Cadmus, and overcome the **phantom** warriors sprouting from the field. Jason would have never performed the difficult tasks without the help of Aeetes' daughter Medea, a famous sorceress and granddaughter of Helios. Eros had done his job by shooting at Medea's heart with an arrow and making her fall in love with Jason madly. After Jason had promised to marry her and take her to Greece, Medea gave him a magic ointment made from saffron that grew out of Prometheus' blood, with which Jason was to cover his body before he attacked the bulls. The ointment protected Jason from the bulls' fiery breath, and then he managed to yoke the bulls, plough the field, and sow the dragon's teeth. From the teeth, an army of armed men immediately sprouted, but Jason, as Medea had told him, threw a stone among them, and the men started to attack and kill each other. As they were paying no attention to Jason, he slew them easily.

However, Aeetes still refused to give Jason the Golden Fleece and threatened to burn the Argo and kill its crew. Medea, who was deep in love with Jason, took him to the place where the Golden Fleece was kept and helped him to take it away. When they hurried away with the Golden Fleece, Medea killed her half-brother Apsyrtus who chased them, and the Argonauts escaped.

After Apsyrtus had been killed, angered Zeus sent a storm to drive the Argo off course. The ship spoke and told Jason and Medea to go to Circe, Medea's aunt, for **purification**. They did as were told. The other adventures of the Argonauts on their way home were similar to those of Odysseus. They passed the island of the Sirens where they would have all died if Orpheus' song wasn't louder than the singing of the Sirens.

On his return to Iolcus, Jason discovered that King Pelias had killed his father, and his mother had died of grief. To revenge, Medea tricked Pelias by offering to rejuvenate him. She claimed that she had a way to make the old young again. To prove this, she took an old ram, put it in boiling water and turned it into a young lamb by using one of her charms. She then convinced Pelias' daughter to place Pelias in boiling water, which eventually led to his death.

After this terrible murder, Jason and Medea went into exile in Corinth. There they had two sons. But soon Jason decided to abandon Medea in order to fulfil his ambitions for power by marrying the princess of Corinth. Desperately, Medea killed the new bride with a poisoned robe and crown which burned the flesh from her body; the king died as well when he came to his daughter's rescue. Then Medea dreadfully killed her own sons by Jason before fleeing to Athens in her grandfather Helios' chariot. There, she married the old king Aegeus.

For the rest of his life, Jason wandered endlessly around Greece, being cursed by the Olympians for breaking his faith with Medea. One day when he was very old, he sat in the shade of the rotting Argo, weeping to think of his past glories, but was killed by the prow which fell suddenly. (851 words)

Story Five

▶ **I. Answer the following questions briefly after your first reading.**

    1. What was Theseus most famous for?
    2. How was Theseus recognized by his father?
    3. How did Theseus get out of the labyrinth?

▶ **II. Decide whether the following statements are TRUE or FALSE after your second reading.**

    _____ 1. Before Aegeus left for Athens, he left a pair of sandals and a sword under a huge rock.

    _____ 2. When Theseus arrived at Athens, Medea helped him to become the heir to Aegeus' throne.

    _____ 3. Minos demanded the tribute of seven maidens and seven youths every nine years to avenge the death of his son.

    _____ 4. Theseus was sent by his father to kill the Minotaur.

    _____ 5. The Aegean Sea was named after Aegeus, who, believing that his son had died, committed suicide by throwing himself into the sea.

Theseus

Theseus was a king of Athens famous for his triumph over numerous monsters, especially the Minotaur, which lived in a complicated labyrinth on the island of Crete. Theseus was the son of Aegeus, king of Athens, and Aethra. Aegeus, in his drunkenness, slept with Aethra and left for his home city of Athens the next day. As he left, he left a pair of sandals and a sword under a large rock; should Aethra bear a male child, she was to send him to Athens to claim his birthright as soon as he was old enough to lift the rock and retrieve the items.

Aethra gave birth to Theseus, who came of age and set off for Athens with the sword and sandals, encountering and defeating six murderous adversaries along the way. When Theseus reached Athens, Medea, the sorceress, had become the wife of Aegeus. She convinced the king to have the young man poisoned. Aegeus recognized Theseus' sword as Theseus was about to drink the poisoned wine and knocked the goblet from his lips at the last second. Theseus was acknowledged by his father, and became the heir to the throne.

Years before Theseus' arrival at Athens, a terrible misfortune had fallen upon the city. Minos, the ruler of Crete, lost his only son who was killed during a visit to Athens. To avenge the death of his son, Minos invaded the city and threatened to *demolish* it unless King Aegeus sent the tribute of seven maidens and seven youths to Crete every nine years. The Athenian victims were to be sacrificed to the Minotaur, a savage creature locked in a labyrinth with the head of a bull and body of a man.

When Theseus learned of the Minotaur and the sacrifice, he decided to end the tribute by killing the Minotaur. Theseus volunteered to go to Crete as one of the victims, promising Aegeus that his ship's black sail would be replaced with a white one if he was *victorious*.

In Crete, Ariadne, Minos' lovely daughter, fell in love with Theseus. She gave him a ball of thread and told him to tie one end of the wool to the entrance so that he would not get lost in the labyrinth. Theseus found the Minotaur and bashed it to death with his fist. He then led the other victims back to the entrance by rolling up the thread into a ball again. Ariadne then left Crete with Theseus. Unfortunately, she died on the way to Athens. Filled with grief over the death of Ariadne, Theseus forgot to switch the black sail with the white one. Aegeus, consequently, watching from afar, believed his son was dead and hurled himself into the sea, which was named the "Aegean" after him. (460 words)

Story Six

▶ **I. Match the major characters in the story with the proper information after your first reading. There may be more than one piece of information to each character.**

1. Laius   a. the person who was abandoned by his parents when he was a baby

2. Jocasta   b. the king of Thebes who was killed by his own son
3. Sphinx   c. the hero who was applauded king after solving a difficult riddle
4. Oedipus   d. the queen of Thebes
               e. the woman who hanged herself after learning that she had unwittingly married her own son
               f. a woman-headed monster

II. Decide whether the following statements are TRUE or FALSE after your second reading.

_____ 1. Oedipus was forsaken by his parents since it was prophesied that he would take the throne away from his father.

_____ 2. Oedipus was brought up in Corinth.

_____ 3. The king and queen of Corinth informed Oedipus of his being adopted after he grew up.

_____ 4. Oedipus left Corinth for Thebes in an attempt to find his real parents.

_____ 5. Oedipus killed his father Laius purposefully.

Oedipus

Oedipus was born to King Laius and Queen Jocasta of Thebes. A prophet warned Laius that the boy would grow up to murder his father and marry his mother. To thwart the prophecy, Laius ordered his loyal shepherd to abandon his newborn baby on the nearby mountain. In those days, it was not unusual to leave an unwanted or **defective** baby in the wilderness. To be extra-sure, the king had his baby's feet **pierced** and tied together.

The sympathetic shepherd, however, could not bring himself to do the evil deed. He then turned the baby over to the care of a fellow shepherd who happened to be the servant of the king of Corinth. The boy was given the name Oedipus. The king and queen of Corinth were childless, so they adopted the foundling. The prince had never doubted his parentage until one day a drunk mentioned his being adopted. Oedipus confronted his parents with the news, but they denied every word. Being troubled, Oedipus visited various oracles to find out whether he was really adopted.

All the oracles told him instead that he was destined to kill his father and marry his mother. The frightened young man decided to turn his back on Corinth and travel all the way to Thebes in his attempt to avoid the fate predicted by the oracle.

On his way to Thebes, Oedipus was involved in a quarrel with a man and killed him by accident, who turned out to be his father.

Soon the young man arrived in Thebes. Round about this time, the kingdom was *endangered* by a woman-headed monster, called Sphinx, who posed a riddle on all the travelers to Thebes. If the travelers were unable to answer her correctly, they would be killed and eaten. Unfortunately, no one knew the answer. The riddle was: "What animal walks on four legs in the morning, two legs at noon, and three legs in the evening?" Oedipus, however, quickly offered the answer: "Man who creeps in babyhood, walks upright in manhood, and supports his steps with a staff in old age." Sphinx was *astounded* to hear Oedipus' answer and then inexplicably killed herself by throwing herself into the sea, freeing Thebes from her harsh rule. The people of Thebes gratefully appointed Oedipus as their king and gave him the recently widowed Queen Jocasta's hand in marriage. He ruled well, and they had four children.

Many years after the marriage of Oedipus and Jocasta, a plague of *infertility* struck Thebes: crops no longer grew on the fields and women did not bear children. Oedipus asserted that he would end the pestilence. He sent a man to the Oracle at Delphi for guidance and the man came back with the message that the murderer of the former King Laius must be found and either be killed or exiled. In the search for the killer, the identity of Oedipus was disclosed. Eventually, Oedipus and Jocasta found out what had really happened. Jocasta hanged herself. Oedipus blinded himself so that he might not look on the sun again. He was driven out of the kingdom and wandered from one city to another. Finally at Athens at the signal of Zeus' thunder, he mysteriously ended his poor earthly life. (541words)

Vocabulary Focus

I. Match the words from *Stories* part with their corresponding definitions.

1. fiery   a. change the route or course
2. pierce   b. a ghostly appearing figure
3. transcend   c. go beyond
4. pestilence   d. like or suggestive of fire; burning strongly
5. phantom   e. epidemic disease
6. divert   f. penetrate or cut through with a sharp instrument
7. embark   g. a state of misfortune or affliction
8. astounded   h. overwhelmingly surprised or shocked
9. adversity   i. set out on
10. scorch   j. make very hot and dry; become burned or destroyed by fire
11. invincible   k. seize and take control without authority and possibly with force
12. usurp   l. incapable of being overcome or subdued

II. Use the words from *Exercise I* to complete the sentences.

1. She was _____ by his arrogance.
2. They vanished down the stairs like two _____.
3. He could never _____ his resentments and his complexes.
4. A helicopter crashed in a _____ explosion a few minutes after its take-off.
5. They decided to _____ that ship to rescue the passengers on the wrecked ship several miles away.
6. One bullet _____ the left side of his chest.
7. Those who do not desert you in time of _____ are real friends.
8. They were crazed by the famine and _____ of that

bitter winter.

9. He is about to _____ on a new business venture.

10. The forces for peace, justice and progress are _____ after all.

11. The meat is likely to _____ if you leave it cooking too long.

12. All organizations and individuals are forbidden to undermine, damage or _____ defence assets.

▶ III. Choose the italicized words from *Stories* part to complete the table.

Verb	Noun	Adjective	Noun (Person)	Antonym
decapitate	1_____	decapitated	decapitator	
2_____	depopulation	depopulated		populate
purify	3_____	purified	purifier	
4_____	demolition		demolisher	
	victory	5_____	victor	
6_____	endangerment	endangered		
	defect/defection	7_____		
	8_____	infertile		fertility

▶ IV. Use the words in the table from *Exercise III* to complete the sentences.

1. Potting up green plants in the house will _____ the air inside.

2. They come in all sizes — from a few hundred students to enough to _____ a city.

3. The discharge of heavy metal ion wastewater is a primary source of water pollution, and has been engendering great _____ for the human society.

4. According to the *Daily Express* of October 10, Swedish scientists are on the brink of a womb transplant which will let _____ women become

101

pregnant.

5. We do not accept merchandise for return unless items are _____, in which case they will be replaced, subject to availability, or refunded at buyers discretion.

6. Captives who fell into the hands of the Amazons were often _____.

7. My family has been displaced by urban _____.

8. In 1978, he played for the _____ Argentinian side in the World Cup.

Vocabulary Development
Collocation (2)
Types of Collocation

There are several different types of collocation. Collocations can be adjective + adverb, noun + noun, verb + noun and so on. Below you can see seven main types of collocation in sample sentences.

1. adverb + adjective

- Invading that country was an **utterly stupid** thing to do.
- We entered a **richly decorated** room.
- My friend is **desperately worried** about her son at the moment.

2. adjective + noun

- The Titanic sank on its **maiden voyage**.
- He was writhing on the ground in **excruciating pain**.
- Heracles became an example of **steady fastness** in adversity.

3. noun + noun

- Let's give Mr. Jones a **round of applause**.
- The **ceasefire agreement** came into effect at 11:00 am.
- Ino arranged to have **seed corn** roasted so that it would not sprout.

4. noun + verb

- The **lion** started **to roar** when it heard the dog barking.
- **Snow was falling** as our **plane took off**.
- The **bomb went off** when he started the car engine.

UNIT 4

5. verb + noun
- The prisoner was hanged for **committing murder**.
- I always try to **do my homework** in the morning, after **making my bed**.
- He has been asked to **give a presentation** about his work.

6. verb + expression with preposition
- We had to return home because we **had run out of money**.
- At first her eyes **filled with horror**, and then she **burst into tears**.
- Their behaviour was enough to **drive anybody to crime**.

7. verb + adverb
- She **placed** her keys **gently** on the table and sat down.
- Mary **whispered softly** in John's ear.
- I **vaguely remember** that it was growing dark when we left.

Now choose the best answer from the four options.

1. They argue _____, but neither could convince the other.
   a. warmly   b. heartedly   c. heatedly   d. keenly

2. My children are _____ addicted to television.
   a. unconditionally   b. hopelessly
   c. illy   d. redeemably

3. A _____ of lions was resting under a tree.
   a. group   b. bunch   c. colony   d. pride

4. The busy bees _____ at the big bear.
   a. buzz   b. alarm   c. moo   d. boom

5. He'd like to study for a degree but is afraid he won't _____ the requirements for university entry.
   a. reach   b. achieve   c. arrive   d. meet

6. The U.S. Congress voted to _____ a long-standing ban on Americans traveling to Cuba.
   a. cancel   b. lift   c. remove   d. withdraw

7. She's always trying to _____ an impression on people with her new clothes.
   a. make   b. set   c. strike   d. let

8. At the age of five, he started to _____ music. He was the musician named Beethoven.
   a. write   b. make   c. build   d. compose

9. I send my _____ regards to him.
   a. good   b. hot   c. warmest   d. well

10. He was very tired and therefore he fell _____ asleep.
 a. deeply   b. sound   c. intensively   d. profoundly

Speaking
Comparison and Contrast (1)
Two People

Comparison and contrast are ways of looking at objects and thinking about how they are alike and different. There are two main reasons that people use comparison and contrast: to explain and to evaluate. We can compare and contrast two objects to help someone understand the characteristics of each one. We can also compare and contrast two objects to show why one object is better than the other.

When we compare and contrast two people, we should firstly examine the ways in which the two people are alike, and then examine the ways in which they are different, or we can do it the other way round. However, regardless of our approach, we should gather as many points of comparison and contrast as possible. Then, once we believe we have gathered sufficient points, we should select the points we believe will most effectively support the main argument we intend to make. Finally, we should decide upon the order in which we will present those points. Here are some expressions to show similarity and difference.

To show similarity:

similarly, likewise, in the same fasion/way, in like manner, like, also, in addition, plus, too, each of, both, as well as, the same

Example 1: Mothers generally believed that by the age of six most children should have their own money to spend. **Similarly / Likewise**, most fathers discussed the terms of receiving an allowance with their six-year-old children.

Example 2: **Like** the middle-class children reported in his study, middle-class children in our study generally thought that they should have to do some household chores in exchange for their allowance.

Example 3: Most middle-class children in his study thought that they should have to do some household chores in exchange for their allowance. **The same** was true for middle-class children in our sample.

To show difference:

in contrast, by contrast, nevertheless, however, although, while, but, yet, whereas, on the other hand, conversely, unlike

Example 1: Over 75% of Britons feel children should receive money on special occasions. ***In contrast***, only 20% of Germans think this is appropriate.

Example 2: ***Unlike*** Germans, Britons feel no restrictions should be imposed on how children spend their money.

Example 3: ***While*** MacKenzie argues that our petroleum reserves will not make it through the next half century, Day believes that reserves will double in the next half century and will last another 100 years.

In addition to the stories of gods and heroes, there are myriad fascinating legends about love, greed, ambition and revenge in Greek myths. Now read the following episodes, and then make a comparison and contrast between Pygmalion and Narcissus, Phaeton and Orpheus.

Episode 1: Narcissus

Narcissus was a beautiful young man, who, by the age of sixteen, had left a trail of broken hearts from rejected lovers. He wanted nothing to do with falling in love with anyone and rejected all attempts at romance. There was a day when Narcissus was walking in the woods. Echo, a mountain nymph who could only repeat the words of the others, saw him and fell deeply in love with him. She commenced to follow him. Narcissus sensed that someone was following him and shouted "Who's there?" Echo repeated "Who's there?" She eventually revealed her identity. She made an attempt to embrace the boy. He stepped away from her and told her to leave him alone. She was heartbroken and spent the rest of her life in lonely glens until nothing but an echo sound remained of her.

Nemesis, the goddess of revenge, learned of this story and decided to punish Narcissus. She lured him to a pool where he saw his own reflection. He was amazed at the beauty of his reflection. He didn't realize his reflection was only an image and fell in love with it. He eventually figured out that his love could not be addressed and committed suicide by plunging a dagger in his heart. Where his blood soaked the earth sprung up the white narcissus flower. (224 words)

Episode 2: Pygmalion

Pygmalion was a king of Cyprus. He saw so much to blame in women that he had no interest in them and resolved to live unmarried. He was a sculptor, and had made with wonderful skill a statue of ivory, so fair and realistic that he fell in love with it. Soon, the festival of Aphrodite came, and Pygmalion made offerings at the altar of Aphrodite. There, too scared to admit his desire, he quietly wished for a bride who would be "the living likeness of my ivory girl". When he returned home, he kissed his ivory statue and found that its lips felt warm. He kissed it again, touched its breasts with his hand and found that the ivory had lost its hardness. Aphrodite had granted Pygmalion's wish. Pygmalion married the ivory sculpture, which was changed to a woman under Aphrodite's blessing. Together, they had a son, Paphos, from whom the island's name is derived. (156 words)

Episode 3: Phaeton

Phaeton was the son of Apollo by Clymene, an Ethiopian princess. The mother had filled the lad's head with so many stories of his father's glory that the youth was quite proud. Wherever he went he told those stories again and again until everybody was tired of him.

But one day he was teased by a playmate, who said that Phaeton had been fooled by his mother and his father was not the sun god. He came back to his mother, confused and ashamed. Unable to do anything for him, she sent her son to pray to Apollo for help.

The sun god graciously received his son and heard the story with interest. Then he took an oath by the Styx, ready to grant his son a wish. But the god was surprised to hear that the boy's hope was to drive his fiery carriage. He told his son of the dangers on the way, but failed to stop the boy from the try. As the god had sworn by the Styx, there was no going back on his word. In his desperate effort to avoid disaster, Apollo warned his son to keep to the middle course and stop the horses in time. Phaeton joyfully jumped on the carriage and set off. Very soon he lost his way. He grew pale at the great height and the vast sky in front of him and behind. The horses ran wild. Unable to hold them, Phaeton dropped them in fear. Straight down to the earth the carriage dashed. Rivers were dried up. Crops hung down and withered. Men's cries of suffering rose up from the burnt earth. The enraged Zeus soon found the cause of the trouble and without hesitation gave one of his most powerful thunderbolts at the proud and careless boy. Phaeton dropped straight down into a river. (308 words)

UNIT 4

Episode 4: Orpheus

Orpheus was the son of Apollo and the Muse Calliope. He was presented by his father with a lyre and taught to play upon it, and he played to such perfection that nothing could withstand the charm of his music.

When his wife Eurydice died of a snake bite, Orpheus was left inconsolable. Orpheus sang his grief to both gods and men, finding it all unavailing, and resolved to seek his wife in the regions of the dead. He descended by a cave and arrived at the Stygian realm. He passed through crowds of ghosts, and presented himself before the throne of Hades and Persephone. Accompanying the words with the lyre, he began to sing. As he sang these tender strains, the ghosts shed tears. Then for the first time, it is said, the cheeks of the Furies were wet with tears. Persephone could not resist, and Hades himself gave way. Orpheus was permitted to take Eurydice away with him on one condition that he should not turn round to look at her till they should have reached the upper air. Under this condition they proceeded on their way, he leading, she following, through passages dark and steep, in total silence, till they had nearly reached the outlet into the cheerful upper world. Orpheus, then, in a moment of forgetfulness, to assure himself that she was still following, cast a glance behind him, when instantly she was borne away.

Orpheus swore he would never love another, and it may have been the steadfastness of this vow which caused certain wild women of Thrace to tear him limb from limb in a fit of jealousy. They threw his head and his lyre into a river, down which they floated, murmuring sad music. His lyre was later placed by Zeus among the stars as the Lyra. (304 words)

Writing
Comparison and Contrast (1) Two People

When we compare and contrast two people in an essay, the aim is to show their similarities and differences, or how someone has changed. If we compare two people, we focus more on their similarities though we may mention their differences shortly. If we contrast two people, we point out the differences between them.

Here are some widely used strategies to organize comparison and contrast papers.

1. Whole-to-Whole, or Block

In this structure, we say everything about one person and then everything about the other. Whole-to-Whole comparison and contrast uses a separate section or paragraph for each person you're discussing.

2. Similarities-to-Differences

In this structure, we explain all the similarities about the two people being compared and then we explain all the differences. Similarities-to-Differences comparison and contrast uses a separate section or paragraph for similarities and differences. In other words, the body of your paper would have two large sections: one for similarities, and another for differences.

3. Point-by-Point

In a Point-by-Point structure, we explain one point of comparison before moving to the next point. Point-by-Point comparison and contrast uses a separate section or paragraph for each point.

In writing a comparison and contrast essay, we are allowed to be creative. For example, instead of simply comparing and contrasting certain attributes, habits, behaviors, etc, in paragraph after paragraph, we can incorporate an anecdote (a story) about an occurrence or event that demonstrates not only the similarities between the two people we have selected but also the differences.

Sample

"Two peas in a pod," that is how my father describes my sister and me; and although it is true that Vicki and I do have much in common, we are, to use another cliché, really as "different as night and day".

Granted, Vicki and I do look alike, at least to a certain extent. We both have our father's high cheekbones, dimpled chin, and wavy hair; however, while my hair is chestnut, Vicki's is the glossy blue-black of a raven's wing. Plus, though we are both tall like our mother, I am slim and wiry, thanks to my aerobics' classes; but Vicki, on the other hand, doesn't like to break a sweat, and her idea of strenuous activity is having to change TV channels without a remote. As a result, unlike mine, her figure is decidedly "curvaceous".

Additionally, Vicki and I share a love of music, a trait we inherited from my father, but while I play the guitar and, as a young girl, dreamed of being a folk singer and traveling the highways and byways of America in a Volkswagen bus, Vicki is an accomplished pianist, who fulfilled her own dream of playing with the Boston Symphony and, last year, recorded her first CD, "Music for Romantics".

To sum up, though Vicki and I share a lot in common, we differ greatly physically and mentally. (227 words)

Now write a comparison and contrast essay of Heracles and Theseus by following the five steps.

Step 1. Review the stories of Heracles and Theseus, and examine the ways in which the two heroes are alike and different.

Step 2. Gather as many points of comparison and contrast as possible, for example, their parentage, what they are celebrated for, the difficulties or frustrations that they have met, the courage, strength and persistence that they have shown in performing their own tasks, their unique characteristics, their limitations.

Step 3. Select the points you believe will most effectively support the main argument you intend to make.

Step 4: Decide upon the organization you are going to use and the order in which you will present those points to the reader.

Step 5: Write the essay.

Further Development

I. Watch the video clip on *Hercules* and fill in the blanks with the words you hear.

1. Classical mythology is loaded with stories of gods who impregnate mortal women and give birth to gods or demi-gods. So this demi-god idea means that this person has some features _____, some divine powers but, at the same time, he is mortal, he can die.

2. I suspected the Greeks invent this idea because they wanted to reach the gods as much as possible to _____ that are closer and closer to the gods.

3. Hercules would grow up to be Greece's model hero. But he has one powerful enemy who wants to _____, Zeus' wife, the goddess Hera.

4. She's the queen of the goddesses and she has wonderful beauty. She's supremely intelligent, she's mighty. But she's also exceedingly jealous because Zeus is always _____.

5. Hera's hatred of Hercules is actually very, very irrational. It's almost as if she knew that he was going to _____ in heaven in some way.

6. One night, while Hercules is still a baby, Hera sends two poisonous snakes into his nursery. He's got one snake in each hand and he's _____.

7. She can make his life wretched but she cannot kill him because destiny says _____.

II. Discuss the following questions based on your watching in *Exercise I*.

1. How were the heroes or demi-gods in Greek myths similar to and different from gods?
2. What qualities of Hercules made him a celebrated hero?
3. What do you think of Hera's hatred of Hercules?

III. In the following story of *Midas*, four sentences have been removed. Choose the most suitable one from the list A–F to fit into each of the blanks. There are two extra choices, which do not fit in any of the gaps.

Midas was a king of great fortune who ruled the country of Phrygia in Asia Minor. He had everything a king could wish for. He shared his life of abundance with his beautiful daughter. _____1_____. His avarice was such that he used to spend his days counting his golden coins!

110

UNIT 4

Occasionally he used to cover his body with gold objects, as if he wanted to bath in them.

One day, Dionysus, the god of wine and revelry, passed through the kingdom of Midas. One of his companions, a satyr named Silenus, got delayed along the way. Silenus got tired and decided to take a nap in the famous rose gardens surrounding the palace of King Midas. There, he was found by the king, who recognized him instantly and invited him to spend a few days at his palace. After that, Midas took him to Dionysus. The god of celebration, very grateful to Midas for his kindness, promised Midas to satisfy any wish of him. Midas though for a while and then he said: "I hope that everything I touch becomes gold." _____2_____. Dionysus could do nothing else and promised the king that from that following day everything he touched would turn into gold.

The next day, Midas woke up eager to see if his wish had become true. He extended his arm touching a small table that immediately turned into gold. Midas jumped with happiness! He then touched a chair, the carpet, the door, his bathtub and a table. All of them turned into gold as the god of wine had promised! Midas kept on running in ecstasy all over his palace until he got exhausted. He then sat at the table to have breakfast and took a rose between his hands to smell its fragrance. When he touched it, the rose became gold. "I will have to absorb the fragrance without touching the roses, I suppose." He thought in disappointment. Without even thinking, he ate a grape but it also turned into gold! The same happened with a slice of bread and a glass of water. Suddenly, he started to sense fear. Tears filled his eyes and at that moment, his beloved daughter entered the room. When Midas hugged her, she turned into a golden statue! _____3_____.

The god of wine heard Midas and felt sorry for him. He told Midas to go to the river Pactolus and wash his hands. Midas did so: he ran to the river and was astonished to see gold flowing from his hands. _____4_____. Midas hugged his daughter in full happiness and decided to share his great fortune with his people.

A. Despaired and fearful, he raised his arms and prayed to Dionysus to take this curse from him

B. Midas became a better person, generous and grateful for all goods of his life

C. When Midas returned home, everything he had touched had become normal again

D. He was actually able to turn everything to gold

E. Even though he was very rich, Midas thought that his greatest happiness was provided by gold

F. Dionysus warned the king to think well about his wish, but Midas was positive

IV. Show your opinions on "Money is the source of happiness".

Suppose you were Midas who had experienced the ecstasy as well as the heartbreak of acquiring the ability to turn everything to gold, and you were invited to give your opinions on the modern notion "Money is the source of happiness". Organize your ideas by completing the following chart. Note that your opinions should be given from two opposing aspects before finally arriving at your conclusion. Then present your speech in your group.

Notion: Money is the source of happiness	
For	Against
Argument 1: e.g.: Money can satisfy one's material necessities as well as spiritual needs.	Argument 1: e.g.: Happiness can not be weighed by material criteria.
Argument 2:	Argument 2:
Argument 3:	Argument 3:
….	…
Conclusion:	

Cultural Exploration

Read the following passage on *Heroism* and finish the tasks.

Heroes in Greek myths were usually descendants of gods who were courageous and smart enough to fight against monsters or evils. Our modern society needs heroes as well. Einstein once said "The world is a dangerous place, not because of those who do bad things, but because of those who look on and do nothing". In fact, heroism is something that is deeply valued across cultures.

On January 2, 2007, approximately 75 people waiting at a busy subway station watched as a young man suffered a seizure and then fell from the platform onto the subway tracks. Onlookers watched in horror yet did nothing, but a man named Wesley Autry took action. Handing his two young daughters to a stranger, he leapt down onto the tracks hoping to have time to drag the man out of the way of an oncoming train. When Autry realized that there was no time to move the other man, he instead held him down between the tracks as a train passed over the top of them.

"I don't feel like I did something spectacular; I just saw someone who needed help. I did what I felt was right," he told *The New York Times* after the incident.

Task 1. Work with a partner to figure out at least five traits (*for example, compassionate, empathetic*) the hero reported in the story might have; then think about whether these traits are echoed in the stories of heroes in Greek myths. If YES, try to find evidence from Greek myths to support your points.

Trait 1	Trait 2	Trait 3	Trait 4	Trait 5
Evidence from heroes in Greek myths:				

Task 2. Comment on the following quotes on or related to heroism and then provide a definition by yourself.

"The characteristic of genuine heroism, is its persistency."
— Ralph Waldo Emerson

"True heroism is remarkably sober, very undramatic. It is not the urge to surpass all others at whatever cost, but the urge to serve others at whatever cost." — Arthur Ashe

"The key to heroism is a concern for other people in need—a concern to defend a moral cause, knowing there is a personal risk, done without expectation of reward." — Philip Zimbardo

"Although we find it true that heroism is in the eye of the beholder, we do acknowledge that people's beliefs about heroes tend to follow a systematic pattern. After polling a number of people, we discovered that heroes tend to have eight traits, which we call The Great Eight. These traits are smart, strong, resilient, selfless, caring, charismatic, reliable, and inspiring. It's unusual for a hero to possess all eight of these characteristics, but most heroes have a majority of them."   — Scott T.

My definition of heroism:

Task 3. One of the biggest questions about heroism comes down to the age-old debate over nature versus nurture. Is heroism something we are born with, or is heroism something that can be learned? Some people argue humans are born good or born bad while others maintain that people are all born with the tremendous capacity to be anything, and they get shaped by the circumstances. What is your opinion? Surf online for information that can be used as evidence to support your view.

My opinion:
Evidence:

Further Reading

Hero and Leander

Leander was a youth of a town of the Asian side of the strait which separates Asia and Europe. On the opposite shore lived the maiden Hero, a priestess of Aphrodite. At a solemn festival of the goddess Aphrodite the two met and fell in love with one another at first sight. Though Hero was dedicated from childhood to the service of the goddess, and forbidden to nurse any ideas of love and marriage, nothing could extinguish the flames of love now. Leander loved her passionately, and each night he swam across the strait to enjoy the company of his beloved. To guide him on this dangerous journey, Hero lighted a torch upon the tower for just this purpose. Leander would stay with his love right until daybreak, and they had a blissful time together. And when one wintry night Leander found himself at sea in the middle of such a windy war, a gust blew out the lamp in Hero's tower, and Leander, being left in the dark without landmarks, lost his way and perished. The day after, Leander's body reached the foot of the tower, and when Hero saw him, she cast herself down from the tower, her dead body remaining beside his. (205 words)

Answer the following questions briefly.

1. What did Leander do every night to be with Hero?
2. In what ways was their love story special?

Tantalus

Tantalus, the king of Sipylos, was a son of Zeus. He was initially known for having been welcomed to Zeus' table in Olympus. There he is said to have misbehaved and stolen ambrosia to bring it back to his people, and revealed the secrets of the gods, thus arousing the anger of the gods.

He was punished by being "tantalized" with hunger and thirst in Tartarus: he was immersed up to his neck in water, but when he bent to drink, it all drained away; luscious fruit hung on trees above him, but when he reached for it, the winds blew the branches beyond his reach.

There was another story about what Tantalus' crime was. The more famous account says that he invited the gods to a banquet and served them the dismembered body of his own son, Pelops. When the gods discovered the trick, they punished Tantalus and restored Pelops to life, replacing with ivory a part of the shoulder which had been eaten by Demeter.

Tantalus' family was an ill-fated one. His daughter, Niobe, lost all her children and was turned to stone. His son, Pelops, was murdered, cooked, and restored to life. His grandsons, Atreus and Thyestes, struggled for power. His great-grandson, Agamemnon, was murdered by another great-grandson, Aegisthus, who was in turn killed by a great-great-grandson, Orestes. (221 words)

Answer the following questions briefly.

1. How was Tantalus punished?
2. How did Tantalus offend the gods?

Passage Three

Sisyphus

Sisyphus was the founder of Corinth. He was sly and evil and used to way-lay travelers and murder them. He betrayed the secrets of the gods and chained the god of death, Thanatos, so the deceased could not reach the underworld. Hades himself intervened and Sisyphus was severely punished.

In the realm of the dead, he was forced to roll a block of stone against a steep hill, which tumbled back down when he reached the top. Then the whole process started again, lasting all eternity. His punishment was depicted on many Greek vases. He was represented as a naked man, or wearing a fur over his shoulders, pushing a boulder. (111 words)

Answer the following questions briefly.

1. How was Sisyphus punished?
2. What does the allusion "the stone of Sisyphus" possibly mean?

UNIT 5

Creation and Pioneers in the Bible

In this unit, you are going to
- outline the stories of creation of the world and human beings;
- identify the origin of Hebrews;
- orally compare and contrast two stories;
- write a comparison and contrast essay on two subjects;
- expand your vocabulary through identifying polysemy.

Pre-information

I. Listen to the passage on *Genesis* and fill in the blanks with the words you hear.

Genesis is the first book of the Bible. Placed at the ____1____ of the Hebrew Scriptures, Genesis is the first of the five books of Moses.

The word Genesis means "the ____2____, source, creation, or coming into being of something". Genesis describes such important beginnings as the ____3____, the fall of man, and the early years of the nation of Israel.

The beginning of salvation history — the story of God and man, sin and

UNIT 5

grace, wrath and _____4_____, ***covenant*** and redemption—also begins in the book of Genesis. These themes are repeated often _____5_____ the rest of the Bible. The book of Revelation is the climax and conclusion of the Bible, and the book of Genesis is the beginning and _____6_____ seed-plot of the Bible. Thus, Genesis is an important book for understanding the meaning of the entire Bible.

II. Listen to the sentences and fill in the blanks with the words you hear. Then work out the meaning of each sentence with a partner.

1. If you try to _____ your misdeed with a fig leaf, you will only make it more conspicuous.

2. If you make a mistake like that again, the boss will certainly raise Cain and give you the _____.

3. While outwardly holding out the _____, they were actually speeding up their war preparations.

4. You must _____ your plan to travel to Africa. It is but the Tower of Babel.

5. We put the same effort in that business, but Benjamin's mess of the _____ went to him.

6. Though that is a small country, its natural resources are as rich as _____.

Stories

I. Match the major characters in the story with the proper information after your first reading.

1. Garden of Eden   a. the first woman in the world taken out of a man

2. Adam   b. a beautiful garden built by God for Adam and Eve to live at the Creation

3. Eve   c. the one who coaxed Adam and Eve to eat the forbidden fruit

4. serpent   d. the thing Adam and Eve sewed together to make coverings for themselves after they ate the forbidden fruit

5. fig leaf   e. the first man created by God

II. Decide whether the following statements are TRUE or FALSE after your second reading.

_____ 1. In the beginning, it was empty, formless and dark, and then God created everything with his hands.

_____ 2. Light was created to serve as signs to mark seasons, days and years.

_____ 3. God created man and gave him every creature and the whole earth to rule over, care for, and cultivate.

_____ 4. God told Adam that he could pick any of the fruit from all kinds of fruit trees except that from the tree of life.

Creation

The story of how God made everything is, naturally, at the very beginning of the Bible:

In the beginning, the earth was empty, and a formless mass cloaked in darkness. Then God said, "Let there be light," and there was light. Then God separated the light from the darkness, calling light "day" and darkness "night".

On the second day, God created an expanse to separate the waters and called it "sky".

On the third day, God created the dry ground and gathered the waters, calling the dry ground "land", and the gathered waters "seas". Then God also created vegetation, plants and trees.

On the fourth day, God created the sun, the moon, and the stars to give light to the earth, and to govern and separate the day and the night.

These would also serve as signs to mark seasons, days, and years.

On the fifth day, God created every living creature of the seas and every winged bird, blessing them to ***multiply*** and fill the waters and the sky with life.

On the sixth day, God created the animals to fill the earth. Then God wanted one more special creature to complete his creation—the human being. He took the dust from the earth and molded it into a man in his own image. When God breathed into the man, he came to life. God named the man Adam. God gave him every creature and the whole earth to rule over, care for, and cultivate. And then God took Adam to the Garden of Eden where God told Adam that he could pick any of the fruit from all kinds of fruit trees except that from the tree of the knowledge of good and evil, otherwise he would die. God also said that it was not good for Adam to be alone. God caused Adam to fall into a deep sleep, and then took a rib from his side. From the rib, God created a woman, Eve, to be Adam's companion. Adam said, "This is now bone of my bones and flesh of my flesh." And he called her "woman", for she was taken out of man.

By the seventh day, God had finished the work he had been doing; so on the seventh day he rested from all his work. And God blessed the seventh day and made it holy, because on it he rested from all the work of creating that he had done.

But later, a serpent, the most tricky and deceitful animal created by God, told Eve that she would not die even if she ate the fruit from the tree of the knowledge of good and evil, and told her that she would be wise like God if she ate the fruit. Eve saw that the fruit was good for food and pleasant to eyes, so she picked a piece of the fruit and shared the fruit with Adam so that he could also be wise. Later that evening, God called them but they didn't answer. They went to hide among the trees where they picked fig leaves to cover their bodies. God was sad and angry, and punished the serpent by cursing its offspring forever to crawl on their bellies in the dust and be enemies of mankind. Then God punished Adam and Eve, and all their descendants, by making their lives hard. No longer could they live in the perfect world of the Garden of Eden. Men would have to struggle and sweat for their existence. Women would have to bear children in pain and be ruled over by their husbands. When they grew old, they would die and their bodies would return to the dust. (614 words)

Story Two

Listen to the story of *Noah and the Flood* and fill in the blanks with the words you hear.

Once Adam and Eve had made a home away from the Garden of Eden, they had two sons—Cain and Abel, ____1____ respectively. Unfortunately Cain killed his brother Abel out of rage because God accepted Abel's offering, but rejected his. Then Cain was *banished*. For many years after, Cain murdered his brother Abel, the earth was corrupt and ____2____. So God decided to wipe mankind from the earth. Since Noah was a righteous man, God told Noah to build an ark of cypress wood and make enough rooms in it for his family and animals. Before the flood came, God told Noah to lead his family into the ark, and bring into the ark ____3____, male and female, to keep them alive with Noah. Noah and his family collected enough food to last many days. Then God came to Noah and told him the time had come to load everything up. A week later, the rain started to come down. It rained for forty days and forty nights. Water began to pour over the roads. It raced through people's houses, covering everything ____4____. Many weeks passed and the water grew deeper until only Noah's ark was left floating on the water.

God remembered Noah and all the wild animals and the livestock that were with him in the ark. He sent a wind over the earth, and the water *receded* until one day they felt the ark ____5____ of Ararat. The water continued to *recede* until the tenth month, and the tops of the mountains became visible.

After forty days, Noah opened the window and sent out a raven, and it kept flying back and forth until the water on the earth had dried up. Then he ____6____ to see if the water had *receded* from the surface of the ground. But the dove could find no place to set its feet because there was water over all the surface of the earth; so it returned to Noah in the ark. Noah waited seven more days and ____7____ from the ark. When the dove returned to him in the evening, there in its beak was a freshly *plucked* olive branch! Noah waited seven more days and sent the dove out again, but this time it did not return to him. That was ____8____ that the land was dry enough to live on again. Then Noah led his people and all the living creatures out of the ark.

After the Flood, Noah offered a sacrifice to God, who promised never again to destroy all life on Earth by flood and created the rainbow as the sign of this "everlasting *covenant* between God and every living creature of all flesh that is on the earth", also known as the Noahic *covenant*. (494 words)

I. Match the major characters, places or objects in the story with the proper information after your first reading.

1. Abraham   a. son of Abraham who was believed by his parents as a promised child
2. Isaac   b. a new land where Abraham was asked to go and live forever with his offspring
3. the ram   c. the person whose name was changed by God to symbolize the covenant promise to multiply his descendants into a great nation and made him the father of many nations
4. Canaan   d. the one that was caught by its horns in a thicket and so was sacrificed as a burnt offering by Abraham in the place of his son

II. Fill in the blanks with the missing information after your second reading.

1. Abraham is _____ of the Jewish nation of Israel.
2. Ishmael, Abraham's son from Hagar, who was a servant girl of Abraham's wife, later became _____ northern Arab people.
3. Abraham and Sarah had a son, Isaac. One day God asked Abraham to bring Isaac to a nearby mountain and _____ as a test for his loyalty.

Abraham and Isaac

The story of Abraham is one of the most important and prominent stories in Islam, Christianity and Judaism. This can be clearly seen by the fact that these three religions are often referred to as the Abrahamic religions. Abraham is often considered the father of the great monotheistic traditions of the world: a crucial figure and a prominent patriarch in the story of God's people, the Israelites, and one of the most important prophets in Islamic tradition.

According to the Bible, Abraham was a descendant of one of Noah's sons and the founding father of Israel. Originally called Abram, his name was changed by God to Abraham as a symbol of the **covenant** promise to **multiply** his descendants into a great nation that God would call his own and make him the father of many nations. God also asked him to leave his city for a new land—Canaan with his wife Sarah and told him that he would bless Abraham and give him that country and it would belong to him and his offspring forever. Abraham then, leading his people, left his homeland and set out for Canaan.

Abraham and his wife Sarah had never been able to have any children and they were afraid they were too old. One night God came to them and promised that Abraham would have as many offspring as there were stars in the sky. Then God told Abraham that he and Sarah would soon have a son. Many years went by after God made the promise to Abraham and still no child had been born. Sarah gave her servant girl Hagar to her husband. Hagar gave birth to a son and named him Ishmael, who later became the ancestor of northern Arab people.

When Abraham was a hundred years old, Sarah **conceived** and bore Abraham a son, who was named Isaac. Abraham and Sarah **rejoiced** over the birth of the promised son. One day God tested Abraham. He asked Abraham to bring Isaac to a nearby mountain and sacrifice him as a burnt offering. So the next morning Abraham took the boy to the mountain as God had asked.

Isaac helped his father lay the stones for the altar. When it was done, Isaac asked where the lamb for the burnt offering was. Abraham answered, "The Lord will provide that." Then he took the wood for the altar and carried the fire and the knife. He bound his son Isaac and laid him on the altar. Then he reached out his hand and took the knife to slay his son. But the angel of God called out to him from heaven.

"Do not lay a hand on the boy," he said. "Now I know that you fear God because you have not *withheld* your son, your only son."

Abraham lifted his son from the altar. He looked up and in a thicket he saw a ram caught by its horns. He went over to take the ram and sacrificed it as a burnt offering instead of his son. The angel of God called to Abraham from heaven a second time and said, "I swear by myself that I will surely bless you and make your descendants as numerous as the stars in the sky and as the sand on the seashore. Your descendants will take possession of the cities of their enemies, and through your offspring all nations on the earth will be blessed." (574 words)

I. Match the major characters in the story with the proper information after your first reading.

1. Esau
2. Jacob

a. His name was changed to Israel.
b. He loved hunting.
c. He was quiet and loved to stay in the tent.
d. He sold his birthright to his brother for a bowl of red pottage.
e. He got blessing from his father in a deceitful way.

II. Fill in the blanks with the missing information after your second reading.

1. One of Isaac's twin sons was named _____, meaning hairy in Hebrew; the other was named _____, which meant grasping the heel.

2. Isaac called for _____ and asked him to hunt some wild animals to prepare him the tasty food so that he might give him _____ before he died.

3. A strange man _____ with Jacob until daybreak, but _____ seemed to win.

Jacob and Esau

Rebekah, Isaac's wife, was pregnant and there were twins in her womb. The babies jostled each other within her. The first to come out was red, and his whole body was like a hairy garment; so they named him Esau, meaning hairy in Hebrew. Then came out his brother, whose hand grasped Esau's heel; so he was named Jacob, which meant grasping the heel.

The boys grew up, and Esau became a skillful hunter, a man of the open country, and was much to Isaac's liking; while Jacob was a quiet man, staying among the tents, and he was *favored* by Rebekah.

Once when Jacob was cooking some red pottage, Esau came in from the open country, *famished*. He said to Jacob, "Quick, let me have some of that red pottage! I'm *famished*!"

Jacob replied, "First sell me your birthright."

Esau swore an oath to Jacob, had some bread and some red pottage, and then left. So Esau despised his birthright.

When Isaac was old and his eyes were so weak that he could no longer see. He called for Esau and asked him to hunt some wild animals to prepare him the tasty food so that he might give Esau his blessing before he died.

When Rebekah heard this, she asked Jacob to go out to the flock and bring her two young goats so that she could help Jacob prepare some tasty food for Isaac, thus Isaac may give his blessing to Jacob.

Then Rebekah took the best clothes of Esau, and put them on Jacob. She also covered his hands and the smooth part of his neck with the goatskins since Esau was a hairy man and Jacob was a man with smooth skin. Jacob went to his father and gave him the food. Isaac touched Jacob but did not recognize him, for his hands were hairy like those of his brother Esau. When Jacob was asked to kiss his father, Isaac caught the smell of Esau's clothes, and he blessed Jacob.

Now Esau came in from hunting, and Isaac knew that he had been *deceived* by Jacob. He had given the special blessing to the wrong son.

Esau was so angry that he decided to kill his brother Jacob, so Jacob went away from his brother and fled to his mother's homeland, where he married two wives and had his sons. Many years after working for his uncle, Jacob decided to return home. As Jacob neared the land of Canaan, he sent messengers ahead to his brother Esau. The messengers returned with the news that Esau was coming to meet Jacob with an army of 400. Jacob became very frightened. So he sent many gifts to Esau and then took his family across the Jordan River to be safe. On the night before Esau was to meet Jacob, Jacob stood alone, worrying and praying. A man came from out of the desert and attacked him. It was dark and Jacob could not see who the man was. The strange man wrestled with Jacob until daybreak, but neither seemed to win.

The strange man said, "Let me go. It will soon be sunrise." Then Jacob knew who he was. Jacob then demanded a blessing, and the man said that from then on, Jacob would be called Israel, meaning "one who has struggled with God".

Jacob was forgiven by his brother Esau and reunited with his father Isaac. After the death of Isaac, Esau, with his family, left his father's house and settled in a new land; Jacob lived in the land where his father had stayed, the land of Canaan. (603 words)

I. Answer the following questions briefly after your first reading.

1. Why was Joseph called "the dreamer" by his brothers?
2. What was Joseph's interpretation to the pharaoh's dreams?

II. Decide whether the following statements are TRUE or FALSE after your second reading.

_____ 1. Joseph was the favorite son of his father because he was the youngest child of the family.

_____ 2. Joseph's brothers were angry at him because they thought Joseph's dreams suggested that he should reign over them.

_____ 3. Joseph was appointed in charge of the government immediately after he was sold by his brothers to Egypt.

_____ 4. Joseph was put into prison because he could not interpret the pharaoh's dreams.

_____ 5. Joseph's whole family moved from Canaan to Egypt to find shelter from famine.

Joseph and His Brothers

Jacob lived in the land where his father had stayed, the land of Canaan. He had twelve sons, but he loved Joseph more than any others, and he made a richly *ornamented* robe for him. Joseph's brothers were jealous of him. The more special treatment he got, the more they hated him. Joseph had told them a dream he had one night. He said they were out in the fields, harvesting the grain. The crops were bundled up in sheaves, and the brothers' sheaves began to bow to Joseph's sheaves. That really made the brothers angry because they thought the dreams meant that Joseph would reign over them. But later Joseph had another dream. In it, he dreamed that the sun, the moon, and eleven stars all bowed to him. His father heard about his dream and was very troubled by it.

One day, Joseph's brothers had gone out into the fields to feed Jacob's animals. They had been gone for some time, and Jacob asked Joseph to go to find them. The brothers saw him coming from far away and said to each other, "Here comes the dreamer. Let's kill him and see what will become of his dreams." But later they changed their minds and didn't kill him; instead, they sold him as a slave to a group of merchants who were on their way to Egypt. The brothers then placed blood on his elegant coat to *deceive* their father into thinking that Joseph was killed by a wild beast. The slave traders took him into Egypt and sold him to one of the pharaoh's officers. Joseph served his master well and gained great favor. But the master's wife tried to seduce Joseph. After he rejected her, she went to her husband with false *accusations*. It resulted in Joseph's *imprisonment*. The prison keeper *befriended* him and learned that Joseph had divine ability to *interpret* dreams.

Two years later, the pharaoh had strange dreams. In his first dream, he was standing by the Nile, when out of the river there came up seven cows, *sleek* and fat, and they gazed among the reeds. After them, seven other cows, ugly and gaunt, came up out of the Nile. The seven ugly and gaunt cows ate up the seven *sleek* and fat ones. The pharaoh woke up, but soon fell asleep again and had a second dream. In the dream, seven heads of grain, healthy and good, were growing on a single stalk. After them, seven other heads of grain *sprouted*, thin and scorched by the wind. The thin heads of grain swallowed up the seven healthy and full heads.

No one could *interpret* the pharaoh's dreams and so Joseph was recommended to the pharaoh. Joseph told the pharaoh that the two dreams were just one and the same. God had *revealed* that seven years of *abundance* would come in Egypt and then seven years of famine would follow them. If the pharaoh put a wise man in charge of the land to collect all the grain of the good seven years and store it up, the country would be saved. Then the pharaoh appointed Joseph in charge of the government.

Just as Joseph's interpretation of the pharaoh's dreams, the famine came after the seven years of *abundance*, and it was severe in the world. All the neighboring countries came to Egypt to buy grain from Joseph, including Joseph's brothers from Canaan, except for the youngest brother Benjamin. When Joseph encountered his brothers, he deliberately concealed his identity. He accused them of being spies and told them to return with their youngest brother or he would not sell them grain. When Joseph's brothers were back to Egypt with Benjamin, they were invited to dine at Joseph's house. Joseph served them delicious food, but Benjamin's mess was five times so much as any of others' since both of them were born from the same mother. After Joseph tested his brothers' characters, he believed they had changed and finally *revealed* his identity.

The pharaoh told Joseph to send word for all his family to come to Egypt and settle there. So Joseph stayed in Egypt, along with his father's family. (697 words)

Vocabulary Focus

I. Match the words from *Stories* part with their corresponding definitions.

1. pluck   a. having a smooth, shiny surface
2. covenant   b. move back or away from a limit, point, or mark
3. conceive   c. a charge of wrongdoing that is made against a person or other party
4. famished   d. pull out from the place of growth, as fruit, flowers, or feathers
5. banish   e. an extremely plentiful or over-sufficient quantity or supply
6. withhold   f. feel joyful; be delighted
7. recede   g. hold back; refuse to hand over or share
8. rejoice   h. a formal solemn agreement between two or more people or groups
9. sleek   i. become pregnant with a child
10. sprout   j. very hungry
11. abundance   k. produce buds and branches
12. accusation l. expel from a place, esp. by an official decree as a punishment

II. Use the words from *Exercise I* to complete the sentences.

1. After all, we should _____ over every step we take toward achieving our goals.

2. Other officials have echoed him in making similar _____ against Google.

3. At the vineyard, workers started _____ white grapes off rows of vines early in the morning.

4. Over the last twenty-five years, thousands of couples have turned

UNIT 5

to the new method for learning how to _____ a boy.

5. America needs oil and Canada has a(n) _____ of it.

6. The spy was found guilty of treason and _____ from the country.

7. Meanwhile, cherry trees began _____ in other U.S. locations.

8. River levels have _____ but the city remains under a state of emergency.

9. The individuals' names are being _____ to protect their identities, they said.

10. The company advertises that this smoothing hair serum provides _____, silky hair in second.

11. After an hour or two of basketball, I am so _____ that I would eat anything.

12. Some say marriage is meant a _____ between a man and a woman until death.

▶ III. Choose the italicized words from *Stories* part to complete the table.

Verb	Noun	Adjective	Noun (Person)	Antonym
1_____	friendship	friendly	friend	
	ornament	2_____	ornamentalist	
3_____		revealed	revealer	
4_____	deception	deceivable	deceiver	undeceive
5_____	favor	favorite	favorite	disfavor
6_____	interpretation	interpretable	interpreter	
7_____	multiplication	multiple		
imprison	8_____	imprisonable		

▶ IV. Use the words in the table from *Exercise III* to complete the sentences.

1. The government report said he used _____ to obtain

131

military landing permission.

2. In other words a legal framework exists, but how it is _____ and applied remains secret.

3. Once a victim is bitten by an animal, the virus _____ slowly and infects the brain and the nervous system.

4. They savored desert sunrises, enjoyed live music, talked to artists and _____ locals.

5. Something interesting has been _____ about the nature of contemporary international relations.

6. They have been married for almost 30 years and are _____ in a relationship held together by hate more than love.

7. I'm glad you pointed out that they were all in _____ of cutting funds for security.

8. Every year before Christmas, I vow not to buy any more _____, and every year I encounter irresistible offerings all over New York.

Vocabulary Development
Polysemy (1)
Introduction

Polysemy refers to the phenomenon that one and the same word acquires different, though obviously related, meanings, often with respect to particular contexts. Look at these examples:

1) Mary *treated* John for his injuries.

2) John *treated* Mary to a nice dinner.

3) Though *treated* cruelly as slaves, the Israelites multiplied and spread.

In example 1), "*treat*" means "to care for or deal with medically or surgically"; in example 2), it means "to provide with free food, drink, or entertainment"; and in example 3), it means "to act or behave in a specified manner toward".

When you learn polysemy:

• You reduce confusion and meaning ambiguity when reading a text.

• You learn a quantitative and qualitative growth of the language's expressive resources.

• You know more about the semantic changes in the system of meanings in the English language.

Now complete the sentences with the proper forms of the words from the box. Please notice that these words may mean differently in different context.

> commit   issue   odd   branch

1. The December _____ of Magazine X features an article on the Tower of the Babel.

2. After telling his brothers about his dreams, Joseph's brothers thought he'd always been _____, but not to this extent.

3. Abraham was faithful to God and _____ his soul to God.

4. He finally found the antique shop in a(n) _____ corner of town.

5. There are unconfirmed reports that he tried to _____ suicide.

6. He cut down a _____ from an old tree, and used it as a stick.

7. I found a(n) _____ sock in the washing machine.

8. I'm sorry, but I can't _____ myself on this matter until I know more details.

9. Senate employees could take their employment grievances to another _____ of government.

10. Dutch belongs to the West Germanic _____ of the Indo-European language family spoken by people in the Netherlands and in the northern half of Belgium.

11. The topic of today's geology lecture was the _____ of water from rivers into oceans.

12. Information about study groups _____ to all members of the class.

Speaking
Comparison and Contrast (2) Two Stories

When we are assigned to compare two stories, we can discuss the plots, or the main characters as another option. In other words, we can find the similarities and differences in what took place in each story, or discuss what the characters did in each story.

The following questions may help us to compare the stories in more detail:

How did each story start?

What happened later?

What was the end of each story?

Who were involved in each story?

What role did each character play in the story?

What did the main characters do in each story?

How did the characters perform the task? Or what methods did the characters use to perform the task?

What was the major conflict or climax in each story?

Why did the main characters do as described in each story?

What theme can we see from each story?

When making comparison, we can use transitions to signal their similarities and differences, for example, "***Both*** Greek myths ***and*** the Bible tell the story of flood"; "The first woman in Greek myths was created to punish man; the first woman in the Bible, ***however***, was made to be man's companion". You can refer to Unit 4 for more transitions and expressions in similarities and differences.

UNIT 5

Now compare the stories of *Creation of Man* in Greek myths and the Bible. Use the techniques and expressions you have learned.

Aspects	Similarities	Differences
Plots	1. 2. ...	1. 2. ...
Characters	1. 2. ...	1. 2. ...

Writing
Comparison and Contrast (2)
Two Subjects

To compare and contrast two subjects in an essay, we can start by stating the topic of the essay, that is, the comparable subjects in this case. The subjects can be introduced in varied ways, one of which is using a general topic sentence of the essay. The general topic sentence states the overall point of the similarities and the differences between the two subjects. Let's take this topic sentence as an example: "Though having a lot in common, Christianity and Judaism are two religions with certain basic differences." With this topic sentence, we reveal the subjects we will discuss in our essay, that is, Christianity and Judaism. Also we show the focus of our essay: the basic differences between Christianity and Judaism, though we will mention some major similarities between the two religions. Therefore, the ideas and the essay will be organized in the format of comparison and contrast pattern.

Under the control of the general topic sentence, we need to organize the ideas logically: usually from a general point to a major support (a specific point supporting the general idea) and to minor supports (detailed explanation or examples relating to the major support). We also need to use transitions when necessary to establish a clear and understandable flow of thoughts.

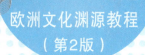

The following is a sample of comparison and contrast essay on Christianity and Judaism. Please read it and see how the points are stated and the ideas are organized.

Sample

Essay	Analysis
Christianity and Judaism The question concerning (1) <u>the similarities and contrasts of Judaism and Christianity</u> has always been a priority in the religious world. It goes without saying that (2) <u>these two religions do have a lot in common,</u> which is (3) <u>primarily due to the fact that Judaism was the forefather of Christianity as well as of Islam.</u> (4) The main base is the same for both religions — the Old Testament. Nevertheless, the influence that Christianity has experienced over the years of its existence has created (5) <u>certain differences in these religions.</u> Both Christians and Jews believe in the existence of God who was the one to create the universe and everything inside it. (6) <u>What differs is the notion of God:</u> (7) Christianity claims the idea of the trinity of God. In Judaism God cannot be divided into different parts but is holistic. For Jews God is unique and is a wholesome entity, which is "solid". The basic difference on the background of general similarities is that Judaism rejects the existence Jesus as one of the three "parts" of God. (8) <u>Another difference between the religions is the attitude towards faith and good deeds.</u> (9) Judaism puts good deeds higher as a complete reflection of faith. Christianity does not consider good deeds be sufficient if a person does not have faith inside. (10) <u>In terms of morals,</u> (11) Jews believe that a person is born neutral and only then shapes his moral values. Christianity states that a person inherits the moral values. (12) There are also numerous other small differences, though both of the religions poses the same message in the core — Love. (260 words)	(1) The topic (2) General point — similarity (3) Major support 1 (4) Minor supports (5) General point — differences (6) Major support 2 (7) Minor supports (8) Major support 3 (9) Minor supports (10) Major support 4 (11) Minor supports (12) Conclusion

http://www.custom-essays.org/samples/Comparison_of_Judaism_and_Christianity.html

Now finish the following outline of an essay on the comparison and contrast between Christianity and Taoism by getting more detailed information online. Then present your work with a complete essay.

Christianity and Taoism

Ⅰ. Introduction

　　Topic of the essay: major similarities and basic differences between Christianity and Taoism

Ⅱ. Body

　　1. Major similarities
　　　a. Belief:
　　　b.
　　2. Basic differences
　　　a. Monotheism or polytheism:
　　　b. History/Origins:
　　　c. Attitudes toward the nature or the world:
　　　d.

Ⅲ. Conclusion

Further Development

I. Watch the video clip on *Cain and Abel* and fill in the blanks with the words you hear.

　　In the Bible and the Koran, it is the first death and ____1____. Consumed with ____2____ and jealousy, Cain kills his brother Abel and is banished, condemned to ____3____ the earth alone.

　　Now this is a sort of story that you can compare to what happened ____4____, what we call the Neolithic Revolution, when these two groups of people, the ____5____ and the ____6____, started to ____7____ with each other. It all began in the ____8____ of civilization, in what is now Iraq. People had begun to move away from Stone Age ____9____ ways and had started ____10____ their environments.

They no longer gathered food, they ____11____ it. There were those who ____12____ animals, the herders, and those who ____13____ plants, the farmers. Experts think ____14____ erupted when bands of herders moved through the countryside and allowed their herds of animals to ____15____ and trample the farmers' fields and crops. The ensuing battles ____16____ and became the stuff of legend.

Once men learned to ____17____ and grow his crops according to his needs, he was able to ____18____ across the lands in search of food to put down roots, build villages and cities, and develop more and more ____19____ that ultimately led to a ____20____ of art, music, and the written word that would endure for all time.

II. Complete the table with the information you've learned from the story of *Cain and Abel* in small groups.

	Cain	Abel
Be good at		
Stand for		
Conflict:		

III. Listen to the story of *the Tower of Babel* and answer the following questions.

1. What made it possible for the people to build a tower reaching the heaven?
2. Why did people decide to build the tower?
3. Why did they fail to build the tower?

UNIT 5

IV. Work in small groups to figure out the meaning of "Tower of Babel" in each sentence based on your understanding of the story.

1. The factories, looming heavy in the black wet night—their tall chimneys rising up into the air like competing **Towers of Babel**.
   Meaning: _____

2. High-speed communications in oncoming years can either produce the most informed generation in history or reduce the globe to a **Tower of Babel**.
   Meaning: _____

3. He is more fond of empty talk than solid work, so all his plans are the **Tower of Babel**.
   Meaning: _____

Cultural Exploration

Read the following passage on *Human Nature* and finish the tasks.

Are humans inherently good or evil? According to Plato, "Evil acts are committed only out of ignorance. As a result, it is inherently against human nature to be evil. Therefore, evil cannot live in the hearts of people." Applying this quote to whether humans are inherently good or evil, and it means that it is impossible for a person to be naturally evil. The evil actions that a person would perform would be a result of ignorance of their environment or of values of their society.

Some Christian churches teach a doctrine of total depravity. *Theopedia* defines this doctrine in this way: "... as a consequence of the Fall of man, every person born into the world is morally corrupt, enslaved to sin and is, apart from the grace of God, utterly unable to choose to follow God or choose to turn to Christ in faith for salvation."

The philosophies of Confucianism and Buddhism value the innate goodness of human nature. Most interpretations of the writings of Confucius maintain that he was "very optimistic" about human nature. As to Confucius, "Their natures are much the same and their habits become widely different" (性相近，习相远) is supposed to be the typical reflection of his idea. He combined the investigation of others with self-examination and found that the main connotation of human nature was kindheartedness and courtesy.

Still, people who hold the Taoist worldview believe that the universe is best seen from the perspective of *yang* and *yin*, an infinite system of opposing elements and forces in balanced dynamic interaction. Two of the forces present in this universe are good and evil. Since humanity is part of the universe, these forces are naturally present in humankind. This view of the good and evil nature of humanity extends the position that people cannot eliminate evil, because it is a natural and necessary part of the universe.

(https://www.debate.org/opinions/is-human-nature-good-yes-or-evil-no
https://www.ukessays.com/essays/philosophy/the-inherint-good-and-evil-of-humans-philosophy-essay.php)

Task 1. Which position do you support? Briefly elaborate your opinions with examples if necessary.

Task 2. Different understanding about the human nature to some extent reflects the cultural differences between the east and the west. Please compare the cultural differences between China and the west, such as social practice or ancient mythology, which you believe originated from the different point of view on human nature, and explain your ideas briefly.

Further Reading

Ishmael

Many years went by after God made the promise to Abraham and still no child had been born. Sarah had a servant girl named Hagar so she gave Hagar to her husband as a second wife.

Abraham went alone with the plan to please Sarah. But when Hagar did become pregnant with a child and gave birth to a son named Ishmael, she was proud and began to show contempt for Sarah, and then Sarah responded by treating Hagar harshly.

Later Sarah gave birth to her son promised by God, and Abraham named the boy Isaac just as God had told him to.

One day Ishmael began to tease Isaac. Sarah saw what happened and was angry. She went to tell Abraham and insisted that Ishmael and his mother, Hagar, be sent away.

"Don't worry about your son, Ishmael," God said to Abraham. "I will care for him and his mother. Ishmael will grow to lead a great nation of his own." So Abraham agreed with Sarah's plan.

Abraham had given Hagar and Ishmael some food and water for their trip, and finally they settled down in the wilderness. Later, Hagar took a wife for her son from the land of Egypt, and Ishmael had his offspring.

The children of Ishmael later formed a mighty nation and called themselves Arabs. Throughout all of history, the Arabs and Isaac's people, the Jews, have fought with one another just as what Ishmael and Isaac did as children. (245 words)

Answer the following questions briefly.

1. Was Ishmael the promised son of Abraham and his wife?
2. Why were Hagar and Ishmael sent away by Abraham?
3. According to the Bible, who were the descendants of Ishmael and Isaac respectively?

Passage Two

Sodom and Gomorrah

Sodom and Gomorrah were wretched cities and full of crimes, so God decided to destroy the two cities. Lot, Abraham's nephew, stayed in Sodom with his people. He was righteous and kind, so God sent his two angels to

Sodom, to save Lot and his family. Lot invited the strangers into his home, and offered them food and a place to stay for the night. The angels agreed, but before they went to their beds that evening, men from across the city surrounded the house, demanding that Lot should bring out his guests. Lot was horrified, but the men were determined and even tried to break down the door. The angels blinded those in the crowd, and told Lot to gather his family quickly and get them out of Sodom, explaining that God was about to destroy the city. With dawn approaching, the angels asked Lot to take his wife and two daughters away from home, or they would be swept away when the city was punished. Lot still hesitated, so the visitors grabbed hold of him, his wife, and his two daughters and rushed them out of the city, urging them to keep running until they reached the mountains and not to look back.

When they were in safety, God rained down burning *sulfur* (硫磺) on Sodom and Gomorrah. The two cities and the entire plain were burning. But Lot's wife was too curious, and she wanted to see the strange scenes. Just as she looked back, she became a pillar of salt.

After the city of Sodom was ruined, trees grew out of the ground. The apples on the trees were beautiful and pleasant to the eyes, but tasted bad and uneatable. (287 words)

Answer the following questions briefly.

1. Where did Lot, Abraham's nephew, stay?
2. What did God plan to do with the two cities in the story, and why?
3. What happened to Lot's wife in the end?

UNIT 6

Exodus and Jewish Kingdoms

In this unit, you are going to
◎ locate the major information in the story of Moses and Exodus;
◎ comment on the merits and the demerits of King David and Solomon;
◎ expand your vocabulary through polysemy;
◎ make a comparison and contrast orally;
◎ write a critical review.

Pre-information

I. Listen to the Passage on *Exodus* and fill in the blanks with the words you hear.

Exodus tells how the Israelites _____1_____ in Egypt through the strength of God. Led by their _____2_____ Moses, the Israelites journeyed through the wilderness to Mount Sinai, where God _____3_____ of Canaan, which was also called the "Promised Land" in return for their faithfulness. Israel entered into a covenant with the God who gives them their _____4_____, known as the Ten Commandments.

Exodus presents the defining features of the Israelites' identity:

memories of a past marked by _____5_____, a binding covenant with God who chooses Israel, and the establishment of the life of the community and the guidelines for sustaining it.

II. Listen to the sentences and fill in the blanks with the words you hear. Then work out the meaning of each sentence with a partner.

1. Forgiveness is always better than _____.

2. If I don't have the data, how can I _____? I can't make bricks without straw.

3. "Did they fire you just because of the minor error after three years of hard work? That's really Egyptian _____!"

4. I needed money _____; it was like manna from heaven when it arrived!

5. Nowadays more and more people are absorbed _____ golden calf; therefore, virtues can hardly find their way in prosperity.

6. Thanks for agreeing with me about the dancing; you're a girl _____.

7. We have many professionals as senior consultants in our company, who are wise as Solomon and _____.

Stories

Listen to the story of the *Birth of Moses* and fill in the blanks with the words you hear.

Joseph and his family settled down in Egypt. Many years after Joseph died, the Egyptians began to be afraid because there were so many of Jacob's *descendants* — Israelites.

A new pharaoh, who did not know about Joseph and his story, came to power in Egypt. When he saw the Israelites had _____1_____, he decided to deal *shrewdly* with them. He was afraid that the Israelites would become even more numerous and, if war broke out, they would join the enemy of Egyptians and fight against them and leave the country.

Though treated cruelly as slaves, the Israelites multiplied and spread; so the Egyptians came to dread the Israelites and _____2_____. The king of Egypt said to the midwives, "When you help the Hebrew women in childbirth, if it is a boy, _____3_____; if it is a girl, let her live. If the boy is born before the midwives come, throw him into the Nile."

Not long after the king put his cruel law into effect, a baby boy was born to the family of Levi. The mother _____4_____. Then she placed the child in a basket and put it among the reeds along the bank of the Nile.

The pharaoh's daughter went down to the Nile, and she saw the basket among the reeds and got it. After she opened it and saw the baby, she felt sorry for him. And she _____5_____ and named him Moses since she drew him out of the water. (211 words)

Story Two

● I. Put a check (√) beside the statements which are true of Moses after your first reading.

_____ 1. was called Prince of Egypt

_____ 2. was born in Egyptian royal family

_____ 3. volunteered to go to the pharaoh to take the Israelites out of Egypt

_____ 4. was summoned by God in the form of a burning bush

_____ 5. requested to observe the annual celebration of Passover

● II. Fill in the blanks with the missing information after your second reading.

1. Though growing up in Egyptian pharaoh's palace, Moses was _____ and took pity of his people.

2. Moses was summoned in Mountain Horeb by God and asked to bring

UNIT 6

the Israelites _____ into Canaan—a land _____.

3. The pharaoh did not believe Moses and made the Israelites _____. So God performed his wonder through Moses and made _____ in Egypt.

4. God _____ all the firstborns in Egypt, and _____ Israeli families with blood on their doors. Ever since that, Israelites _____ the day of the Passover every year.

Moses

Moses grew up in Egyptian pharaoh's palace, but he knew he was an Israelite and he took pity on his people who were at their hard labor. One day, Moses killed an Egyptian who was beating an Israelite slave. When the pharaoh heard of this, he tried to kill Moses. So Moses fled to a nearby land called Midian, and married a daughter of a priest.

Moses became a **shepherd** for his father-in-law. One day when he led the flock to the far end of the desert and came to Horeb, the mountain of God, he saw that the bush was on fire, but it did not burn up. A voice began to speak to him from out of the fire. It was God. Then God told Moses that he had seen the misery of Israelites in Egypt. So he was sending Moses to bring them up out of Egypt into a good and spacious land, Canaan—a land flowing with milk and honey. And God promised to give Moses the power to show the signs to the people so they would know that God was with Moses. Since Moses didn't believe he had been able to speak well, God sent Aaron, Moses' brother to meet him on his way back to Egypt to speak for him.

When Moses was in Egypt and told the pharaoh what God asked him to do, the pharaoh didn't believe a word of him and made the Israelites suffer more. The pharaoh even punished the Israelites by telling his overseers not to give the people straw to make brick as they did before; instead, let them gather straw for themselves. On the contrary, the pharaoh still required the same daily output of bricks as before. So God performed his wonder through Moses and made nine plagues in Egypt: Frogs; Gnats; Flies; Livestock diseased; Boils; Thunder and hail; Locusts; Darkness. But the miracles only made the pharaoh more **stubborn**, and he refused again and again to let the Israelites go. So God decided to bring one more plague on the pharaoh and on Egypt — about midnight he would go throughout Egypt to kill every firstborn son in Egypt, including the firstborn son of the pharaoh and of the cattle as well. But the Israelites would be kept safe and would not be harmed. Moses went to tell his people that each family must find a lamb without defect and kill it. Then they were to take some of the blood and put it on the sides and tops of the doorframes of the houses. After that, they should roast the lamb's flesh and prepare it for a feast.

At midnight the Lord struck down all the firstborns in Egypt, and passed over Israelites families with blood on their doors. Shortly after midnight, there was loud wailing in Egypt, for there was not a house without someone dead. Therefore, the pharaoh told Moses to leave Egypt with his people. On that very day, Moses began to lead the people of Israel out of Egypt, back toward the Promised Land. Then God also instructed them to observe the Passover celebration every year on the anniversary of their Exodus. (531 words)

I. Match the items in the story with the proper information after your first reading.

1. Beside the Red Sea   a. The people of Israel complained to Moses for lack of water.

2. In the wildness   b. God gave Moses the Ten Commandments inscribed on two tablets.

3. Through the desert   c. Moses separated the water into two halves for Israelites to walk on dry land.

4. On Mount Sinai   d. The people of Israel found quail and the bread called manna outside their tent.

II. Fill in the blanks with the missing information after your second reading.

1. The pharaoh ordered his army to _____ after Moses led his people in desert.

2. Moses separated the Red Sea into two halves. The Israelites

UNIT 6

_____ and crossed the sea, but behind them, the Egyptian army _____ after Moses covered the dry land with water.

3. The people of Israel _____ to Moses in the wildness when they could not find water and food.

4. On Mount Sinai, God gave Moses the Ten Commandments which were God's _____ to the people.

The Exodus and the Ten Commandments

After the Passover, Moses led the people of Israel away from Egypt. But after the Hebrews left Egypt, the king changed his mind and was angry that he had lost his source of slave labor. He summoned his 600 best chariots, all the other chariots in the land, and marched his massive army in pursuit. The Israelites seemed to be trapped when they realized they were chased by Egyptian army — Mountains stood on one side, the Red Sea in front of them. **Terrified**, they **complained** they would rather be slaves again than die in the desert. The angel of God, in a pillar of cloud, stood between the people and the Egyptians, protecting the Hebrews. Then Moses stretched his hand out over the sea. A strong east wind blew all night, **separating** the waters and turning the sea floor into dry land. During the night, the Israelites fled through the Red Sea, a wall of water to their right and to their left. The Egyptian army charged in after them. Once the Israelites were safe on the other side of the sea, Moses stretched out his hand again, and then the sea rolled back in and became **normal**, covering the Egyptian army, its chariots and horses.

Thereafter, Moses and the Israelites walked for many days through the desert without water. When they did find water, it tasted so bitter that they could not drink it. They cried to Moses, asking him what to do. God told Moses to throw a piece of wood into the water, and the water turned sweet.

Later in the wildness people ran out of the food they brought with them, and began to grumble, recalling the tasty meals they had enjoyed when they were slaves. Moses prayed to God, and God told Moses he would rain down bread from heaven for the people. That evening quail came and covered the camp. The next morning when the people looked outside their tents, they saw white, flaky dew — later called manna by the people of Israel, covering the ground. Moses instructed the people to gather an omer (Note: an ancient unit of measure used in the era of the ancient Temple in Jerusalem) for each person each day. When some of them tried to save extra, it became wormy and spoiled. Manna appeared for six days in a row. On Saturday, the Israelites were to gather a double portion, and none at all could be found on the seventh day. Moses stated that the double portion was to be consumed on Sabbath, and that God instructed him that no one should leave his place on that day so that the people could rest during it. In this way, Sabbath was reinstituted the first week manna appeared.

Then the Israelites traveled through the desert and set up camp at the foot of Mount Sinai. God called to Moses from that mountain with a message to tell the people of Israel that he had brought them out of Egypt, so now it was time for them to obey him. He would tell them some special rules they would have to follow.

Then Moses went up the mountain and there God gave him the Ten **Commandments** which were *inscribed* on two stone **tablets**. Moses kept these as reminders of God's laws for his people.

    1. I am your God, and you must not worship other gods.

    2. Do not make up any idols or images to worship or serve.

    3. Do not misuse the name of God.

    4. Remember the Sabbath day and keep it holy.

    5. Honour your father and mother.

    6. You shall not murder.

    7. You shall not *commit* adultery.

    8. You shall not steal.

    9. You shall not give false *testimony* against your neighbor.

    10. You shall not *covet* your neighbor's house.

The Ten Commandments were God's most important instructions to the people. They were the rules to help guide the Israelites in their daily lives.

In addition, God also gave people other laws to live by. As to personal injuries, he said, "If men struggle with each other and strike a woman with child so that she gives birth prematurely, yet there is no injury, he shall surely be fined as the woman's husband may demand of him, and he shall pay as the judges decide. But if there is any further injury, then you shall *appoint* as a penalty: life for life, eye for eye, tooth for tooth, hand for hand, foot for foot, burn for burn, wound for wound, bruise for bruise".

Moses stayed on the mountain for forty days and nights, copying down what God told him. People asked Aaron to make them a god during the long absence of Moses on Mt. Sinai. Aaron told them to bring their wives' and daughters' golden earrings to him, and melted them down and molded a golden calf. Then they built an altar in front of it to bring offerings to their new god. Upon returning from the mountain with the *tablets* of the Law and seeing the people worshipping the golden calf, Moses broke the *tablets* and had the idol melted down. Then he ground it into powder, scattered it on the water and made the Israelites drink it. Finally he killed a lot of traitors. (883 words)

I. Match the major characters in the story with the proper information after your first reading.

1. David   a. the first king of Jewish Kingdom, who was later rejected by God
2. Saul   b. a Jewish King who had reigned for forty years
3. Goliath   c. wife of Uriah, then wife of David, and mother of Solomon
4. Bathsheba   d. a giant Philistine warrior who challenged the Israelites to come out and fight him

II. Fill in the blanks with the missing information after your second reading.

1. Being a shepherd provides free time for David to develop two other skills, that of _____.

2. One of the most famous incidents of David is _____ Goliath as a shepherd boy during the reign of Saul.

3. David decided to bring _____ and the tablets on which Moses had written down the laws of God, to Jerusalem.

4. David died and was buried beside his forefathers in Jerusalem, the

city he had made _____ and called the City of David.

King David

The first king of Jewish Kingdom was Saul, who was rejected by God because of his disobedience in his later years and died in a battle. David was the second king of Jewish Kingdom after Saul.

David was a **shepherd** from an early age, and developed his courage and fighting skills by **defending** the flocks from the wild animals, including lions and bears. The free time that being a **shepherd** provided also allowed him to develop two other skills, that of music and poetry.

One of the most famous incidents of David was his defeating Goliath as a **shepherd** boy during the **reign** of Saul. When the Israelites were at war with the Philistines, the two armies faced each other from opposite hills with a valley between them. Every morning for forty days, the mighty Goliath, who might be over nine feet tall, challenged the Israelites for someone to come out and fight him, but none would go out. One day, David, who was actually then too young for the army, arrived with some foods for his older brothers. He heard Goliath and immediately volunteered to fight him. King Saul put a coat of armour and a bronze helmet on him, but David refused because he was not used to them. As Goliath moved closer to attack him, David ran quickly toward the battle line to meet him. Then David reached into his bag, took out a stone and slung it, striking Goliath on the forehead, and he fell facedown on the ground. The success made David very popular in Israel and then God **appointed** David king after Saul.

David was thirty years old when he became the king, and he **reigned** forty years. One of the things he did was to capture the city of Jerusalem and make it Israel's new capital. Then David decided to bring the Ark of the Covenant and the **tablets** on which Moses had written down the laws of God, to Jerusalem.

As a king, David was secure enough on his throne that he no longer had a need to go to war to prove his military power as what King Saul had done. He could send his generals instead. Thus King David could stay in his palace when his soldiers were at war with the Ammonites. One afternoon, when David walked on a palace balcony, he saw a beautiful woman bathing. Through his messengers, David learned that she was Bathsheba, wife of Uriah, who had gone to battle for David. David sent messengers to get Bathsheba, and she came to him and got pregnant. David then recalled Uriah from battle and pretended that Uriah was the father of Bathsheba's baby. However, Uriah refused to go home to his wife, so David wrote a letter to Joab, the commander in the front line, "Set Uriah in the forefront of the hardest fighting, and then draw back from him, so that he may be struck down and die." Uriah was killed. David then married Bathsheba. Bathsheba's child died. Later Bathsheba and David soon conceived a second son, Solomon.

When King David was old in years, he chose Solomon to succeed him. Later David died and was buried beside his forefathers in Jerusalem, the city he had made Israel's capital and called the City of David. (550 words)

I. Put a check (√) beside the statements which are true of Solomon after your first reading.

_____ 1. was the first king of Jewish Kingdom.
_____ 2. was famous for his wisdom.
_____ 3. made Jerusalem Israel's capital.
_____ 4. built the original Temple of God in Jerusalem.
_____ 5. placed heavy taxation on the people.

II. Fill in the blanks with the missing information after your second reading.

1. God gave Solomon _____ heart as well as riches and honour.

2. Solomon was chosen to be David's _____, although he wasn't the oldest son.

3. Solomon had grown great through his wisdom, but his power became dangerous and he was _____ by it.

4. Solomon's empire was lost and his kingdom was _____ after he died.

Solomon

King Solomon was the last of the Biblical kings of the United Monarchy period. He was the child of King David and Bathsheba, and chosen to be David's successor, although he wasn't the eldest son. One day after Solomon became the king, the Lord appeared to him during the night in a dream, and said, "Ask for whatever you want me to give you." Solomon asked for "a *discerning* heart to govern the people and to distinguish between right and wrong". God gave him a wise and *discerning* heart as what he asked for. Moreover, God gave him what he had not asked for — both riches and honour — so that in his lifetime he would have no equal among kings.

The most famous incident of his wisdom as a judge was when two women came to his court with a baby whom both women claimed as their son. Solomon threatened to split the baby in half. One woman was prepared to accept the decision, but the other begged the king to give the baby to the other woman. Solomon then knew the second woman was the mother.

Solomon was also famous for building the *original* Temple of God in Jerusalem to serve as a permanent place to house the Ark of the Covenant, containing the Ten Commandments, as well as a pot of manna and Aaron's staff.

For nearly 500 years, the Ark of the Covenant, containing the *tablets* and scrolls of the law, had been carried around by the people of Israel. Ever since Moses had put the *tablets* into the Ark, it had been kept and had travelled from deserts to villages until at last King David had brought it to Jerusalem, intending to build it a permanent home.

It was the fourth year of Solomon's *reign*, and already he was richer and more powerful than any king before him. He built a great Temple for the Lord's Ark with the finest materials and by the most skillful craftsmen in the world, which had taken a little more than seven years to finish.

Solomon had grown great through his wisdom; he remained great through his power over people. However, this power became dangerous and the king was *corrupted* by it. Solomon's downfall came in his old age. He had taken many foreign wives, whom he allowed to worship other gods. He even built shrines for the sacrifices of his foreign wives. Within his kingdom, Solomon placed heavy taxation on the people, who became bitter. He introduced a form of slavery which the Israelites hated.

Solomon died in Jerusalem after 40 years as ruler of Israel. He was buried in the City of David. His son succeeded him as king. Under his rule, Solomon's empire was lost and his kingdom was divided into two parts — the northern Kingdom of Israel and the southern Kingdom of Judah. (477 words)

Vocabulary Focus

I. Match the words from *Stories* part with their corresponding definitions.

1. reign
2. sling
3. tablet
4. shrewdly
5. discerning
6. commit
7. testimony
8. corrupt
9. shepherd
10. stubborn
11. inscribe
12. covet

a. unreasonably, often perversely unyielding; bullheaded
b. evidence given by a witness
c. one who herds, guards, and tends sheep
d. mark, carve, or engrave (words or letters) on or in a surface
e. the flat pieces of clay or stone suitable for bearing an inscription
f. wish or long for, especially for the property of another person
g. cause to become dishonest, unjust and unable to be trusted
h. hurl with a weapon consisting of a looped strap in which a stone is whirled and then let fly
i. perform an act, usually with a negative connotation
j. characterized by keen awareness, sharp intelligence
k. the period during which a king, queen or emperor, etc. rules
l. able to judge which things are good and which are bad

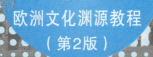

II. Use the words from *Exercise I* to complete the sentences.

1. The _____ and his dog gathered in the sheep.

2. It was once seen as a universal truth that those who were caught in a wildfire were _____ people who refused to evacuate when ordered.

3. Some galleries commemorate donors by _____ their names on the walls.

4. Police are investigating the latest robbery to see if the burglars are the same as the ones who _____ a similar crime last week.

5. Archaeologists reckon the road was built in about the year 125 A.D., during the _____ of the Emperor Hadrian.

6. He eyed them _____ with his twinkling eyes set in his grimy, sweaty face.

7. Xi'an Stone Forest Museum is an art treasure-house containing the largest and richest collection of stone _____ of ancient China.

8. It is the job of the press and _____ readers to compile and synthesize these messy facts and statements into a coherent narrative.

9. The prosecutor cited this _____ several times in his closing arguments.

10. It is sad to see a man so _____ by the desire for money and power.

11. Microsoft _____ Apple's understanding of consumer electronics, tech culture and entertainment ubiquity.

12. He took off his jacket and _____ it into the back seat.

UNIT 6

III. Choose the italicized words from *Stories* part to complete the table.

Verb	Noun	Adjective	Noun (Person)	Antonym
1_____	defence/defense	defensive	defendant	
2_____	terror	terrified/terrifying	terrorist	
descend	descending	descending	3_____	
4_____	separation	separate	separatist	inseparate
normalize	normalization	5_____		abnormal
originate	origin	6_____		unoriginal
7_____	appointment	appointed	appointer	
8_____	complaint	complaining	complainer	

IV. Use the words in the table from *Exercise III* to complete the sentences.

1. Readers pointed these errors out so I corrected them soon after the _____ version was published.

2. All the ingredients, including water, have to be listed in _____ order by weight.

3. For greater efficiency, recyclable materials need to be _____ at the site.

4. Opinion columnist talked about extreme weather that puts the _____ realities of climate change right in front of us.

5. The hospital claimed they were simply following their _____ procedure.

6. Doctors also _____ about the increasing pressures that were being placed on them.

7. The _____ is the first bank executive to be tried in the country for actions taken during the global financial crisis.

8. Meyer laid out his plans after he was _____ full-time CEO on Tuesday.

157

Vocabulary Development
Polysemy (2)
Multiple Meaning Verbs

English is a language with a huge vocabulary. To make matters even more confusing, many of these words have more than one meaning. For example, the verb "to run" can be used with the meaning of "to move quickly", "to manage a business", "to offer a service" etc., and "to take" can mean "to go with someone to guide them", "to buy", "to eat/drink", or "to write down" etc.; in addition, "to get" is also one of the most frustrating verbs for people learning English to use.

Learning the different meaning of those verbs helps people understand others better.

Now choose from the ten different words that could be used instead of "get" in this conversation.

> prepare take make buy receive annoy arrive
> hear understand catch become hit

A: Look at this present I've just *got* _____1_____ from dad.

B: But your birthday was last week.

A: Yes, but it only *got* _____2_____ here today. You see how poor dad is; he *got* _____3_____ flu.

B: What's the present?

A: It's a radio. Wait till I get _____4_____ it out of the box. Oh, sorry. I got _____5_____ you on the chin.

B: That's OK.

A: Oh Yes! I wonder how many stations we can *get* _____6_____ on it.

B: What's that hole for? I don't *get* _____7_____ it.

A: That's where it plugs in. Let's see if we can *get* _____8_____ it

UNIT 6

to work. What a funny noise!

B: It's getting ____9____ worse. Turn it off. The noise really gets ____10____ me. You'll have to get ____11____ a different plug or something.

A: I'll try and fix it while you get ____12____ the supper.

Speaking
Comparison and Contrast (3)
Compare and Comment

I. Review the stories of Moses, David and Solomon, and match the stories with the pictures below. Describe the pictures, and tell the stories to your partners.

Moses	David	Solomon

(1)   (2)   (3)

II. Comment on the three important biblical figures through comparison and contrast. Your comments will include: (1) a summary of your comparison and contrast; (2) your opinions based on the similarities and differences.

	Moses	David	Solomon
Similarities			
Differences			
Your Comment			

Writing
Critical Review (1)

When we write a critical review, we usually summarize and evaluate a text. We have to read the selected text in detail and also read other related texts so that we can present a fair and reasonable evaluation of the selected text. The critical review can be of a book, a chapter, or a journal article.

To be critical does not mean to criticize in a negative manner. Rather it requires writers to question the information and opinions in a text and present the evaluation or judgment of the text. To do this well, we should attempt to understand the topic from different perspectives (i.e. read related articles) and in relation to the theories, approaches, frameworks and points of view of the topic.

To write a critical review, we may consider such elements as: what we are interested in, why are we interested in it, what are the evidence, and what is our point of view, etc.

Generally, whenever people read anything, they are likely to ask:
- Why should I read this?

UNIT 6

- What is the point?

Specifically, they may think about it a lot, and they are likely to ask:
- Why are these articles interesting to me?
- Do they present a new procedure/idea?
- Do these articles contribute important new knowledge to the field?
- Are these articles mistaken?
- Am I agreeing or disagreeing with them?

Sample

In Homer's classics *Iliad*, Agamemnon was the king of Mycenae and the leader of Greek forces in the Trojan War.

The controversial issue raised by historians and critics is the extent of guilt ascribed to Agamemnon's deeds and character. In addition, it is rather interesting to investigate whether Homer himself provided us with an accurate account of Agamemnon's character in his classical work.

Homer presents the character of Agamemnon as a man empowered with virtually unlimited and enormous power as well as a rather powerful social position in the society. However, his personal features did not deserve such a high status. Homer's Agamemnon made most of his decisions while ruled by over-wrought emotions.

Overall, Homer's Agamemnon represents a deeply flawed character overwhelmed by inner desires and emotions. His authoritative position was always predetermined by personal whims as well as individual needs which were put atop of the genuine community interests. Such was the main controversy masterly depicted by Homer.

On the one hand, Agamemnon appears as a highly accomplished warrior, though as a king he often demonstrates the features incompatible with the ideals of true kingship, such as selfishness, which makes the epical character of Agamemnon as a person that is righteous to an extent though morally flawed.

Right from the beginning, the character of Agamemnon appears as a courageous and great warrior that heroically destroyed the powerful army as well as Troy. For the sake of his selfish ambitions and revenge for Paris' crime, he decides to sacrifice Iphigenia, his daughter, for the favourable wind to set sail for Troy.

Another flawed expression of Agamemnon is depicted through his arrogant and disrespectful attitude towards his wife. Utter infidelity and ignorance is seen in Agamemnon's disrespectful and rather condemned words to her. His dishonorable actions led to her embarrassment in front of the chorus as well as before his new mistress, Cassandra. Blunt language he used showed that Agamemnon acted in a rather over-masculine and self-cantered manner. (326 words)

(http://www.custom-essays.org/examples/Iliad_essay_Agamemnon_the_King.html)

Analyze the critical review essay by filling in the table below.

1. The figure whom the author is interested in	
2. The reason why the figure is interesting to the author	
3. The author's claim	
4. The reason for the claim	
5. The evidence to support the claim	
6. Whether the essay is fact-based, or emotional	
7. Whether the essay aims to make the audience see something different or to make the audience act on the information in a specific way	

Further Development

I. Fill in the blanks with the proper forms of the words from the box.

> dress   negative   physical   raze   archeological   legacy

Did King Solomon and his empire really not leave behind any ____1____ footprint? Archeologically, whether King Solomon existed? To be fair with you, the answer, if we are strictly speaking about archeology, the answer should be ____2____. But here in Jerusalem, the faithful believe that Solomon built the first temple and that it was ____3____ and then built again, and destroyed again. These people anxiously await the time when the third incarnation of the original temple can be built inconveniently, where the beautiful Islamic Mosque was standing. The temple, more than anything, is Solomon's most lasting ____4____, in faith, at least. But what about cold, hard stones? The book of King is replete with details of the temple. ____5____ masonry with interlaced cedar beams, quarry-dressed stones, elaborate columns, rooms with carved olivewood cherubs and an inner sanctum made of pure gold. So we are left with a very full Biblical description of a glorious temple but no ____6____ temple on earth in Jerusalem or even nearby.

II. Discuss the following questions after finishing Exercise I.

1. What is the significance of the Temple to the religious believers?
2. What role does the temple play in Israeli-Palestinian conflicts?

III. Watch the four video clips on *Truth of Exodus* and fill in the blanks with the words you hear.

(Clip 1)

The book of Exodus is a book of ____1____, which culminates in the ____2____ of the Ten Commandments. The Exodus story is the ____3____ for Judaism and Christianity. It's literally a story of the underdog that rises up ____4____ and gets out from under that and establishes them as people of God.

(Clip 2)

The ten plagues are the ten ____5____ events that brought horror and death to the land, suggested by some scientists as a description of ____6____.

(Clip 3)

The Hebrews reached the ____7____, and the pharaoh's army caught up with them. Then Moses stretched out his hands then the red sea ____8____. Some scientists believe it could have happened if all

_____9_____ were right. Oceanographer suggests that the parting of the red sea was a rare meteorological _____10_____ called "wind setdown", the phenomenon taking place at the shallow water.

(Clip 4)

From the ten Plagues of the Egypt to the parting of the Red Sea, to the mountain of the God itself, the miracles of Exodus can be explained as _____11_____. That does not make the story any less miraculous. Exodus speaks about the underdog, through faith and _____12_____, actually can overcome whatever oppression and whatever troubles it might be facing in life.

IV. Discuss the following questions based on your watching in *Exercise III*.

You believe it and why	You doubt it and why
e.g.: The miracles of Exodus can be explained as scientific phenomena.	e.g.: It's just a story told by the faithful based on the hardships endured by the Israelites.

Cultural Exploration

Read the following passage on *Justice and Revenge* and finish the tasks.

The expression "an eye for an eye and a tooth for a tooth" has been widely used to justify vengeful feelings. Does the "eye-for-eye" principle promote the merciless execution of justice?

The understanding of the story in this chapter about "eye for eye" seems to be two folded. For some, it promotes the principle of vengeance which is a reprehensible or unworthy motivation and that, as a result, pursuing revenge should not be the method of choice when giving out punishment for crimes. But others doubt whether these approaches to punishment are really more just than the retributive or vengeance model.

Task 1. The following are examples of using "an eye for an eye" in modern time. Tell your partner what you've learned about "an eye for an eye".

Example 1: A conversation

Andy: Brannon hit me!

Devin: Hit him back. An eye for an eye.

Example 2: News

1) "Some of our people are saying an eye for an eye, a tooth for a tooth, a life for a life," Barron said. – *NY Post*

2) "An Eye for An Eye – In 1972, In Munich, Another Terrorist Attack" – *CBS News*

Task 2. What principle is underlying the phrase "an eye for an eye"?

Task 3. In addition to "an eye for an eye", there is also phrase like "An eye for an eye will only make the whole world blind". Please list more expressions conveying similar ideas with them in Chinese culture, and then talk with other students as to the different ideas people hold towards "taking revenge".

Further Reading

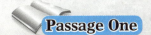

The Entry into Canaan

After Moses had died, God said to Joshua, "Now it is the time for you to leave the wildness and cross the river Jordan into the Promised Land. Everywhere you go will be yours; I am giving it to you, as I promised Moses I would. From the desert to the river *Euphrates*(幼发拉底河), and onwards to the Mediterranean Sea shall be your land. No one will ever be able to stand against you; be strong and full of courage, and above all—obey my commandments. If you obey me, I will protect you wherever you

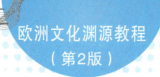

go."

Joshua called the people together to tell them what God had said. Then Joshua said to them, "In three days' time, we will cross the river Jordan. Twelve men from the tribes of Israel, one from each tribe, will lead you. The priests will walk in front of you, carrying the Ark of the Covenant of God, and the river dry up to let you pass."

On the third day, the people gathered together on a hill, and the priests and the twelve men, one from each tribe, began carrying the Ark down to the water's edge. When they reached it, Joshua held up Moses' staff, and the priests and the twelve men moved forward. As their feet touched the water, the water piled up into a great wall on either side and the priests were able to step down into the dry river bed. When they reached the middle of the Jordan, the priests stood still and lifted the Ark up high, for everyone to see. Meanwhile, each of the twelve men chose a large stone from the middle of the river bed, carried it across to the far side, and set it up there as a memorial to God.

At a sign from Joshua, the people of Israel surged forward and crossed the river Jordan, shouting and singing to God as they went. When the last man had crossed to the other side, Joshua commanded the priests carrying the Ark to follow on. Slowly they marched to the other side. When they too were on high ground, the waters closed up behind them, and the river flowed on as before.

That night the Israelites celebrated the feast of the Passover. They baked unleavened bread, collecting the wheat from the fields around them, and grinding into flour. From that day on, the manna from heaven stopped, and they ate the food they gathered from the land. (419 words)

Answer the following questions briefly.

1. Who did God choose to succeed Moses as the leader of Israel?

2. What instruction did God give to Joshua?

3. What happened to the Israelites when they carried the Ark of Covenant to the water's edge?

4. What did the Israelites eat the night they entered Canaan?

Passage Two

The Story of Saul

Saul was the first king of Israel. He was the son of Kish of the tribe of Benjamin. He became king at about the time that Samuel had retired as the last Judge of Israel. Although the land of Israel had been ruled by judges, the people were *clamoring*(喧闹) to have a king, like other nations. Samuel asked God for advice. God directed Samuel to Saul and to *anoint* (通常指宗教仪式在……上涂油) him as the first king.

Saul and his army defeated the Philistines in their first battle. However Saul did not obey God, and kept some of the *loot* (抢劫) after defeating the Amalekites. For this, God rejected Saul as king of Israel, and had Samuel anoint young David as the next king.

After David killed Goliath, Saul made David his special assistant, and as David succeeded in everything he did, Saul grew extremely jealous. Saul became possessed by an evil spirit, went into fits of anger and tried to kill David several times. He even threw a spear at his own son, who had become David's close friend. So David fled away from Saul.

Saul set out in person to hunt David down and in the hills Saul finally picked up David's trail. David and his men had hidden themselves in a cave when, by chance, the king came into it, alone and undefended. David was persuaded by his men to kill the King but he refused since David believed that Saul was anointed as king by God. Instead, David cut off a piece of the king's cloak and spared Saul's life.

After Samuel died, the Philistines invaded Israelite territory and gathered forces. Saul had a *foreboding* (预感) of his fate, and as he did not have Samuel to ask God for advice, he traveled to consult a witch about the outcome of the battle. The result of the *seance* (会议) confirmed his worst fears. He was told that the entire Israel army would be routed by the Philistines, and that he and his three sons would be killed.

The Israelite army had no chariots and could not withstand the assault of the heavy Philistine *weaponry* (兵器). Saul and his three sons were killed. Their bodies were brought to Jabesh where they were *cremated* (火葬). After learning of Saul's death, David moved to Hebron and was crowned king of the Judean *confederacy* (联盟). (429 words)

Answer the following questions briefly.

1. Who is Saul?
2. Did Saul get along well with young David?
3. What happened to Saul finally?

UNIT 7

Life Stories of Jesus

欧洲文化渊源教程
（第2版）

In this unit, you are going to
◎ identify major information in the life of Jesus;
◎ describe pictures pertaining to life stories of Jesus;
◎ write a critical review;
◎ expand your vocabulary through the collocations.

Pre-information

I. Listen to the passage on the *New Testament* and fill in the blanks with the words you hear.

The New Testament is a collection of works written at different times by different writers. It has 27 books and _____1_____ three sections: the Gospels (Matthew, Mark, Luke and John); the Letters written by various _____2_____ leaders to provide guidance for the earliest church communities; and the final Book of Revelation. The Gospels are written to present the life and _____3_____ of Jesus in ways that would be appropriate to _____4_____ and for that reason are not all the same. In the gospel accounts, towards the end of the final week in

Jerusalem, Jesus had the Last Supper with his disciples, and the next day was _____5_____. The trial ended in his crucifixion and death. Three days after his burial, he was resurrected and appeared to his disciples over a 40-day period, after which he ascended to Heaven.

II. Listen to the sentences and fill in the blanks with the words you hear. Then work out the meaning of each sentence with a partner.

1. The old baron was hard enough on his people but the son who _____ him tried to out-Herod Herod.

2. When he said he had some extremely important information and must talk to the chief _____, no one suspected it was meant to be a Judas kiss.

3. The negative associations with 13 can be traced to the number of diners at _____ before the betrayal of Jesus.

4. A modern equivalent of _____ is I would if I could but I can't.

5. The police asked a good Samaritan who intervened during a(n) _____ to come forward and testify.

6. He's a real _____ Thomas —he simply wouldn't believe I'd won the car until he saw it with his own eyes.

7. Phil seemed cold and distant, and now she was very afraid that he would _____ her.

Stories

Story One

Listen to the story of the *Birth of Jesus* and fill in the blanks with the words you hear.

This is how the birth of Jesus Christ came about: His mother Mary was pledged to be married to Joseph, but before they came together, she was found to be with child through the Holy Spirit. Because Joseph, her husband, was a righteous man and did not want to _____1_____, he had in mind to divorce her quietly. But after he had considered this, an angel appeared to him in a dream and said, "Joseph, son of David, do not be afraid to take Mary home as your wife, because _____2_____ is from the Holy Spirit. She will give birth to a son, and you are to give him the name Jesus, because he will _____3_____." When Joseph woke up, he did what the angel had commanded him and took Mary home as his wife. But he had no union with her until she gave birth to a son.

In those days, Caesar Augustus _____4_____ that a census should be taken of the entire Roman world. And everyone went to their own town to register. So Joseph also went up from Nazareth to Bethlehem because he belonged to the house and line of David. He went there to register with Mary, who was pledged to be married to him and was _____5_____. When Joseph and Mary got to Bethlehem, there was no place for them to stay because the inn was already full. They ended up spending the night in a stable, a place where animals were kept. While they were there, the time came for the baby to be born, and she gave birth to her firstborn, a son. She wrapped him in cloths and placed him in a manger, because there was no guest room available for them. (312 words)

I. Match the major characters in the story with the proper information after your first reading.

1. Jesus   a. were inspired by the star to travel to Jerusalem.
2. The Magi   b. fled to Egypt with his wife Mary and infant son.
3. King Herod   c. survived Herod's slaughter of the innocents.
4. Joseph   d. saw the baby Jesus as a threat and wanted to murder him.

UNIT 7

II. Decide whether the following statements are TRUE or FALSE after your second reading.

_____ 1. The Magi recognized Jesus Christ as the Messiah while he was still a child and came to worship him with valuable gifts.

_____ 2. The Magi met King Herod on their way to worship Jesus. King Herod succeeded in tricking them into revealing the child's location in Bethlehem on their way home.

_____ 3. When Herod learned he had been outwitted by the Magi, he became furious, ordering the slaughter of all the boys.

_____ 4. Joseph did not return to Israel until Herod had died.

The Magi's Visit and the Escape to Egypt

After Jesus was born in Bethlehem in Judea, during the time of King Herod, the Magi from the east came to Jerusalem and asked, "Where is the one who has been born king of the Jews? We saw his star when it rose and have come to worship him." When King Herod heard this, he was disturbed. Then he called together all the people's chief priests and teachers of the law, and asked them where the Messiah was to be born. "In Bethlehem in Judea," they replied, "for this is what the prophet has written." Then Herod called the Magi secretly and found out from them the exact time the star had appeared. He sent them to Bethlehem and said, "Go and search carefully for the child. As soon as you find him, report to me, so that I too may go and worship him." After the Magi had heard the king, they went on their way, and the star they had seen when it rose went ahead of them until it stopped over the place where the child was. On coming to the house, they saw the child with his mother Mary, and they bowed down and worshiped him. They opened their treasures and presented him with gifts of gold, frankincense and myrrh. And having been warned in a dream not to go back to Herod, they returned to their country by another route.

When the Magi had gone, an angel appeared to Joseph in a dream. "Get up," the angel said, "take the child and his mother and escape to Egypt. Stay there until I tell you, for Herod is going to search for the child to kill him." So Joseph got up, took the child and his mother during the night and left for Egypt, where he stayed until the death of Herod.

When Herod realized that he had been *outwitted* by the Magi, he was furious, and he gave orders to kill all the boys in Bethlehem and its *vicinity* who were two years old and under, in accordance with the time he had learned from the Magi.

After Herod died, an angel appeared in a dream to Joseph in Egypt and said, "Get up, take the child and his mother and go to the land of Israel, for those who were trying to take the child's life are dead." So he got up, took the child and his mother and went to the land of Israel. But when he heard that Archelaus was reigning in Judea in place of his father Herod, he was afraid to go there. Having been warned in a dream, he withdrew to the district of Galilee, a region in northern Israel, and he went and lived in a town called Nazareth. (461 words)

Story Three

I. Answer the following questions briefly after your first reading.

1. Who recognized Jesus as the Messiah and baptized him?
2. What is a parable?

II. Decide whether the following statements are TRUE or FALSE after your second reading.

　　_____ 1. The baptism by John the Baptist marks the beginning of Jesus' public ministry.

　　_____ 2. Jesus used his parables to get his point across and make his hearers think.

　　_____ 3. The miracles of Jesus are the supernatural deeds of Jesus in the course of his ministry.

　　_____ 4. Jesus' disciples were delighted when they saw he was walking on the water.

　　_____ 5. Jesus' parables usually have a double meaning.

UNIT 7

Jesus' Miracles and Parables

According to the gospels, the ministry of Jesus started with his Baptism by John the Baptist in the River Jordan, when he was about thirty years old. Most notably, John the Baptist was the one who recognized Jesus as the Messiah and baptized him.

Empowered and led by the Holy Spirit, Jesus spent forty days fasting in the desert in preparation for his ministry, which his baptism *inaugurated*. Jesus then began preaching in Galilee and gathered disciples.

The following story tells how Jesus calls Philip and Nathanael. The next day Jesus decided to leave for Galilee. Finding Philip, he said to him, "Follow me." Philip found Nathanael and told him, "We have found the one Moses wrote about in the Law, and about whom the prophets also wrote—Jesus of Nazareth, the son of Joseph." "Nazareth! Can anything good come from there?" Nathanael asked. "Come and see," said Philip. When Jesus saw Nathanael approaching, he said of him, "Here truly is an Israelite in whom there is no deceit." "How do you know me?" Nathanael asked. Jesus answered, "I saw you while you were still under the fig tree before Philip called you." Then Nathanael declared, "Rabbi, you are the Son of God; you are the king of Israel."

Jesus' activities in Galillee also included a number of miracles and teachings. He traveled from town to town, healing the sick and preaching about the coming kingdom of God. He promised a wonderful eternal life after death for those who would put their trust in God and obey his commandments. Jesus reinforced his teaching by miracles and parables.

These miracles may be categorized into four groups: cures where an *ailment* is cured, exorcisms where demons are cast away, resurrection of the dead, and control over nature. The story of Jesus walking on the water is one of the key miracles. One day, Jesus made his disciples get into a boat and go ahead of him to the other side of the Sea of Galilee. Several hours later in the night, the disciples encountered a storm. Then they witnessed Jesus walking toward them across the surface of the water. They were frightened, thinking they were seeing a spirit, but when Jesus told them not to be afraid, they were reassured.

Jesus' parables are short stories that teach a moral or spiritual lesson by *analogy* or similarity. It can be a figure of speech or comparison, such as "the kingdom of God ... is like a mustard seed ... or like yeast" (Luke 13). More commonly it is a short story told to bring out a lesson or moral. Jesus used simple stories or images to convey important doctrines, and lessons *pertaining* to the way of life and happiness. Jesus' parables have a double meaning. First, there is the literal meaning, apparent to anyone who has experience with the subject matter. But beyond the literal meaning lies a deeper meaning — a beneath-the-surface lesson. His parables often have an unexpected twist or surprise ending that catches the reader's attention. The parable of the Good Samaritan is a case in point:

A traveler was beaten, robbed, and left half dead along the road. First a priest and then a Levite came by, but both passed by on the other side. Finally, a Samaritan came by. He bandaged his wounds, took him to the inn, and then he even footed the bill for him.

Samaritans were considered a low class of people by the Jews since they had intermarried with non-Jews and did not keep all the law. People would expect the Samaritan man to be the one who just passed by without helping. Instead, this Samaritan man took pity on the injured Jewish man and showed love and compassion. (624 words)

I. Match the major characters in the story with the proper information after your first reading.

1. Jesus   a. denied knowing Jesus three times.
2. Judas   b. shared a meal with his disciples before he was crucified.
3. Peter   c. betrayed Jesus.

II. Answer the following questions briefly after your second reading.

1. What's the significance of the Last Supper?
2. What festival was the Last Supper related to?
3. What do the bread and wine stand for?

UNIT 7

The Last Supper

Jesus' final ministry in Jerusalem is sometimes called the Passion Week and begins with his triumphal entry into Jerusalem. The four Gospels all state that the Last Supper took place towards the end of the week and that Jesus and his disciples shared a meal shortly before Jesus was crucified at the end of that week. During the meal Jesus predicted his betrayal by one of the disciples present and foretold that Peter would deny knowing him three times. The Last Supper contains many significant principles and continues to be an important part of Christian lives throughout the world. It is described in three of the four New Testament Gospels, Matthew, Mark and Luke.

The Last Supper was held on the evening of preparation for the Jewish Passover, a very holy time for the Jewish nation in remembrance of when God spared the Jews from the plague of death of every firstborn child in Egypt. Jesus arranged the dinner purposely by instructing his disciples where to host it. The disciples did just as Jesus asked, and they found a place and got ready for the Passover. The following is what the Gospel of Matthew recorded.

When evening came, Jesus was reclining at the table with the twelve disciples. And while they were eating, he said, "Truly I tell you, one of you will betray me." They were very sad and began to say to him one after another, "Surely you don't mean me?" Jesus replied, "The one who has dipped his hand into the bowl with me will betray me. The Son of Man will go just as it is written about him. But *woe* to that man who betrays the Son of Man! It would be better for him if he had not been born." Then Judas, the one who would betray him, said, "Surely you don't mean me, Rabbi?" Jesus answered, "You have said so." While they were eating, Jesus took bread, and when he had given thanks, he broke it and gave it to his disciples, saying, "Take and eat; this is my body." Then he took a cup, and when he had given thanks, he gave it to them, saying, "Drink from it, all of you. This is my blood of the covenant, which is poured out for many for the forgiveness of sins. I tell you, I will not drink from this fruit of the vine from now on until that day when I drink it new with you in my Father's kingdom."

The Last Supper, a late 15th century mural painting by Leonardo da Vinci, represents the scene of the Last Supper of Jesus with his disciples. Leonardo depicted the consternation that occurred among the twelve disciples when Jesus announced that one of them would betray him. (463 words)

The Last Supper by Leonardo da Vinci

I. Match the major characters in the story with the proper information after your first reading.

1. Judas   a. was the high priest who plotted to kill Jesus.
2. Caiaphas   b. was the Roman governor.
3. Jesus   c. was mocked by Roman soldiers who placed a crown of thorns upon his head.
4. Pilate   d. returned the money to the priests.

UNIT 7

II. Fill in the blanks with the missing information after your second reading.

1. _____ is infamously known for his kiss and betrayal of Jesus in exchange for a payment of thirty pieces of silver coins.

2. Judas ended up _____ out of remorse and guilt.

3. The chief priests used the money returned by Judas to buy _____ as a burial place for foreigners.

4. Following the custom of _____ before Passover, Pilate suggested pardoning Jesus but the crowd protested and demanded the release of another prisoner.

5. Pilate _____ to show that he was not responsible for the execution of Jesus and reluctantly sent him to his death.

The Death of Jesus

Jesus was very popular with the crowds of people in Jerusalem. His claims of divine *authority* and his refusal to follow some Jewish religious rules were usurping the *authority* of the religious establishment. This conflict ultimately led to Jesus' execution by crucifixion only three years after he had begun his ministry.

The chief priests and the elders of the people *assembled* in the palace of Caiaphas, the high priest, and they *schemed* to arrest Jesus secretly and kill him. Then one of the twelve disciples — the one called Judas Iscariot — went to the chief priests and asked, "What are you willing to give me if I deliver him over to you?" So they counted out for him thirty pieces of silver. From then on Judas watched for an opportunity to hand him over.

After the Passover meal, Jesus went with his disciples to a place called Gethsemane. At some point, Jesus took three of them — Peter, James and John — to a place separated from the rest. Jesus prayed in the Garden, returning twice to his disciples, only to find them sleeping. He urged them to pray that they would not fall into temptation and commented, "The spirit is willing, but the flesh is weak." And then he returned to his own *agonizing* prayer. After this, Judas Iscariot, the betrayer, arrived with a *multitude* of soldiers, high priests, Pharisees, and servants to arrest Jesus. Judas identified him by the prearranged signal of a kiss which he gave to

Jesus. Then the men stepped forward, seized Jesus and arrested him.

When Judas saw that Jesus was condemned, he was seized with *remorse* and returned the thirty pieces of silver to the chief priests and the elders. "I have sinned," he said, "for I have betrayed innocent blood." "What is that to us?" they replied. "That's your responsibility." So Judas threw the money into the temple and left. Then he went away and hanged himself. The chief priests picked up the coins and said, "It is against the law to put this into the treasury, since it is blood money." So they decided to use the money to buy the potter's field as a burial place for foreigners. That is why it has been called the Field of Blood to this day.

Then it was the governor's custom at the festival to *release* a prisoner chosen by the crowd. At that time they had a *notorious* prisoner whose name was Barabbas. So when the crowd had gathered, Pilate asked them which one to *release* for he knew it was out of self-interest that they had handed Jesus over to him. While Pilate was sitting on the judge's seat, his wife sent him this message, "Don't have anything to do with that innocent man, for I have suffered a great deal today in a dream because of him." But the chief priests and the elders persuaded the crowd to ask for Barabbas and to have Jesus executed. "Which of the two do you want me to *release* to you?" asked the governor. "Barabbas," they answered. "What shall I do, then, with Jesus who is called the Messiah?" Pilate asked. They all answered, "*Crucify* him!" "Why? What crime has he committed?" asked Pilate. But they shouted all the louder, "*Crucify* him!" When Pilate saw that he was getting nowhere, but that instead an uproar was starting, he took water and washed his hands in front of the crowd. "I am innocent of this man's blood," he said. "It is your responsibility!" All the people answered, "His blood is on us and on our children!" Then he *released* Barabbas to them, but had Jesus flogged, and handed him over to be crucified.

Then the governor's soldiers stripped him and put a scarlet robe on him, and then twisted together a crown of thorns and set it on his head. After they had mocked him, they took off the robe and put his own clothes on him. Then they led him away to *crucify* him.

Two rebels were crucified with him, one on his right and one on his left. From noon until three in the afternoon darkness came over all the land. About three in the afternoon Jesus cried out in a loud voice, "My

God, my God, why have you *forsaken* me?" And when Jesus had cried out again in a loud voice, he gave up his spirit.

Before sunset, Jesus was taken down by Joseph of Arimathea. Joseph took the body, wrapped it in a clean linen cloth, and placed it in his own new tomb that he had cut out of the rock. He rolled a big stone in front of the entrance to the tomb and went away. (786 words)

I. Answer the following questions briefly after your first reading.

1. What did the angel tell Mary Magdalene and the other Mary?
2. What were the reactions of the disciples when they saw Jesus on the mountain in Galilee?

II. Fill in the blanks with the missing information after your second reading.

1. _____ is the festival which celebrates the resurrection of Jesus.
2. It is commonly supposed that Jesus was crucified on _____ and resurrected on Sunday.
3. According to the New Testament, Jesus _____ forty days after his resurrection.

The Resurrection of Jesus

The resurrection of Jesus is the Christian belief that Jesus Christ miraculously returned to life on the Sunday following the Friday on which he was executed by crucifixion. It has long been central to Christian faith and appears within diverse elements of the Christian tradition, from feasts to artistic depictions to religious *relics*. Easter is the most important festival which celebrates the resurrection of Jesus. The following is adopted from Matthew 28:

After the Sabbath, at dawn on the first day of the week, Mary

Magdalene and the other Mary went to look at the tomb. There was a violent earthquake, for an angel of God came down from heaven and, going to the tomb, rolled back the stone and sat on it. His appearance was like lightning, and his clothes were white as snow. The guards were so afraid of him that they shook and became like dead men.

The angel told the women that Jesus had risen from the dead. So the women hurried away from the tomb, afraid yet filled with joy, and ran to tell his disciples. Suddenly Jesus met them. "Greetings," he said. They came to him, clasped his feet and worshiped him. Then Jesus said to them, "Do not be afraid. Go and tell my brothers to go to Galilee; there they will see me."

While the women were on their way, some of the guards went into the city and reported to the chief priests everything that had happened. When the chief priests had met with the elders and devised a plan, they gave the soldiers a large sum of money, telling them, "You are to say, 'His disciples came during the night and stole him away while we were asleep.' If this report gets to the governor, we will satisfy him and keep you out of trouble." So the soldiers took the money and did as they were instructed. And this story has been widely *circulated* among the Jews to this very day.

Then the eleven disciples went to Galilee, to the mountain where Jesus had told them to go. When they saw him, they worshiped him, but some doubted. Then Jesus came to them and said, "All *authority* in heaven and on earth has been given to me. Therefore go and make disciples of all nations, baptizing them in the name of the Father and of the Son and of the Holy Spirit, and teaching them to obey everything I have commanded you. And surely I am with you always, to the very end of the age."

Jesus *ascended* into heaven 40 days after he was resurrected. During those 40 days he appeared to his followers, taught them and commissioned them to continue his earthly ministry. The ascension of Jesus was an event that shocked the disciples. Jesus had just finished talking with them and he went up into the clouds and was hidden from view. A few angels came by and told the disciples to move along. Jesus had *ascended* into heaven and he would return in the same way. (510 words)

UNIT 7

Vocabulary Focus

▶ I. Match the words from *Stories* part with their corresponding definitions.

1. scheme   a. get the better of by superior cleverness
2. crucify   b. gather together
3. relic   c. widely and unfavorably known
4. ailment   d. devise systematic plan of action
5. multitude   e. free from confinement
6. assemble   f. put (someone) to death by nailing or binding them to a cross
7. inaugurate   g. have reference or relation; relate
8. outwit   h. a surrounding or nearby region
9. release   i. an object surviving from an earlier time
10. notorious   j. an illness
11. pertain   k. mark the beginning or first public use of
12. vicinity   l. a large number

▶ II. Use the words from *Exercise I* to complete the sentences.

1. They are aggressive birds that consistently _____ the tools utilized to scare them away.

2. The society was officially _____ on 11th January, 1861 with 14 members.

3. We call upon the police to cease these illegal actions immediately and to _____ the people who have been illegally detained.

4. Spiders are _____ hunters, luring prey into their sticky webs or ambushing them from behind a leaf.

5. He is currently interested in all the laws _____ to adoption.

6. A large crowd had _____ outside the American embassy.

183

7. There were a hundred or so hotels in the _____ of the station.

8. The terrorists _____ to bring about the collapse of the government.

9. After performing the miracle of walking on the water on the Sea of Galilee, Jesus and his disciples anchored their boat on the shore at Gennesaret. The residents saw Jesus and went to him to be miraculously healed of a variety of _____.

10. It is possible for a _____ man to take five days to die.

11. The building stands as the last remaining _____ of the town's cotton industry.

12. Addiction to drugs can bring a _____ of other problems.

III. Choose the italicized words from *Stories* part to complete the table.

Verb	Noun	Adjective	Noun (Person)	Antonym
	1_____	remorseful		
2_____	forsakenness	forsaken	forsaker	
agonize	agony	3_____		
analogize	4_____	analogous		
	5_____	woeful		
authorize	6_____	authoritative	authorizer	
7_____	circulation	circular		
8_____	ascension	ascending		descend

IV. Use the words in the table from *Exercise III* to complete the sentences.

1. Their pay would be raised to support their _____ status.

2. Society sees the few people making a spectacle, not the many who _____ in secret.

3. My colleague has shown no _____ for his harsh words and has not changed his views or his ways.

4. China called for concerted efforts to tackle financial _____.

5. She drew a(n) _____ between running the economy and a housewife's weekly budget.

6. Rumours were already beginning to _____ that the project might have to be abandoned.

7. It could be the first school library, public or private, to _____ ink and paper in favor of e-books.

8. It ended as a statement, _____ and lasting.

Vocabulary Development
Collocation (3)
Unique, Strong and Weak Collocations

Some collocations are unique collocations which cannot usually be changed. Some words have a very limited number of collocates. We call these "strong collocations". They are often highly idiomatic. Other words have a larger number of possible collocates. We call these "weak collocations". Weak collocations are on the verge of the area we define as collocation. They are more common than strong collocations.

1. Unique collocations

1) I'll be back *in a flash*.

2) My boss usually arrives at eight o'clock *on the dot*.

3) The children arrived *safe and sound*.

4) Who's going to *foot the bill* for the damage?

5) The reason most people aren't excited about the election is that both candidates leave them *shrugging their shoulders*.

2. Strong Collocations

1) She seemed to have gone *stark raving mad*.

2) The outbreak of violence served as a *stark reminder* of how fragile the peace was.

3) He came to the door *stark naked*.

4) You're *bone idle*.

5) This soil is *bone dry*.

6) Such is human nature that everybody present **was moved/reduced to tears**.

3. Weak Collocations

1) accumulate/acquire/amass/flaunt/display their wealth

2) abandon/be involved in/dabble in/enter/go into/ engage in politics

3) prices dropped/fell/fluctuated/remained steady/rose/soared/spiraled/went through the roof

Some collocations can be changed by using different grammatical forms or adding other words.

1) We're in danger of *pricing* ourselves *out of the* (property) *market*.

2) She's been *gaining* (an awful lot of) *weight* recently.

3) to *purify* water/a water *purifying* gadget/water *purification*

However, some collocations cannot make these changes without sounding very unnatural. For example, we usually say "a tidal wave" but not "the wave was tidal".

Now finish the following exercises.

I. Complete the sentences with the words in the box. You may need to use some words more than once.

> heavy   idle   severe   strong   vain   plain   straight   hard

1. The _____ weather meant that hundreds of schools had to be closed.

2. The Second World War yielded much _____ casualties than had ever been known before.

3. He said he would throw us out, but it was just a(n) _____ threat.

4. It was a very _____ meal—far too much meat and not enough vegetables or salads.

5. Martina Hingis has always exerted a(n) _____ influence on the way I play tennis.

6. Pray for unity and world peace, so that these precious losses will not have been in _____.

186

UNIT 7

7. The _____ truth is that I hate my job.

8. It was a(n) _____ exam and the final question was really _____ — it was a(n) _____ nut to crack!

9. We are under _____ pressure to reduce the wage bill and make 500 workers redundant.

10. I lost my temper and told him _____ that I hadn't been looking for any job.

11. She speaks English quite well but with a(n) _____ French accent.

12. They rushed the victim to hospital, in the _____ hope of saving her life.

II. Think of as many collocations as you can and fill in the following blanks, then compare your answers with the collocations from *Stories* part in the textbook.

1. In the _____ of God, stop that noise!
2. Let us now look at some _____ of speech used in the Bible.
3. They ended up _____.
4. (v.) _____ a prisoner
5. as white as _____ (n.)

Speaking
Interpreting the Artwork

Painting interpretation is a very tricky subject, and that's just because each person has a different answer. It is more subjective than the others, as you are expected to use your analysis of the piece of art to apply your own supposition to the artist's intended purpose for the artwork. Try to accomplish some of the following things when formulating your interpretation:

1. Communicate the artist's statement

Describe what you think the artist is trying to say through the work of art. When it comes to the people, you can interpret what the facial expression and body language of a character tell you about, for example, how he is feeling or thinking, what he intends to do, his relationship with the others in the picture. As for places and objects, you can tell the audience what kind of place it is, why the people are there, what is happening now, or what will happen later.

2. Expound on the feeling conveyed by the artwork

Art is a human expression of life and feeling and seeks to imitate either the tangible or the abstract. Describe what the artwork means to you and explain why. For example, the painting of *Saturn Devouring His Son* is so powerful and grotesque that it is difficult to inspect closely.

Saturn Devouring His Son by Francisco Goya, 1746—1828, Spanish painter

3. Examine the techniques and how they possibly relate to the artist's intended purpose

The techniques include the line, color, texture, etc. For example, color presents us with an additional range of expressive nuances. Reds, yellows, and oranges are sometimes referred to as "warm colors", and they very often connote active movement or intensity. Blues, greens, and purples are the so-called "cool colors", and they tend to connote harmony, tranquility, or sadness. Black, white, grays, and browns are the "neutral colors", and they are very often used either as a backdrop to set off more striking colors, or as a means of adding touches of realism to a work. You can also identify symbols in the artwork and describe how they contribute to the artist's execution of the intended purpose.

4. State what you think the artwork's value is

Explain where you feel the artwork has strong value and where you think it falls short. For example, its value may be to evoke nostalgia, to incite anger or to impart beauty. And then, explain why you feel this way.

Remember, there are no incorrect interpretations when you critique artwork. Your goal is not to say whether or not the art is good, but rather to impart as best you can the visceral response the artwork incites.

Here are some useful structures for you to interpret:

"From her facial expression, I can assume that…"

"From the wrappers on the floor, I can tell that…"

"I believe…"

"Perhaps this man is about to…"

Now read the episodes below from the stories of Jesus and match each episode with its picture. Then describe the pictures to your partner and interpret the pictures to show your understanding.

a._____   b._____   c._____   d._____

Episode 1: Jesus was baptized

John the Baptist is regarded as the precursor of Jesus Christ. A very well-known preacher, he gave sermons about the proximity of God's Final Judgment. People went out to him from Jerusalem and all Judea and the whole region of the Jordan. Confessing their sins, they were baptized by him in the Jordan River. Then Jesus came from Galilee to the Jordan to be baptized by John. But John tried to deter him, saying, "I need to be baptized by you, and do you come to me?" Jesus replied, "Let it be so now; it is proper for us to do this to fulfill all righteousness." Then John consented. As soon as Jesus was baptized, he went up out of the water. At that moment heaven was opened, and he saw the Spirit of God descending like a dove and lighting on him. And a voice from heaven said, "This is my Son, whom I love; with him I am well pleased." After the baptism, Jesus is believed to have left to preach in Galilee, while John continued preaching in the Jordan valley. (183 words)

Episode 2: Jesus was tempted

According to the Gospels, after being baptized, Jesus fasted for forty days and nights in the Judaean Desert. During this time, the devil appeared to Jesus and tempted him. Jesus having refused each temptation, the devil departed and angels came and brought nourishment to Jesus. The following is from Matthew 4:

The tempter came to him and said, "If you are the Son of God, tell these stones to become bread." Jesus replied with Scripture, telling Satan man does not live by bread alone. Then the devil took him to the holy city and had him stand on the highest point of the temple. "If you are the Son of God," he said, "throw yourself down. For it is written: 'He will command his angels concerning you, and they will lift you up in their hands, so that you will not strike your foot against a stone.'" Jesus answered him, "It is also written: 'Do not put the Lord your God to the test.'" Again, the Devil took Jesus up and showed him all the kingdoms of the world, saying they were all under his control. He promised Jesus to give them to him, if Jesus would bow down and worship him. Jesus said to him, "Away from me, Satan! For it is written: 'Worship the Lord your God, and serve him only.'" Then the devil left him, and angels came and attended him. (234 words)

Episode 3: Jesus entered Jerusalem

As they approached Jerusalem and came to Bethphage on the Mount of Olives, Jesus sent two disciples, saying to them, "Go to the village ahead of you, and at once you will find a donkey tied there, with her colt by her. Untie them and bring them to me. If anyone says anything to you, tell him that God needs them, and he will send them right away." The disciples went and did as Jesus had instructed them. They brought the donkey and the colt, placed their cloaks on them, and Jesus sat on them. A very large crowd spread their cloaks on the road, while others cut branches from the trees and spread them on the road. The crowds that went ahead of him and those that followed shouted, "Blessed is he who comes in the name of God!" When Jesus entered Jerusalem, the whole city was stirred and asked, "Who is this?" The crowds answered, "This is Jesus, the prophet from

Nazareth in Galilee." (166 words)

Episode 4: Doubting Thomas

The resurrected Jesus made a series of appearances to his disciples. Thomas, one of the Twelve, was not with the disciples when Jesus came. So the other disciples told him, "We have seen the God!" But he said to them, "Unless I see the nail marks in his hands and put my finger where the nails were, and put my hand into his side, I will not believe." A week later the disciples of Jesus were in the house again, and Thomas was with them. Though the doors were locked, Jesus came and stood among them and said, "Peace be with you!" Then he said to Thomas, "Put your finger here; see my hands. Reach out your hand and put it into my side. Stop doubting and believe." Thomas said to him, "My Lord and my God!" Then Jesus told him, "Because you have seen me, you have believed; blessed are those who have not seen and yet have believed." (160 words)

Writing Critical Review (2)

Structure of a Critical Review

Critical reviews usually have a similar structure. A review should have an introduction, summary, critique, and conclusion.

Introduction

Introduction of any essay should be no longer than 1/10 of its length. The contents of an introduction always has a deductive nature, as it leads the reader from the general views or positions on the analyzed topics to the specific narrow theme of the essay. You can include a few opening sentences that announce the author(s) and the title, briefly explain the topic of the text, present the aim of the text and summarize the main issues or key argument raised by the author of the text, and conclude the introduction with a brief statement of your evaluation of the text.

Summary

The summary of the author's view on the work analyzed includes:
1) The delivery of the main idea of the work;
2) The list of the most important facts the author bases his thesis

upon;

3) A presentation of the author's conclusion or suggestions for action.

You can also briefly explain the author's intentions throughout the text and you may briefly describe how the text is organized. The summary should only make up about a third of the critical review.

Critique

The critique should be a balanced discussion and evaluation of the strengths, weakness and notable features of the text. Remember to base your discussion on specific criteria. Good reviews also include other sources to support your evaluation (remember to reference).

You can choose how to sequence your critique. Here are some examples to get you started:

1) Most important to least important conclusions you make about the text.

2) If your critique is more positive than negative, then present the negative points first and the positive last.

3) If your critique is more negative than positive, then present the positive points first and the negative last.

4) If there are both strengths and weakness for each criterion you use, you need to decide overall what your judgment is. For example, you may want to comment on a key idea in the text and have both positive and negative comments. You could begin by stating what is good about the idea and then concede and explain how it is limited in some way. While this example shows a mixed evaluation, overall you are probably being more negative than positive.

5) You can also include recommendations for how the text can be improved in terms of ideas, research approach; theories or frameworks used can also be included in the critique section.

Conclusion

This is usually a very short paragraph. You can restate your overall opinion of the text and briefly present recommendations.

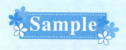

Review	Structure
Review: Turkle, Sherry (2011). Alone Together: Why We Expect More from Technology and Less from Each Other. New York: Basic Books (Extract from Chapter 1 — Connectivity and Its Discontents)	Title
The last 20 years have seen a revolution in the way we communicate, all brought about by the quite extraordinary developments that have occurred in the field of information and communications technologies. There is no doubt that the way people interact with each other nowadays is drastically different from the way things were done in the not-so-distant pre-digital past. But have these developments been positive ones? Can we say that human relations have improved as a result of these changes? Sherry Turkle in her book *Alone Together: Why We Expect More from Technology and Less from Each Other* is quite sure that this is not the case.	Introduction
In her study, based on interviews with users of technology across a wide spectrum of society, Turkle argues that while it may appear that people are more in touch with each other, the effect paradoxically of all this new communication is that people are becoming more socially alienated. Turkle quotes many stories from her interviews to illustrate her basic argument.	Summary— main idea 1
Another major concern of the author is the way that communications technology has come to overwhelm our lives. Turkle points out that it used to be the case that we kept computers busy; now the relationships is reversed, and it is they that keep us busy. This is seen in the growing phenomenon of multitasking.	Summary— main idea 2
Turkle's argument is an interesting and challenging one, and she manages to draw on numerous real life stories to vividly illustrate her points. Many of these stories are familiar ones, and capture well the frustrations and annoyances many of us can feel when confronted with some of the less impressive uses of digital communications.	Evaluation— positive feature

Review	Structure
There are some problems, however, with Turkle's argument. One of these concerns the evidence she uses to support her case. As noted, the main data used in her study are interviews with people from various walks of life about their experiences of digital technology. We note, however, that virtually all the stories recounted in the chapter are ones that illustrate some personally dissatisfying experience. One has the impression that Turkle is only interested in the negatives of the virtual world, and in this sense the study seems a biased one.	Evaluation—negative feature
In summary, while Turkle's book—at least the extract I read—is an interesting and lively account of life in the digital age, it does offer a fairly one-sided view of her subject, and fails to recognize the many benefits that digital culture has brought. One thought I had in writing this review, is that without these technologies, I would not have had such easy access to Turkle's book to read in the first place. (441 words)	Conclusion

Now read an article or book about European civilization and write a review according to the following steps.

Step 1. Read the article/book to gain a general idea of what it is about. Write down the general ideas or themes.

Step 2. Read the article/book again, highlight the important sections such as the conclusions of the writer and the arguments and data that the writer provides in order to reach his or her conclusions, and make notes.

Step 3. Check the main points with the article/book once more. Make sure your notes agree with the points raised by the writer.

Step 4. Write your introduction to the review.

Step 5. Write the body of the review. This must consist of summary and criticism sections in roughly equal proportions.

Step 6. Write the conclusion.

Step 7. Carefully edit and proofread it before submitting it.

UNIT 7

Further Development

I. Watch the video clip on *Herod* and fill in the blanks with the words you hear.

Narrator: Herod the Great was _____1_____. A powerful king, he ruled the land of Judea for over thirty years. His legacy includes _____2_____. He is remembered today as the tyrant who tried to kill the infant Jesus. Ironically, although he failed, many historians now take the view that Herod actually _____3_____.

Prof. Warren Carter: "Herod has embodied Roman rule in a way that has caused much misery and much pain and much hardship for much of the population. There has been considerable resistance that has built up. There is longing amongst some for a very different way of life. The teaching of Jesus taps into this unrest, he envisages a different sort of society."

Narrator: The teachings of Jesus _____4_____ to people who had been oppressed for more than a generation. At the same time, Herod's connections with Rome allowed Christianity to _____5_____.

II. Present your opinions on the following topics in small groups.

The process of becoming civilized is a long and painful one. In the video you've just watched, King Herod initiated a murder of all the infants in Bethlehem at will. Historically, many cultures practiced abandonment of infants called "infant exposure". Although such children would survive if taken up by others, exposure is often considered a form of infanticide. However, Christianity rejects infanticide. And child abandonment is a criminal offense under the laws in the civilized society. Retell some examples of infanticide and child abandonment in what you have learned to your partner and try to find more examples illustrating the process of civilization.

195

	In History	In Modern Time
Infanticide		
Child Abandonment		

III. Fill in the blanks with the proper forms of the words from the box.

> hand   seek   specify   resist   actually   away

Without understanding the parables, it is impossible to fully understand Jesus and his teachings. Let's take the maxim "an eye for an eye, a tooth for a tooth" as an example. The Old Testament law ____1____ equal revenge for equal wrong: "an eye for an eye, a tooth for a tooth" (Exodus 21, Leviticus 24). Jesus cites the text verbatim in Matthew 5. However, he does not endorse the principle; instead he ____2____ repeals it and teaches that it is important not to ____3____ revenge when other people wrong you. After quoting the authoritative line from Exodus, he goes on to say, "But I tell you, do not ____4____ an evil person. If anyone slaps you on the right cheek, turn to them the other cheek also. And if anyone wants to sue you and take your shirt, ____5____ over your coat as well. If anyone forces you to go one mile, go with them two miles. Give to the one who asks you, and do not turn ____6____ from the one who wants to borrow from you."

IV. Discuss the following questions after you finish the above passage.

1. When you know that someone spoke evil of you behind your back, what would you do?

2. Which is a better policy, "an eye for an eye" or "turn the other cheek"?

Cultural Exploration

Read the following passages on *Prejudice* and finish the tasks.

Location factors heavily into our assumptions and judgments about people. Imagine you are told about a group of people: one person grew up in Texas, another in Manhattan in New York City, another in Wisconsin, and another from rural Nevada. In all likelihood you have already come up with some concept of who these people are based on their location of origin and raising. This tendency is nothing new; it went on in first century Israel as well. People would be judged based upon whether they grew up in more urbanized areas or more rural areas. And, then as now, the more remote and less urbanized the location is, the more likely people from there were to be looked down on. So it is with Nazareth in Galilee in Story Three. Galilee itself was seen as remote, away from the epicenter of Judaism in Jerusalem. It is now believed that Nazareth was a village of no more than 500 in the days when Jesus grew up there. It is evident why Nazareth would easily be despised in the eyes of others: it is a remote and undeveloped area, a small village.

Task 1. Read Story Three and tell your partner what you can learn about prejudice from Nathanael.

Task 2. Read the two famous quotes and work out a definition of prejudice with your partner.

Everyone is a prisoner of his own experience. No one can eliminate prejudices — just recognize them.　　　　　　　　—Edward R. Murrow

Prejudices, it is well known, are most difficult to eradicate from the heart whose soil has never been loosened or fertilized by education; they grow there, firm as weeds among rocks.　　　　　　—Charlotte Bronte

Task 3. Prejudice can be based on a number of factors including sex, race, age, sexual orientation, nationality, socioeconomic status, and religion. List some examples of prejudice in China and the western society, exchange your results with your partners, identify their similarities and differences, and discuss the possible causes.

	Prejudice in China	Prejudice in the West
Examples		
Similarities		
Differences		

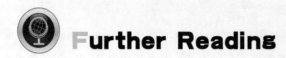

Further Reading

Judas: Hero or Traitor?

Judas, the disciple blamed for betraying Jesus Christ to the Romans, was a hero, a newly released ancient text says.

National Geographic revealed Thursday what it calls the Gospel of Judas, a 1,700-year-old text which reverses the accepted view of the religious villain.

"Jesus Christ asks Judas to betray him to the authorities," *National Geographic* said in a story about the 26-page text posted on its website.

In the Bible's New Testament Gospels, Judas betrayed Jesus for 30 pieces of silver, and then stricken by remorse, returned the bribe and committed suicide.

But the *codex* (古书手抄本) says Jesus asked Judas to betray him.

In the text Jesus tells Judas: "'You will exceed all of them.'"

In that passage, "Jesus says it is necessary for someone to free him finally from his human body, and he prefers that this liberation be done by a friend rather than by an enemy," said Rodolphe Kasser, a clergyman, a former professor at the University of Geneva in Switzerland and head of the translation team.

"So he asks Judas, who is his friend, to sell him out, to betray him. It's treason to the general public, but between Jesus and Judas, it's not treachery."

The 1,700-year-old script is written in *Coptic*(科普特语的), an ancient Egyptian language. (Associated Press)

The text is expected to be controversial because it contradicts the Christian thought which has lasted for nearly 2,000 years.

National Geographic said in the early days of Christianity there were competing doctrines, and the codex probably reflects the thinking of the Gnostics, a group that hid its writings when they were denounced by the established church.

The manuscript was mentioned around A.D. 180 by Bishop Irenaeus of Lyon, who called it *fictitious* (编造的).

"Let a vigorous debate on the significance of this fascinating ancient text begin," Rev. Donald Senior, president of the Catholic Theological Union of Chicago, told the Associated Press.

Appears real

The text, written in Coptic script, is believed to be a translation of an original Greek text written by Christians before A.D. 180.

It was found in Egypt in the 1970s, and an antique dealer tried to sell it several times, including to Yale University. But Yale declined, doubting its *provenance* (出处).

The codex was finally transferred to the Maecenas Foundation for Ancient Art, based in Basel, Switzerland, which worked with the National Geographic Society and the Waitt Institute for Historical Discovery in California to restore, translate and publish the book.

The University of Arizona carbon-dated five tiny samples of *papyrus* (纸莎草纸) and leather binding to between A.D. 220 and A.D. 340, and other tests backed up that conclusion.

Pages were put on display at the National Geographic Society's headquarters in Washington, which has also published Coptic and English

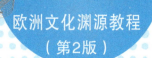

versions of the text. The codex will later be sent to Egypt. (492 words)

Answer the following questions briefly.

1. What did Judas do according to the 1,700-year-old text?
2. Why is the text likely to give rise to public disagreement?
3. What have been done to check the authenticity of the text?

Beliefs of Christianity

Although different sects of Christianity have different focuses on their doctrines, they agree on and observe some basic ones.

Creation: Christianity believes that God creates the world, thus, he is said to know everything, to be everywhere. He is the supreme master of the universe.

Trinity: In Christianity, the (Holy) Trinity is the existence of God in three forms (the Father, the Son and the Holy Spirit).

God the Father is the fountainhead of the Holy Trinity. It is from the Father that the Holy Spirit eternally proceeds. God the Father created all things through the Son, and sent his Son to give humans everlasting life.

Jesus Christ is the Second Person of the Holy Trinity, eternally born of the Father. He becomes man. His coming to earth is foretold in the Old Testament by the prophets. He is the one who has been described as "the coming king", "Christ", etc. in the Old Testament and the one who is sent from God to save the world from the ruling of Satan. Also, the Son of God redeems human nature, which is a redemption accessible to all who are joined to him in his glorified humanity.

The Holy Spirit is called the "promise of the Father" which is given by Christ as a gift to the Church to empower the Church for service to God.

Sin: Human sins when Adam and Eve pervert what God has given them good and are driven out of Eden. The sin from Adam and Eve is said to be the origin of human sins. Therefore, in Christianity, human beings are born with sin.

Salvation: It refers to the coming of Jesus Christ "in the flesh". Christianity believes that since humans have the original sin and cannot save themselves, God sends his Son to the world to die for them and save them.

In his mercy, God forgives human sins when human beings confess them, giving them strength to overcome sin in lives. Salvation begins with these three steps: repent, be baptized, and receive the gift of the Holy Spirit. Salvation demands faith in Jesus Christ. People cannot save themselves by their own good works. Salvation is "faith working through love." It is believed to be an ongoing, life-long process.

Heaven and Hell: Christianity believes that the world is full of sins. Jesus comes from the Heaven to judge the alive and the dead in the world. The souls of people who have been faithful to God will go to Heaven as a reward, while wicked people are punished after death in Hell. (426 words)

Answer the following questions briefly.

1. What is trinity?
2. What is the origin of human sins according to the passage?
3. What are the fates of the faithful and the wicked respectively according to Christian beliefs?

Appendix I Proper Terms

Unit 1 — Unit 4

Achilles [əˈkiliːz] A Greek hero; the son of Peleus and the sea goddess Thetis. In the *Iliad* he was the foremost of the Greek warriors at the siege of Troy.

Adonis [əˈdəunis] A handsome youth loved by both Aphrodite and Persephone.

Aeetes [ˈiːtiːz] A king of Colchis and son of the sun-god Helios. He was also the brother of Circe, and father of Medea.

Aegeus [ˈiːdʒiəs] A king of Athens and the father of Theseus.

Aeneas [iˈniːəs] A Trojan prince; the son of Anchises and Aphrodite, who escaped the sack of Troy and sailed to Italy via Carthage and Sicily. After seven years, he and his followers established themselves near the site of the future Rome.

Aeolus [ˈiːəuləs] The god of the winds.

Agamemnon [ægəˈmemnən] A king of Mycenae who led the Greeks at the siege of Troy. On his return home he was murdered by his wife Clytemnestra and her lover Aegisthus.

Ajax [ˈeidʒæks] The son of Telamon; a Greek hero of the Trojan War who killed himself in vexation when Achilles' armour was given to Odysseus.

Alcmene [ælkˈmiːni] Amphitryon's wife, who gave birth to Hercules after being seduced by Zeus.

Amazon [ˈæməzn] A tribe of female warriors who lived east of the Greek regions in Asia Minor.

Andromeda [ænˈdrɔmidə] An Ethiopian princess and daughter of Cassiopeia. She was fastened to a rock and exposed to a sea monster that was sent by Poseidon, but was rescued by Perseus and became his wife.

Aphrodite [æfrəˈdaiti] The goddess of love and beauty. She was the daughter of Zeus, or was born from the sea foam. She was identified with Roman Venus.

Apollo [əˈpɔləu] Greek god of light, prophesy, poetry, music and healing. He was son of Zeus and Leto, and twin brother of Artemis.

Apsyrtus [æpˈsjuətəs] The son of Aeetes and brother of Medea.

Arcas [ˈɑːkəs] The son of Zeus and Callisto. He was set among the stars with his mother as the Little Bear and the Great Bear respectively.

Ares [ˈeəriːz] Greek god of war. He was son of Zeus and Hera, and identified with Roman Mars.

Argo [ˈɑːgəu] The ship in which Jason sailed in search of the Golden Fleece.

Argonauts [ˈɑːgənɔːts] Those who sailed with Jason on the Argo in search of

Appendix I

the Golden Fleece.

Argus [ˈɑːgəs] (1) A giant with 100 eyes, who was guardian of the heifer Io and was slain by Hermes. (2) A son of Phrixus and builder of the Argo.

Ariadne [æriˈædni] The daughter of Minos and Pasiphae who gave Theseus the thread with which he found his way out of the Minotaur's labyrinth.

Artemis [ˈɑːtimis] The virgin goddess of the hunt and the moon. She was daughter of Zeus and Leto, and twin sister of Apollo. She was identified with Roman Diana.

Asia Minor [ˈeiʃəˈmainə] A peninsula in southwestern Asia that forms the Asian part of Turkey.

Athamas [ˈæθəmæs] A Boeotian king. His first wife was Nephele, a cloud nymph, and second wife Ino.

Athena [əˈθiːnə] The goddess of wisdom, useful arts and prudent warfare; the guardian of Athens. She was identified with Roman Minerva.

Atlas [ˈætləs] One of the Titans, and brother of Prometheus and Epimetheus. He was forced to support the sky on his shoulders as punishment for rebelling against Zeus.

Augeas [ɔːˈdʒiːæs] The mythical Greek king who for 30 years did not clean his stables which contained his vast herd of cattle.

Aulis [ˈɔːlis] An ancient town in East central Greece, in Boeotia. Traditionally the harbour from which the Greeks sailed at the beginning of the Trojan War.

Bacchus [ˈbækəs] The Roman god of wine; equivalent of Dionysus.

Briseis [braiˈsiːis] A captive of Achilles, later taken by Agamemnon and the famous quarrel resulted.

Cadmus [ˈkædməs] A Phoenician prince; son of Agenor and the brother of Phoenix, Cilix and Europa. He founded the Greek city of Thebes.

Calliope [kəˈlaiəpiː] The Muse of epic poetry.

Callisto [kəˈlistəu] A nymph and follower of Artemis. She was transformed into a bear and set among the stars.

Calypso [kəˈlipsəu] The sea nymph who detained Odysseus for seven years.

Caucasus Mountains [ˈkɔːkəsəs ˈmauntins] A mountainous region between the Black Sea and the Caspian Sea.

Centaur [ˈsentɔː] A mythical being that is half man and half horse.

Cerberus [ˈsəːbərəs] A three-headed dog guarding the entrance to Hades.

Ceres [ˈsiəriːz] Roman goddess of agriculture; counterpart of Greek Demeter.

Chaos [ˈkeiɔs] A state of utter confusion and disorder before the universe came into being in Greek myths.

Charon [ˈkərən] The ferryman who brought the souls of the dead across the river Styx or the river Acheron to Hades.

Chiron [ˈkaiərən, ˈkairən] The wise centaur and the head of Centaur tribe. He tutored Achilles, Hercules, Jason, and other heroes.

Circe [ˈsəːsi] A goddess who turned Odysseus's men temporarily into swine but later gave him directions for their journey home. Daughter of Helios, aunt of Medea.

Colchis [ˈkɔlkis] A region on the Black Sea south of the Caucasus that was the site of an ancient country where Jason sought the Golden Fleece.

Crete [kriːt] An island in the east of the Mediterranean Sea.

Cronus [ˈkrəunəs] The supreme god until Zeus dethroned him. He was the son of Uranus and Gaea, and was identified with Roman Saturn.

Cupid [ˈkjuːpid] Roman god of love; counterpart of Greek Eros.

Cyclopes [ˈsaiklɔps] (sing. Cyclops) The giant beings, each with a single, round eye in the middle of his forehead. (1) They were the three sons of Gaea and Uranus. (2) They were the sons of Poseidon in the story of the Odyssey, one of whom is Polyphemus.

Cyprus [ˈsaiprəs] An island in the eastern Mediterranean.

Danae [ˈdænəiː] A princess of Argos and daughter of Acrisius. She was the mother of Perseus who was imprisoned by her father in a bronze chamber.

Daphne [ˈdæfni] A nymph who was transformed into a laurel tree to escape the amorous Apollo.

Delphi [ˈdelfai, ˈdelfi] An ancient Greek city on the slopes of Mount Parnassus; site of the oracle of Delphi.

Demeter [diˈmiːtə] Goddess of fertility and protector of marriage in ancient mythology; counterpart of Roman Ceres.

Deucalion [djuːˈkeiljən] Son of Prometheus. He and his wife Pyrrha were the only survivors on the earth after the great flood sent by Zeus.

Diana [daiˈænə] Roman virgin goddess of the hunt and the moon; counterpart of Greek Artemis.

Diomedes [daiəˈmiːdiːz] One of the Greek heroes of the Trojan War.

Dione [daiˈəuni] A Titan goddess; mother of Aphrodite by Zeus.

Dionysus [daiəˈnaisəs] God of wine, fertility and drama. He was identified with Roman Bacchus.

Echo [ˈekəu] A nymph who, spurned by Narcissus, pined away until only her voice remained.

Epimetheus [epiˈmiθjuːs, -θiːəs] Brother of Prometheus. He and Pandora were the parents of Pyrrha, wife of Deucalion.

Erebus [ˈeribəs] Personification of the darkness of the Underworld and the offspring of Chaos. In later myths, Erebus was the dark region beneath the earth through which the shades must pass to the realm of Hades below.

Eris [ˈeris] The goddess of discord, sister of Ares.

Eros [ˈirɔs, ˈerɔs] (1) The god of love; son of Aphrodite. He was identified with Roman Cupid. (2) A divine being who emerged self-born from Chaos at the beginning of time to make procreation possible.

Europa [juə'rəupə] A Phoenician princess abducted to Crete by Zeus in the form of a bull. She had the continent of Europe named for her.

Eurydice [juə'ridisi:] A dryad married to Orpheus, who sought her in Hades after she died. She could have left Hades with him had he not broken his pact and looked back at her.

Eurystheus [juə'risθju:s, -θiəs] King of Mycenae, who set Heracles to the twelve labors.

Furies ['fjuri:z] The hideous snake-haired monsters (usually three in number) who pursued unpunished criminals.

Gaea ['dʒi:ə] The goddess of the earth, or Mother Earth. She was one of the most ancient divinity in Greek myths.

Geryon ['geriən] A mythical monster with three heads that was slain by Heracles.

Gorgon ['gɔ:gən] A monstrous feminine creature whose appearance would turn anyone who laid eyes upon it to stone. There were three of them: Euryale ("far-roaming"), Sthenno ("forceful"), and Medusa ("ruler"), the only one of them who was mortal. They lived in the ultimate west, near the ocean, and guarded the entrance to the underworld.

Hades ['heidi:z] The god of the underworld; brother of Zeus and husband of Persephone.

Harmonia [hɑ:'məunjə] The goddess of harmony and concord; daughter of Aphrodite and Ares.

Hebe ['hi:bi] The goddess of youth and spring; wife of Heracles; daughter of Zeus and husband of Persephone.

Hecatoncheires [hekə'tɔŋkəri:z] The giants, each with fifty heads and one hundred hands. They are the three sons of Gaea and Uranus.

Hector ['hektə] The eldest son of Priam, and was killed by Achilles during the Trojan War.

Helen ['helən] The beautiful daughter of Zeus and Leda, whose abduction by Paris from her husband Menelaus caused the Trojan War.

Helios ['hi:liɔs] The Titan god of the sun, who drove his chariot daily across the sky.

Helle ['heli] A daughter of Athamas and Nephele, sisiter of Phrixus. When riding on the flying golden ram with her brother, she fell off the ram into the Hellepont, which was named after her, and died.

Hephaestus [hi'fi:stəs] Son of Zeus; the lame god of fire and the forge, and patron god of smiths and weavers. He was identified with Roman Vulcan.

Hera ['herə, 'hiərə] Queen of the Olympian gods; sister and wife of Zeus. She was remembered for her jealousy of the many mortal women Zeus fell in love with. She was identified with Roman Juno.

Heracles ['herəkli:z] A great hero. He was the son of Zeus and Alcmene, and was famous for his enormous strength and twelve fulfilled tasks. He was identified with Roman Hercules.

Hermes [ˈhəːmiːz] The messenger of the gods, and the guide of dead souls to the underworld. He was the god of commerce and theft. He was identified with Roman Mercury.

Hero [ˈhiərəu] A priestess of Aphrodite, who killed herself when her lover Leander drowned while swimming across the Hellespont to visit her.

Hesiod [ˈhiːsiɔd] One of the earliest Greek poets. Two of his complete epics have survived, the *Theogony* and the *Works and Days*.

Hestia [ˈhestiə] The virgin goddess of the hearth. She was sister of Zeus, and identified with Roman Vesta.

Hippolyta [hiˈpɔlitə] The Amazonian queen who possessed a magical girdle she was given by her father Ares, the god of war. The girdle was a waist belt that signified her authority as queen of the Amazons.

Homer [ˈhəumə] Ancient Greek epic poet who is believed to have written the *Iliad* and the *Odyssey*.

Hydra [ˈhaidrə] The many-headed monster that was slain by Heracles.

Iapetus [aiˈæpətəs] The Titan who was the father of Atlas, Epimetheus and Prometheus.

Ida [ˈaidə] Mt. Ida, a mountain in Northwest Turkey. It is located in the southeast of the site of ancient Troy.

Iliad [ˈiliəd] A Greek epic poem (attributed to Homer) describing the siege of Troy.

Ino [ˈainəu] A daughter of Cadmus and Harmonia. She was married to Athamas, but hated the two children, Phrixus and Helle, by Athamas's first wife. She planned to kill them so that her sons could inherit. From her story came the Golden Fleece.

Io [ˈaiəu] A maiden seduced by Zeus. She was turned into a white heifer by Zeus when Hera was about to discover them together. She was the ancestor of Heracles.

Ionian Sea [aiˈəunjən, -niən siː] An arm of the Mediterranean Sea between western Greece and southern Italy.

Iphigenia [ifidʒiˈnaiə] The daughter of Agamemnon, taken by him to be sacrificed to Artemis, who saved her life and made her a priestess.

Ithaca [ˈiθəkə] A Greek island in the Ionian Sea; the smallest of the Ionian Islands; regarded as the home of Homer's Odysseus.

Jason [ˈdʒeisən] The husband of Medea and leader of the Argonauts who sailed in quest of the Golden Fleece.

Jocasta [dʒəuˈkæstə] A queen of Thebes; the wife of Laius, who married Oedipus without either of them knowing he was her son.

Juno [ˈdʒuːnəu] Supreme goddess of Romans; wife and sister of Jupiter;

Appendix I

counterpart of Greek Hera.

Jupiter ['dʒu:pitə] Supreme god of Romans; counterpart of Greek Zeus.

Laius ['laijəs] A king of Thebes, killed by his son Oedipus, who did not know of their relationship.

Leander [li:'ændə] A youth of Abydos, who drowned in the Hellespont in a storm on one of his nightly visits to Hero, his beloved.

Leda ['li:də] A queen of Sparta who was the mother of Helen and Pollux by Zeus, who visited her in the form of a swan.

Leto ['li:təu] Wife or mistress of Zeus and mother of Apollo and Artemis.

Maia ['meijə, 'maiə] A goddess and the mother of Hermes by Zeus.

Mars [mɑ:z] Roman god of war and agriculture; counterpart of Greek Ares.

Medea [mi:'diə] A princess and sorceress of Colchis who aided Jason in taking the Golden Fleece from her father. Later she became the wife of Jason, but took revenge when Jason betrayed her.

Medusa [mi'dju:zə] A woman transformed into a Gorgon by Athena; she was slain by Perseus.

Menelaus [menə'leiəs] King of Sparta and the brother of Agamemnon. He was the husband of Helen, whose abduction led to the Trojan War.

Mercury ['mə:kjuri] Messenger of Jupiter; Roman god of commerce; counterpart of Greek Hermes.

Metis ['metis] The Titan goddess of prudence, good counsel, wisdom and craftiness. She was the first wife of Zeus. Zeus swallowed her for fear that her son would dethrone him.

Midas ['maidəs] King of Phrygia who was given the power by Dionysus of turning everything he touched to gold.

Minerva [mi'nə:və] Roman goddess of wisdom; counterpart of Greek Athena.

Minos ['mainɔs] A son of Zeus and Europa; king of ancient Crete. He ordered Daedalus to build the labyrinth. After death Minos became a judge in the underworld.

Minotaur ['mainətɔ:] A mythical monster with the head of a bull and the body of a man; slain by Theseus.

Muse [mju:z] Any of the nine daughters of Zeus. They were the goddesses of music and song, and the source of inspiration to artists and poets.

Mycenae [mai'si:ni:] An ancient city in southern Greece; center of the Mycenaean civilization.

Myhhra ['mi:rə] A princess of Cyprus who had incestuous relations with her father and was changed into a myrrh tree by the gods. Their child, Adonis, was bron from the split trunk of the tree.

Narcissus [nɑ:'sisəs] A beautiful youth who fell in love with his reflection in a pool and pined away, becoming the flower that bears his name.

Nemean lion ['ni:miən lain] An enormous lion strangled by Hercules as the first of his 12 labours.

Nemesis [ˈnemisis] The goddess of divine retribution and vengeance.

Nephele [ˈnefəli] A cloud nymph; mother of Phrixus and Helle.

Neptune [ˈneptjuːn] Roman god of the sea; counterpart of Greek Poseidon.

Niobe [ˈnaiəbi] The daughter of Tantalus. Her pride in her children provoked Apollo and Diana, who slew them all. Niobe herself was changed by the gods into stone.

Nyx [niks] Greek goddess of the night; daughter of Chaos; counterpart of Roman Nox.

Oceanid [əuˈsiːənid] The sea nymph who was a daughter of Oceanus and Tethys.

Oceanus [əuˈsiənəs] A Titan, the god of the stream that flowed around the earth. He was the father of Styx.

Odysseus [əˈdisjuːs, əuˈdisjuːs] A famous mythical Greek hero; his return to Ithaca after the siege of Troy was described in the *Odyssey*.

Odyssey [ˈɔdisi] A Greek epic poem (attributed to Homer) describing the journey of Odysseus after the fall of Troy.

Oedipus [ˈiːdipəs] The son of Laius and Jocasta, the king and queen of Thebes. He killed his father, being unaware of his identity, and unwittingly married his mother, by whom he had four children. When the truth was revealed, he put out his eyes and Jocasta killed herself.

Ogygia [əuˈdʒidʒiə] An island mentioned in Homer's *Odyssey* as the home of the nymph Calypso, the daughter of the Titan Atlas.

Olympians [əuˈlimpiəns] The group of gods headed by Zeus, who lived on the top of Mount Olympus.

Olympus [əuˈlimpəs] Mount Olympus, a place where Greek gods are believed to live. Heaven.

Orestes [ɔˈrestiːz] The son of Agamemnon and Clytemnestra, who killed his mother and her lover Aegisthus in revenge for their murder of his father.

Orpheus [ˈɔːfjuːs] The famous mythic Thracian poet; son of the Muse Calliope, and husband of Eurydice. His music had the power to move even inanimate objects and who almost succeeded in rescuing his wife Eurydice from Hades.

Pan [pæn] The god of fields, woods, shepherds and flocks. He was represented as a man with goat's legs and horns. He was identified with Roman Faunus.

Pandora [pænˈdɔːrə] The first woman. She was made by gods and given to human beings as a punishment. She was the wife of Epimetheus.

Paris [ˈpæris] A prince of Troy, whose abduction of Helen from her husband Menelaus started the Trojan War.

Parnassus [paːˈnæsəs] A mountain in central Greece, where Deucalion's ship landed after the flood.

Parthenope [paːˈθenəpi] One of the sirens, who drowned herself when Odysseus evaded the lure of the sirens' singing. Her body was said to have

been cast ashore at what became Naples.

Patroclus [pə'trɔkləs] A friend of Achilles, killed in the Trojan War by Hector. His death made Achilles return to the fight after his quarrel with Agamemnon.

Peleus ['peliəs] A king of the Myrmidons; father of Achilles.

Pelias ['piːliæs,'pe-] A son of Poseidon and Tyro. He feared his nephew Jason and sent him to recover the Golden Fleece, hoping he would not return.

Penelope [pi'neləpi] The wife of Odysseus and mother of Telemachus.

Persephone [pə:'sefəni] Daughter of Zeus and Demeter. She was abducted by Hades and made queen of the underworld.

Perseus ['pəːsjuːs] A legendary hero; son of Danae and Zeus; husband of Andromeda. He killed the Gorgon Medusa.

Phaeton ['feitn, 'feiətən] A son of Apollo who begged his father to let him drive the chariot of the sun.

Phrixus ['friksəs] A son of Athamas and Nephele. In consequence of his stepmother's intrigue, he was to be sacrificed, but at the last moment was rescued and taken away by a magical flying ram with his sister Helle.

Phrygia ['fridʒiə] An ancient country in western central Asia Minor.

Pluto ['pluːtəu] The god of the underworld; brother of Zeus and husband of Persephone.

Polydectes [pəlai'dekts] The ruler of the island of Seriphos. He fell in love with Danae when she and her son Perseus were saved by his brother.

Polyphemus [pɔli'fiːməs] The Cyclops who confined Odysseus and his companions in a cave until Odysseus blinded him and escaped.

Poseidon [pɔ'saidən] The god of the sea and earthquakes; brother of Zeus. He was identified with Roman Neptune.

Priam ['praiəm] The last king of Troy, killed at its fall. He was father by Hecuba of Hector, Paris, and Cassandra.

Prometheus [prə'miθjuːs, -θiəs] A god from Titans, who is said to steal the fire and make the first generation of human beings.

Psyche ['saiki] A beautiful princess loved by Eros who visited her at night and told her she must not try to see him; became the personification of the soul.

Pygmalion [pig'meiljən] A king of Cyprus, who fell in love with the statue of a woman he had sculpted and which his prayers brought to life as Galatea.

Pyrrha ['pirə] Daughter of Epimetheus and Pandora, wife of Deucalion.

Rhea [riə; 'riːə] A Titaness, wife of Cronus and mother of Zeus.

Scyros ['sairəs] An island in the Aegean Sea; birth place of Peleus.

Semele ['semili] Daughter of Cadmus and Harmonia. She was the mortal mother of Dionysus by Zeus.

Silenus [sai'liːnəs] Chief of the satyrs and foster father to Dionysus; often depicted riding drunkenly on a donkey.

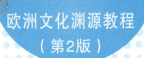

Siren [ˈsaiərin] One of a group of sea nymphs who by their sweet singing lured mariners to destruction on the rocks surrounding their island.

Sisyphus [ˈsisifəs] A king of Corinth, punished in Hades for his misdeeds by eternally having to roll a heavy stone up a hill: every time he approached the top, the stone escaped his grasp and rolled to the bottom.

Sparta [ˈspɑːtə] An ancient Greek city in the South Peloponnese, famous for the discipline and military prowess of its citizens and for their austere way of life.

Sphinx [sfiŋks] A riddling winged monster with a woman's head and breast on a lion's body; daughter of Typhon.

Styx [stiks] The goddess of the underworld river, or the river itself, across which Charon carried dead souls. The oath sworn in her name or by her river was the most unbreakable one.

Tantalus [ˈtæntələs] A king; the father of Pelops, punished in Hades for his misdeeds by having to stand in water that recedes when he tries to drink it and under fruit that moves away as he reaches for it.

Tartarus [ˈtɑːtərəs] The deepest region in the underworld; a place of punishment in hell.

Telemachus [tiˈleməkəs] The son of Odysseus and Penelope, who helped his father kill Penelope's suitors.

Tethys [ˈtiːθis] A Titaness and sea goddess; wife of Oceanus, and mother of Styx.

Thebes [θiːbz] An ancient city in east-central Greece, northwest of Athens.

Themis [ˈθiːmis, ˈθemis] A Titaness, daughter of Uranus and Gaea. She was the mother of Prometheus by Iapetus, and the mother of the three Fates by Zeus. She was the goddess in charge of law and justice.

Theogony [θiːˈɔgəni] A poem by Hesiod describing the origins and genealogies of the Greek gods.

Theseus [ˈθiːsiəs, ˈθisjuːs] A hero and king of Athens who was noted for his many great deeds. He killed Procrustes and the Minotaur, defeated the Amazons, and united Attica.

Thetis [ˈθetis] One of the Nereids and mother of Achilles by Peleus.

Thrace [θreis] A region and ancient country and wine-producing region in the east of the Balkan Peninsula north of the Aegean Sea; colonized by ancient Greeks; later a Roman province; now divided between Bulgaria and Greece and Turkey.

Titan [ˈtaitən] One of a group of gods given birth by Gaea and Uranus. They are also offspring of Titans, such as Prometheus.

Trojan [ˈtrəudʒən] A native of ancient Troy.

Troy [trɔi] An ancient city in Asia Minor that was the site of the Trojan War.

Typhon [ˈtaifɔn] The last son of Gaia, fathered by Tartarus. He was known as the father of many monsters.

Ulysses [juːˈlisiːz] The Roman name for Odysseus.

Uranus [ˈjuːərənəs] One of the most ancient gods in ancient Greek stories. The ruler of the universe, or god of the Heavens. He was the son of Gaea, and later became her husband.

Venus [ˈviːnəs] Roman goddess of love and beauty; counterpart of Greek Aphrodite.

Vulcan [ˈvʌlkən] Roman god of fire and metal working; counterpart of Greek Hephaestus.

Zeus [zjuːs] The supreme god of the Olympians; son of Rhea and Cronus whom he dethroned; brother and husband of Hera; father of many gods and heroes; counterpart of Roman Jupiter.

Unit 5 — Unit 7

Aaron [ˈɛərən] The brother of Moses; the first High Priest of the Hebrews. He there gained a name for eloquent and persuasive speech.

Ark [ɑːk] (1) Noah's Ark, a large vessel built at God's command to save Noah, his family, and stock of all the world's animals from the flood. (2) The Ark of the Covenant, a chest described in the book of Exodus as containing the Tablets of Stone on which the Ten Commandments were inscribed.

Abel [ˈeibəl] The second son of Adam and Eve, born after the Fall of Man.

Abraham [ˈeibrəhæm] A man featured in the book of Genesis. Jewish, Christian and Muslim traditions regard him as the founding patriarch of the Israelites, Ishmaelites and Edomite peoples.

Adam and Eve [ˈædəm ˈænd ˈiːv] The first man and his wife created by God.

Ammonites [ˈæmənaits] A nomadic tribe living east of the Jordan; a persistent enemy of the Israelites.

Ararat [ˈærəræt] A mountain in the eastern Turkey where Noah's Ark landed after the Great Flood.

Babel [ˈbeibəl] A structure featured in the book of Genesis; an enormous tower intended as the crowning achievement.

Bathsheba [ˈbæθʃibə; bæθˈʃiːbə] The wife of Uriah the Hittite and later of David, king of the United Kingdom of Israel and Judah. She was the mother of Solomon, who succeeded David as king.

Benjamin [ˈbendʒəmin] The youngest son of Jacob and the forebear of one of the tribes of Israel.

Bethlehem [ˈbeθlihem] A small town south of Jerusalem. It was the native city of King David and the birthplace of Jesus.

Caesar Augustus [ˈsiːzə ɔːˈgʌstəs] The first emperor in the ancient Roman Empire.

Caiaphas [ˈkaiəfæs] A Jewish high priest. According to the Gospels, he presided at the council that condemned Jesus to death.

Cain [kein] The first son of Adam and Eve, born after the Fall of Man.

Canaan ['keinən] The promised land to Israelites by God, which was described as "the land flowing with milk and honey" in the Bible.

David ['deivid] The second king of Judah and Israel. He slew the Philistine giant Goliath and succeeded Saul as the king.

Eden ['i:dən] Garden of Eden, a beautiful garden built by God for Adam and Eve to live at the Creation.

Esau ['i:sɔ:] Son of Isaac, twin brother of Jacob. The name was given on account of the hairy covering on his body at birth: "all over like a hairy garment".

Galilee ['gæləli] A northern region of ancient Palestine.

Gethsemane [geθ'seməni] A garden in the east of Jerusalem near the foot of the Mount of Olives. It was the scene of Jesus' agony and betrayal.

Goliath [gə'laiəθ] The Philistine warrior, famous for his battle with the young David, the future king of Israel.

Hagar ['heigɑ:] The Egyptian servant of Abraham's wife, Sarah. With Abraham she had a son, Ishmael.

Hebrew ['hi:bru:] A language that was spoken by Jews in former times. A modern form of Hebrew is spoken now in Israel; belonging to or relating to the Hebrew language or people.

Herod ['herəd] King of Judea who (according to the New Testament) tried to kill Jesus by ordering the death of all children under age two in Bethlehem.

Horeb ['hɔ:reb] Mount Horeb, or Mount Sinai in some versions. It is the place at which the Hebrew Bible states that the Ten Commandments were given to Moses by God. It is described as the Mountain of God.

Isaac ['aizək] The son of Abraham and Sarah, and the father of Jacob and Esau. The Christian church views Abraham's willingness to follow God's command to sacrifice Isaac as an example of faith and obedience.

Ishmael ['iʃmɛəl, 'iʃmeil] In the Old Testament, the son of Abraham who was cast out after the birth of Isaac. He is traditionally considered to be the forebear of the Arabs.

Israel ['izreiəl] (1) In the Old Testament, he is also known as Jacob, son of Issac. (2) An ancient kingdom of Palestine founded by Saul 1025 B.C. After 933 it split into the Northern Kingdom, or kingdom of Israel, and the kingdom of Judah to the south.

Israelite ['izriəlait] A native or inhabitant of the ancient Northern Kingdom of Israel. A descendant of Jacob; a Jew. A member of a people regarded as the chosen people of God.

Jacob ['dʒeikəb] Son of Isaac with Rebekah; the twin brother of Esau, and grandson of Abraham. He is also known as Israel, the third Biblical patriarch.

Jerusalem [dʒe'ru:sələm] The capital of Israel. It has been the holiest city in Judaism and the spiritual center of the Jewish people since the 10th

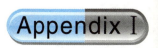

century B.C., contains a number of significant ancient Christian sites, and is considered the third-holiest city in Islam.

Jesus Christ ['dʒi:zəs 'kraist] A teacher and prophet born in Bethlehem and active in Nazareth. His life and sermons form the basis for Christianity.

Joab ['dʒəuæb] The captain of David's army who also took part in David's murder of Uriah.

Jordan ['dʒɔ:dən] River Jordan, a river in Palestine that empties into the Dead Sea. John the Baptist baptized Jesus in the Jordan.

Joseph ['dʒəuzif] Son of Jacob, famous for his coat of many colors and his God-given ability to interpret dreams.

Joshua ['dʒɔʃwə] A biblical Israelite leader who succeeded Moses. He was one of the twelve spies sent on by Moses to explore the land of Canaan who would later lead the conquest of that land, the Bible's Promised Land. Joshua was appointed by Moses to succeed him as leader of the Israelites upon Moses' death.

Judas Iscariot ['dʒu:dəs isˈkæriət] The disciple who betrayed Jesus of Nazareth according to the Christian Bible. He was one of the original 12 disciples.

Judea [dʒu:ˈdiə] An ancient region of southern Palestine comprising present-day southern Israel and southwest Jordan.

Koran [kɔˈra:n] The sacred writings of Islam revealed by God to the prophet Muhammad during his life at Mecca and Medina.

Lot [lɔt] The nephew of Abraham.

Magi ['meidʒai] The Wise Men from the east who brought gifts to the infant Jesus.

Mary ['meəri] Mother of Jesus and the principal saint of many Christian churches.

Messiah [miˈsaiə] A spiritual savior prophesied in the Hebrew Bible. Christians believe Jesus to be the Messiah (Christ).

Midian ['midiən] The place to which Moses fled when running away from the Pharaoh.

Moses ['məuziz] The Hebrew prophet who led the Israelites from Egypt across the Red Sea on a journey known as the Exodus. He received the Ten Commandments from God on Mount Sinai.

Nazareth ['næzəriθ] A town located in Israel's Galilee region. In the New Testament, the city is described as the childhood home of Jesus.

Nile [nail] The world's longest river (4150 miles) which flows northward through eastern Africa into the Mediterranean. The Nile River valley in Egypt was the site of the world's first great civilization.

Noah ['nəuə] The tenth and last of the Patriarchs before the flood. Noah saved his family and animals from God's flood. He received a covenant from God, and his sons repopulated the earth.

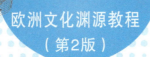

Pharaoh ['feərəu] A king of ancient Egypt.

Pharisee ['færisi:] A member of an ancient Jewish sect that emphasized strict interpretation and observance of the Mosaic law in both its oral and written form.

Philistine ['filistain] People who inhabited the southern coast of Canaan. There was almost perpetual war between the Philistines and the Israelites.

Pilate ['pailət] The Roman prefect of Judaea who presided at the trial of Jesus and gave the order for his crucifixion.

Samaritan [sə'mæritn] A member of a people inhabiting Samaria in biblical times.

Sarah ['sɛərə] Wife of Abraham and mother of Isaac.

Saul [sɔ:l] The first king of the ancient United Kingdom of Israel and Judah.

Sinai ['sainai] The place at which the Ten Commandments were given to Moses by God.

Sodom and Gomorrah ['sɔdəm 'ænd gə'mɔrə] Cities of sinfulness and sexual deviation which were destroyed by God.

Solomon ['sɔləmən] Son of David and king of Israel noted for his wisdom (10th century B.C.).

Uriah [ju(ə)'raiə] A soldier in King David's army. David had him killed after David's apparent adultery with his wife Bathsheba.

Appendix II
Keys to the Exercises

Unit 1

Pre-information

I . 1. origins 2. make sense of 3. structure and order
4. account 5. composed 6. in the eighth century B.C.
7. violently seized 8. conflict and war

II . 1. customer service 2. the end of the last Ice Age 3. set free
4. find an opportunity 5. benefit mankind 6. digital revolution

Allusions:

1. titan: a person of exceptional importance and reputation

2. Deucalion: the son of Prometheus who with his wife, Pyrrha, was the only survivor on earth of a flood sent by Zeus (Deucalion's flood). The couple became the ancestors of the renewed human race.

3. Prometheus: the Titan who stole fire from Olympus and gave it to mankind

4. Promethean gift: very good or precious gift

5. Pandora's Box: a source of many unforeseen and unmanageable problems

6. golden age: a time period when some activity or skill was at its peak; any period (sometimes imaginary) of great peace and prosperity and happiness

Stories

Story One
I. 1. c   2. b   3. d   4. a   5. e
II. 1. Eros   2. Uranus   3. Cyclopes   4. Titans

Story Two
I. 1. Cronus — Zeus' father, Rhea — Zeus' mother

2. Zeus slipped his father, Cronus, a specially prepared drink, and made his father vomit up his siblings.

II. 1. F   2. T   3. T   4. T   5. F

Story Three
1. the most powerful gods in the universe
2. not very well civilized
3. his own flesh and blood
4. end up marrying one another
5. good enough for our family

Story Four
I. 1. Prometheus who shaped man out of mud.
   Athena who breathed life into the clay figure.

2. Zeus was angry at Prometheus for three things: tricking him on sacrifices, stealing fire for man, and refusing to tell Zeus which of Zeus' children would dethrone him.

II. 1. making man stand upright as the gods did and giving them fire
   2. the Caucasus Mountains; a giant eagle
   3. Chiron; Heracles

Story Five
1. innocence and happiness
2. Labor was not necessary
3. suffering hardship and decay
4. displeasure and discomfort
5. had to be built
6. war and violence
7. blood and glory
8. violence and hatred

Vocabulary Focus

I. 1. d   2. i   3. a   4. f   5. j   6. l
   7. k   8. b   9. c   10. e   11. g   12. h

II. 1. ambush   2. potion   3. void   4. conceal
    5. sickle   6. prevails   7. gigantic   8. revolt
    9. decreed   10. slipping   11. vomit   12. exile

III. 1. furious   2. prophesy   3. prudence   4. swiftness
     5. defy   6. successive   7. immortality   8. dominate

Ⅳ. 1. swift 2. dominate 3. prophecy 4. immortal
   5. succession 6. fury 7. defy 8. prudent

Vocabulary Development

1. cycle 2. pandemic 3. amused 4. hectare
5. chronological 6. geometry 7. chronic 8. panorama

Further Development

Ⅰ. 1. mortal 2. depicted 3. represented 4. determined
   5. altered 6. subject

Ⅲ. 1. entire cities and civilizations
   2. stories were invented
   3. reach the peak
   4. collective memory
   5. violently submerging

Cultural Exploration

Task 3.

In Greek myths, great flood is the result of gods' wrath and gods' punishment of humans. In Chinese myths, great flood results from natural causes.

In Greek myths, the end of the great flood story is sweeping away evils and the rebirth of humans. In Chinese myths, the end of the great flood story is the mitigation of the disaster and the technical progress in controlling water.

In Greek myths, human beings survived because of gods' mercy. In Chinese myths, human beings survived because of their efforts.

In Greek myths, human piety and god's power are emphasized in the story. In Chinese myths, human heroic deeds are emphasized.

Unit 2

Pre-information

Ⅰ. 1. supernatural 2. human 3. play tricks 4. jealous
   5. made up 6. passed down 7. residence 8. every aspect

Ⅱ. 1. failed to rescue 2. the most handsome 3. proud of
   4. delivered 5. blush 6. accused

Allusions:

1. Hades: the underworld, hell
2. Adonis: a handsome young man
3. Diana: a woman who remains unmarried
4. Hermes: a messenger
5. Daphne: a shy girl
6. laurel: a symbol of victory

Appendix II

Stories

Story One

I. 1. Poseidon 2. Hera 3. Athena 4. Aphrodite
   5. Artemis 6. Hephaestus 7. Demeter 8. Dionysus
   9. Apollo 10. Hermes

Story Two

1. wisdom 2. prophesied 3. overthrow 4. at her ease
5. prudence 6. ended up 7. advice 8. developed
9. split open 10. inevitably

Story Three

I. 1. c 2. a 3. b
II. 1. a myrrh tree 2. two-thirds 3. rose

Story Four

1. in the underworld 2. disappearance started the cycle
3. no longer gave birth 4. part of the underneath
5. for every seed she ate 6. rejoices

Story Five

I. 1. Because Daphne was struck by Eros' leaden arrow, which made her hate the thought of love.
   2. A laurel tree.
II. 1. F 2. T 3. F 4. T

Story Six

I. 1. F 2. T 3. F 4. F
II. 1. invisible 2. the River Styx
    3. burnt to death 4. immortality

Story Seven

I. 1. b, c, f 2. a, d 3. e, h 4. g
II. 1. T 2. F 3. F 4. T

Vocabulary Focus

I. 1. d 2. h 3. e 4. a 5. i 6. b
   7. g 8. l 9. j 10. c 11. k 12. f

II. 1. hurled 2. despised 3. masculine
    4. subdue 5. flatter 6. wrath
    7. shatter 8. entrusted 9. oath
    10. wither 11. viciously 12. ecstasy

III. 1. illegitimate 2. persecute 3. charitable 4. grieve
     5. divine 6. rage 7. confer 8. mischief

IV. 1. persecute 2. grieving 3. enraged 4. legitimate
    5. confer 6. divine 7. mischievous 8. charity

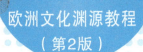

Vocabulary Development

1. amplified 2. commemorate 3. preventable
4. vegetarian 5. plausible 6. excavate
7. inappropriate/ irresponsible 8. contemporary
9. eject 10. immigrant

Further Development

I. 1. summoned 2. aid 3. sworn 4. lightly
   5. feed 6. boundary

III. 1. mortal woman within their family tree
   2. abundant fertility
   3. ultimate betrayal
   4. combined power of all of the Olympian gods
   5. come to his rescue
   6. condemned to hard labor

Cultural Exploration

Task 3.

Chinese gods:

Character: Showing bravery in the desire of controlling, or making peace with the nature; stressing virtues in contributing to people's welfare; loving peace by establishing harmony among people... Chinese myths were developed in the very early period of Chinese history, when people were frightened by natural forces, and tried to survive by struggling with the nature; Chinese put more importance on families or clans, in which the ones with good virtues won respect; Chinese civilization was developed mainly on the basis of agriculture on a big continent, in which people settled in certain areas, and stressed harmony among different clans or tribes; ...

Greek gods:

Character: Showing desire for seizing power; pursuing individual freedom; fulfilling individual desire; being emotional or even bad-tempered... Greek myths were developed in a period when humans have established the social structure, thus social features like seizure of power were reflected in myths; Greeks lived on islands, and Greek civilization was developed when facing fierce and unpredictable sea. This made Greeks more outward and adventurous. Greek economy developed by trading and conquering land. Adventurous life and unknown outside world left them much space to pursue their individual freedom and desire.

Pre-information

I. 1. coastline 2. being described 3. credited
   4. emotional 5. a series of 6. reunited with

218

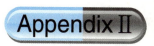

II. 1. an apple of 2. Greek gifts 3. heel
4. Helen 5. live under 6. the twists and turns
7. working on 8. outer space

Allusions:

1. Apple of discord: any subject of disagreement and contention, the root of the trouble, dispute

2. Greek gift(s): a gift with some sinister purposes of the enemy, one given with intent to harm

3. Achilles' heel: a weak point in something that is otherwise without fault; the weakest spot

4. Helen (of Troy): a beautiful girl or woman, a beauty who ruins her country, a terrible disaster brought by sb. or sth. you like best

5. Circe's wand: symbol of feminism

6. Penelope: a faithful wife

7. Penelope's web: slow or endless work

8. Odyssey: a series of adventures and vicissitudes. *Odyssey* is originally a Greek epic poem in 24 books probably composed before 700 B.C. attributed to Homer. It recounts the adventures of Odysseus after the fall of Troy.

Stories

Story one

1. the wedding banquet 2. the destruction of the city
3. act as the judge 4. the most beautiful woman
5. the athletic games 6. as a royal guest

Story two

I. 1. Thetis was shocked by a prophecy that her son would die in war. To save her son, the sea goddess dipped her baby in the waters of Styx which could protect the human body from the fire and sword.

2. The artful Odysseus. He had come to fetch the hero and he had not laboured in vain.

II. 1. F 2. T 3. T 4. F

Story Three

I. 1. b 2. e 3. d 4. a 5. c
II. 1. Achilles' armour 2. his wife
3. the wooden horse 4. Roman race

Story Four

I. 1. Ten years 2. In order not to be found by Polyphemus while escaping.
II. 1. F 2. F 3. T 4. T

Story Five

I. 1. c 2. a 3. b 4. d
II. Penelope 2. the palace 3. suitors 4. an olive tree trunk

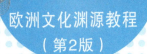

Vocabulary Focus

I. 1. e   2. c   3. f   4. a   5. h   6. b
    7. j   8. k   9. l   10. d   11. g   12. i

II. 1. summoned   2. discord   3. pasture   4. revenge
     5. suitor   6. oath   7. graze   8. warrior
     9. expedition   10. retrieve   11. armour   12. vulnerable

III. 1. artful   2. detach   3. foretell   4. abduction
     5. adventurous   6. ridicule   7. avenge   8. captive

IV. 1. detached   2. adventurous   3. artful   4. avenger
     5. foretell   6. captive   7. abduct   8. ridiculous

Vocabulary Development

1. wide   2. deep   3. fully   4. vitally   5. terrible
6. hard   7. gain   8. start   9. strong   10. observe
11. heavy   12. catch

Further Development

I. 1. exhausted   2. losing   3. immortal
    4. seducing   5. furious   6. reluctantly

II.

Calypso, in Greek mythology, seduced Odysseus and kept him for years away from his wife, Penelope, until Athena intervened; eventually Calypso had to let him go and even helped him to build his boat. She has both negative and positive connotation in Greek mythology: as a concealer and seductress, Calypso is a negative symbol, but as a rescuer she is a positive one. She is always compared with Penelope and thus ended up being a force of diversion and distraction.

Cultural Exploration

Task 1.

History: a chronological record of significant events (such as those affecting a nation or institution) often including an explanation of their causes. Those events usually proved by a lot of historical relics or documents.

Legend: a story coming down from the past, especially one popularly regarded as historical although not verifiable.

Task 3.

History requires concrete evidence while legend is more of people's emotional desires and sometimes is developed from historical events.

Appendix II

Unit 4

Pre-information

I．1. demi-gods or heroes
  2. supernatural courage and strength
  3. live an extraordinary life
  4. showed courage and bravery
  5. the emotions and culture

II．1. hint of their coming   2. the rock concert
  3. international companies   4. solving this problem
  5. sowed the dragon's teeth   6. with satisfaction
  7. all touched   8. Oxford English Dictionary
  9. expensive gifts   10. relying on

Allusions:

1. Hydra: something difficult to root out; or a recurring problem
2. Augean stable: an extremely dirty place
3. golden fleece: treasure obtained after innumerous untold hardships
4. Ariadne's thread: a solution to a confusing problem
5. sow the dragon's teeth: provoke war by spreading words or dispute; or cultivate warriors or monsters
6. Midas touch: good luck or ability to make a fortune
7. Orphean: pleasant to hear; of or relating to Orpheus
8. Herculean: extremely difficult; requiring the strength of a Hercules
9. Oedipus complex: Mother Complex
10. ambitious Phaeton: a person whose ambition is beyond his power

Stories

Story One
1. F   2. T   3. F   4. F   5. F

Story Two
I．1. e   2. c   3. b   4. a   5. d
II．1. Hera, kill him   2. Pleasure, Virtue
  3. insane/mad   4. Hera
  5. its pelt was proof against any weapons
  6. no sooner was one head crushed than two or three more grew in its place
  7. diverting two nearby rivers

Story Three
1. became jealous of them
2. would not sprout
3. required the sacrifice
4. carried both children off

    5. Jason arrived to claim it

Story Four

  Ⅰ.1. c 2. d 3. b 4. a

  Ⅱ.1. Chiron   2. the Golden Fleece

    3. Argonauts   4. he possessed the Golden Fleece.

    5. throwing a stone among them 6. rejuvenate him

Story Five

  Ⅰ.1. Theseus was most famous for the killing of Minotaur/the triumph over Minotaur.

  2. Theseus was recognized by his father with the sword he carried, which was left under a huge rock by his father before his birth.

  3. Theseus got out of the labyrinth with the thread Ariadne had given to him.

  Ⅱ.1. T 2. F 3. T 4. F 5.T

Story Six

  Ⅰ.1. b 2. d,e 3. f 4. a,c

  Ⅱ.1. F 2. T 3. F 4. F 5. F

Vocabulary Focus

  Ⅰ.1. d 2. f 3. c 4. e 5. b 6. a

  7. i 8. h 9. g 10. j 11. l 12. k

  Ⅱ.1. astounded 2. phantoms 3. transcend 4. fiery

    5. divert   6. pierced   7. adversity 8. pestilence

    9. embark   10. invincible 11. scorch   12. usurp

  Ⅲ.1. decapitation 2. depopulate 3. purification 4. demolish

    5. victorious   6. endanger   7. defective   8. infertility

  Ⅳ.1. purify   2. populate   3. endangerment 4. infertile

    5. defective   6. decapitated 7. demolition   8. victorious

Vocabulary Development

  1. c 2. b 3. d 4. a 5. d

  6. b 7. a 8. d 9. c 10. b

Further Development

  Ⅰ.1. that are very godly   2. create images of themselves

    3. see him destroyed   4. running after other women

    5. challenge her favor   6. squeezing them to death.

    7. he will become immortal

  Ⅲ.1. E 2. F 3.A 4. C

Cultural Exploration

  Task 1.

  Possible traits: strong, smart, compassionate, empathetic, caring, reliable,

charismatic, inspiring...

Evidence from heroes in Greek myths:

Heroes in Greek myths were usually physically strong enough. A typical example was Heracles, who strangled the Nemean lion, overcame the nine-headed snake, captured the wild boar and Cretan savage bull, and subdued the man-eating horses with incredible strength.

Heroes in Greek myths were smart as well, which is well exhibited in the story of Heracles, who cleaned the dirty stables by diverting two nearby rivers and getting the fruit from the golden-apple tree by tricking Atlas. This trait is also shown in the story of Oedipus, who brilliantly solved the riddle of Sphinx.

Some heroes showed compassion as part of their character. For example, Theseus risked his own life by volunteering to be one of the victims to be sacrificed to the Minotaur.

Task 3.

Opinion: I agree that we get shaped by our circumstances—by the family or the culture or the time period in which we happen to grow up; whether we grow up in a war zone versus peace; if we grow up in poverty rather than prosperity. So I believe heroism is something that can be cultivated.

Evidence: American psychologist Philip Zimbardo believes that heroism can be taught and has developed a program designed to help children learn to be heroes. The program helps students overcome such problems as the darker side of human nature, prejudice, and the bystander effect by building empathy. Zimbardo suggests that one of the major reasons we fail to help other people is due to our tendency to believe that they deserve what is happening to them. By making students aware of this fallacy, they are less likely to blame the victim and more likely to take actions.

Pre-information

    1. opening   2. origin   3. Creation

    4. mercy   5. throughout   6. essential

Ⅱ. 1. cover up   2. sack   3. olive branch

    4. give up   5. profit   6. corn in Egypt

Allusions:

1. fig leaf: the covering of one's embarrassment

2. raise Cain: cause an angry fuss

3. hold out the olive branch: emblem of peace; to make a compromise

4. the Tower of Babel: a sheer illusion

5. Benjamin's mess: a particular large portion, or the largest portion or share

6. corn in Egypt: extremely abundant, plentiful

Stories

Story One

Ⅰ. 1. b 2. e 3. a 4. c 5. d
Ⅱ. 1. F 2. F 3. T 4. F

Story Two

Ⅰ. 1. a crop farmer and a shepherd 2. filled with violence
3. two of all living creatures 4. in its path
5. rested on the mountain 6. sent out a dove
7. again sent out the dove 8. a sign to Noah

Story Three

Ⅰ. 1. c 2. a 4. d 6. b
Ⅱ. 1. the founding father 2. the ancestor of
3. offer him as a burnt offering

Story Four

Ⅰ. 1. b/d 2. a/c/e
Ⅱ. 1. Esau, Jacob 2. Esau, the blessing
3. wrestled, neither

Story Five

Ⅰ. 1. Joseph had two dreams in which he ruled over not only his brothers but his parents, which annoyed his brothers. So they called him "Joseph the dreamer".

2. Joseph told Pharaoh that the two dreams of the Pharaoh were just one and the same. God had revealed that seven years of abundance would come in Egypt and then seven years of famine would follow them.

Ⅱ. 1. F 2. T 3. F 4. F 5. T

Vocabulary Focus

Ⅰ. 1. d 2. h 3. i 4. j 5. l 6. g
7. b 8. f 9. a 10. k 11. e 12. c

Ⅱ. 1. rejoice 2. accusation 3. plucking
4. conceive 5. abundance 6. banished
7. sprouting 8. receded 9. withheld
10. sleek 11. famished 12. covenant

Ⅲ. 1. befriend 2. ornamented 3. reveal
4. deceive 5. favor 6. interpret
7. multiply 8. imprisonment

Ⅳ. 1. deception 2. interpreted 3. multiplies
4. befriended 5. revealed 6. imprisoned
7. favor 8. ornaments

Vocabulary Development

1. issue 2. odd 3. committed 4. odd
5. commit 6. branch 7. odd 8. commit

9. branch   10. branch   11. issue   12. was issued

Further Development

I. 1. the first murder   2. rage   3. wander
4. around 7000 B.C.   5. farmers   6. shepherds
7. get into conflict   8. cradle   9. hunter gatherer
10. controlling   11. produced   12. domesticated
13. domesticated   14. violence   15. feed on
16. left many dead   17. control nature   18. stop wandering
19. advanced technologies   20. sophisticated culture

III. 1. The people of the world spoke one language and one dialect.

2. They wanted to make a name for themselves and not to be scattered all over the earth.

3. God confused those people's language, and the tower was left unfinished.

Cultural Exploration

Task 2.

More examples for the comparison:

1) Chinese culture: human nature is good — value virtue, and mythological heroes are models virtue; Western culture: human nature is evil — mythological heroes have both strength and shortcomings, who are not models of virtue.

2) social institution in Chinese traditional culture: people should be ruled by a person of great virtue, who instructed people to live a virtuous life through their behaviors as well as their words.

Social institution in Western culture: "tripartite" political system, the intention of which is to prevent the concentration of unchecked power by providing for "checks" and "balances" to avoid autocracy, over-reaching by one branch over another.

Pre-information

1. leave slavery   2. prophet   3. promised them the land
4. laws and instructions   5. hardship and escape

II. 1. eye for eye   2. carry out the analysis
3. punishment   4. so desperately
5. in the worship of   6. after my own heart
7. rich in experience

Allusions:

1. eye for eye: to take revenge on

2. make bricks without straw: to perform a task without essential materials or means.

3. Egyptian punishment: great disasters

4. like manna from heaven: an unexpected and beneficial gift

5. the worship of golden calf: worship of money

6. after my own heart: according to one's own willing, to one's liking, agreeable

7. wise as Solomon: extraordinary wise

Stories

Story One

1. become much too numerous
2. work them ruthlessly
3. kill him
4. hid him for three months
5. took the boy as her son

Story Two

Ⅰ. 1. 4

Ⅱ. 1. an Israelite
   2. out of Egypt; flowing with milk and honey
   3. suffer more; ten plagues
   4. struck down; passed over; observe

Story Three

Ⅰ. 1. c   2. d   3. a   4. b

Ⅱ. 1. bring Israelites back   2. walked on dry land; was drowned
   3. complained   4. most important instructions

Story Four

Ⅰ. 1. b   2. a   3. d   4. c

Ⅱ. 1. music and poetry   2. his defeating
   3. the Ark of the Covenant   4. Israel's capital

Story Five

Ⅰ. 2. 4. 5

Ⅱ. 1. a wise and discerning   2. successor
   3. corrupted   4. divided into two parts

Vocabulary Focus

Ⅰ. 1. k   2. h   3. e   4. j   5. l   6. i
   7. b   8. g   9. c   10. a   11. d   12. f

Ⅱ. 1. shepherd   2. stubborn   3. inscribing   4. committed
   5. reign   6. shrewdly   7. tablets   8. discerning
   9. testimony   10. corrupted   11. covets   12. slang

Ⅲ. 1. defend   2. terrify   3. descendant   4. separate
   5. normal   6. original   7. appoint   8. complain

Ⅳ. 1. original   2. descending   3. separated   4. terrifying
   5. normal   6. complained   7. defendant   8. appointed

Vocabulary Development

1. received
2. arrived
3. caught
4. take
5. hit
6. hear
7. understand
8. make
9. becoming
10. annoys
11. buy
12. prepare

Writing

1. The figure whom the author is interested in	It is rather interesting to investigate whether Homer himself provided us with an accurate account of Agamemnon's character in his classical work.
2. The reason why the figure is interesting to the author	Agamemnon's personal features did not deserve such a high status. Homer's Agamemnon made most of his decisions while ruled by over-wrought emotions.
3. The author's claim	Homer's Agamemnon represents a deeply flawed character overwhelmed by inner desires and emotions.
4. The reason for the claim	1. Agamemnon appears as a highly accomplished warrior, though as a king he often demonstrates the features incompatible with the ideals of true kingship, such as selfishness. 2. Another flawed expression of Agamemnon is depicted through his arrogant and disrespectful attitude towards his wife.
5. The evidence to support the claim	For Claim 1: For the sake of his selfish ambitions and revenge for Paris' crime, he decides to sacrifice Iphigenia, his daughter for the favorable wind to set sail for Troy. For Claim 2: Utter infidelity and ignorance is seen in Agamemnon's disrespectful and rather condemned words to her.
6. Whether the essay is fact-based, or emotional	Fact-based.
7. Whether the essay aims to make the audience see something different or to make the audience act on the information in a specific way	Make the audience see something different—seeing Agamemnon in a different way.

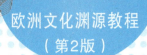

Further Development

Ⅰ. 1. archeological　　2. negative　　3. razed
　　4. legacy　　5. Dressed　　6. physical

Ⅲ. 1. miracles and freedom　　2. delivery
　　3. foundation story　　4. from oppression
　　5. devastating　　6. natural phenomena
　　7. shoreline　　8. parted
　　9. the conditions　　10. phenomenon
　　11. scientific phenomena　　12. perseverance

Cultural Exploration

Task 1.

It means: If someone wrongs or hurts another person, that person should be punished by having the same thing done to him or her. It is used to express that the punishment for a criminal or wrongdoer should be the same as the crime or misdeed. It is most commonly used to refer to getting revenge or justice for a crime or wrongdoing.

Task 2.

The concept of "an eye for eye," is part of the Mosaic Law used in the Israelites' justice system. The principle is that the punishment must fit the crime and there should be a just penalty for evil actions. Justice should be equitable; excessive harshness and excessive leniency should be avoided.

Task 3.

· Phrases similar with "an eye for an eye":

　　Seek revenge for the smallest grievance (睚眦必报)

　　Do onto them as they do unto us (以其人之道还治其人之身)

· Phrases similar with "an eye for an eye will only make the whole world blind":

　　Vengeance has a way of rebounding upon oneself/ There is never an end taking revenge (冤冤相报何时了)

Different expressions may reflect different perspectives people take towards "taking revenge"— valuing ruling by laws or the importance of justice, or valuing ruling by virtue, as influenced by Confucianism in Chinese culture.

Unit 7

Pre-information

Ⅰ. 1. falls into　　2. Christian　　3. teachings
　　4. different readerships　　5. betrayed, arrested and tried

Ⅱ. 1. succeeded　　2. in person　　3. the Last Supper
　　4. the spirit is willing but the flesh is weak　　5. attempted robbery
　　6. doubting　　7. wash his hands of

Allusions:

1. out-Herod Herod: to surpass even Herod in evil and cruelty.

2. Judas kiss: a deceitful and treacherous kiss; an act of betrayal, especially one disguised as a gesture of friendship.

3. the Last Supper: the final meal that Jesus shared with his disciples in Jerusalem before his crucifixion.

4. The spirit is willing but the flesh is weak: One would like to undertake something but hasn't the energy or strength to do so.

5. a good Samaritan: a person who gives help and sympathy to people who need it.

6. a doubting Thomas: someone who will refuse to believe something without direct, physical, personal evidence; in other words, a skeptic.

7. wash one's hands of someone or something: to end all involvement with someone or something.

Stories

Story One
1. expose her to public disgrace
2. what is conceived in her
3. save his people from their sins
4. issued a decree
5. expecting a child

Story Two
Ⅰ. 1. c 　　2. a 　　3. d 　　4. b
Ⅱ. 1. T 　　2. F 　　3. F 　　4. T

Story Three
Ⅰ. 1. John the Baptist.

2. They are short stories that teach a moral or spiritual lesson by analogy or similarity.

Ⅱ. 1. T 　　2. T 　　3. T 　　4. F 　　5. T

Story Four
Ⅰ. 1. b 　　2. c 　　3. a

Ⅱ. 1. The Last Supper contains many significant principles and continues to be an important part of Christian lives throughout the world.

2. The Passover.

3. Jesus gave His followers symbols of remembrance for His body and His blood sacrificed.

Story Five
Ⅰ. 1. d 　　2. a 　　3. c 　　4. b

Ⅱ. 1. Judas Iscariot　　2. hanging himself
　　3. the potter's field　　4. releasing a prisoner chosen by the crowd
　　5. washed his hands

Story Six
Ⅰ. 1. The angel told the women that Jesus had risen from the dead.

2. When they saw him, they worshiped him, but some doubted.

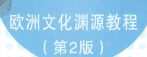

Ⅱ. 1. Easter   2. Friday   3. ascended into heaven

Vocabulary Focus

Ⅰ. 1. d   2. f   3. i   4. j   5. l   6. b
   7. k   8. a   9. e   10. c   11. g   12. h

Ⅱ. 1. outwit   2. inaugurated   3. release   4. notorious
   5. pertaining   6. assembled   7. vicinity   8. schemed
   9. ailments   10. crucified   11. relic   12. multitude

Ⅲ. 1. remorse   2. forsake   3. agonizing   4. analogy
   5. woe   6. authority   7. circulate   8. ascend

Ⅳ. 1. ascending   2. agonize   3. remorse   4. woes
   5. analogy   6. circulate   7. forsake   8. authoritative

Vocabulary Development

Ⅰ. 1. severe   2. heavier   3. idle/vain   4. heavy
   5. strong   6. vain   7. plain   8. hard, hard, hard
   9. heavy/strong/severe   10. straight   11. strong/heavy
   12. vain

Ⅱ. 1. name   2. figures
   3. spending the night in a stable/ living in a nursing home/ in jail/ nowhere
   4. release/ torture/ capture/ catch/ kill
   5. a sheet/ a ghost/ snow

Further Development

Ⅰ. 1. a giant of the ancient world
   2. fine architecture and impressive engineering
   3. created the conditions for Christianity to flourish
   4. offered hope and a better world
   5. spread out across the wider world

Ⅲ. 1. specifies   2. actually   3. seek
   4. resist   5. hand   6. away

Cultural Exploration

Task 1.

In the story of Nathanael, Nathanael asks his famous question: can any good thing come out of Nazareth? We can see clearly that Nathanael is judging the situation based upon the stereotype and/or geographic prejudice. Nathanael's story provides good reminders for us about judgment. It is easy to fall prey to snap judgments about people based upon many factors.

Task 3.

Prejudice in China: In the past, the Han Chinese considered themselves more advanced and civilized than other ethnic groups in China. Therefore, aboriginal tribes

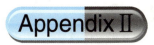

or minority nationality in the remote areas of ancient China were named as man yi(蛮夷) which means barbarians. Physical features such as height and looks can play a role in who would get a job and how much they earn.

Prejudice in the western society: In the United States, black people could not sit in the front of buses or use the same water fountains as white people until the 1950s and 1960s. After 9/11, anyone who looked Middle Eastern was looked at suspiciously and was often the victim of prejudice. Some parents will not approve their offspring marrying anyone of a different religion.

Further Reading

Passage one

1. Judas was asked by Jesus Christ to betray him to the authorities.

2. Because it contradicts the Christian thought which has lasted for nearly 2,000 years.

3. The University of Arizona carbon-dated five tiny samples of papyrus and leather binding to between A.D. 220 and A.D. 340, and other tests backed up that conclusion.

Passage two

1. In Christianity, the (Holy) Trinity is the existence of God in three forms (the Father, the Son and the Holy Spirit).

2. The sin from Adam and Eve is said to be the origin of human sins.

3. The souls of people who have been faithful to God will go to Heaven as a reward, while wicked people are punished after death in Hell.

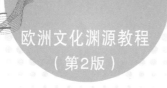

Appendix III
Map of the Book

	Unit	Task/Topic	Page
Listening	1	Pre-information | I	2
		Pre-information | II	3
		Story Five | Five Ages of Man	10
	2	Pre-information | I	28
		Pre-information | II	29
		Story Two | Birth of Athena	34
	3	Pre-information | I	56
		Pre-information | II	57
		Story One | Origin of the Trojan War	58
	4	Pre-information | I	86
		Pre-information | II	87
		Story Three | Golden Fleece	92
	5	Pre-information | I	118
		Pre-information | II	119
		Story Two | Noah and the Flood	122
		Further Development | III	138
	6	Pre-information | I	144
		Pre-information | II	145
		Story One | Birth of Moses	145
	7	Pre-information | I	170
		Pre-information | II	171
		Story One | Birth of Jesus	171
Watching	1	Story Three | Cronus	7
		Further Development | III	22
	2	Story Four | Hades Kidnapped Persephone	36
		Further Development | III	50

232

续表

	Unit	Task/Topic	Page
Watching	3	Further Development | III	80
	4	Further Development | I	109
	5	Further Development | I	137
	6	Further Development | III	163
	7	Further Development | I	195
Vocabulary	1	Vocabulary Focus	11
		Vocabulary Development | Word Roots	13
	2	Vocabulary Focus	42
		Vocabulary Development | Prefixes and Suffixes	44
	3	Vocabulary Focus	66
		Vocabulary Development | Collocation (1) Introduction	68
	4	Vocabulary Focus	100
		Vocabulary Development | Collocation (2) Types of Collocation	102
	5	Vocabulary Focus	130
		Vocabulary Development | Polysemy (1) Introduction	132
	6	Vocabulary Focus	155
		Vocabulary Development | Polysemy (2) Multiple Meaning Verbs	158
	7	Vocabulary Focus	183
		Vocabulary Development | Collocation (3) Unique, Strong and Weak Collocations	185
Speaking	1	Retelling a Story (1)	15
	2	Retelling a Story (2)	46
	3	Describing a Picture	70
	4	Comparison and Contrast (1) Two People	104
	5	Comparison and Contrast (2) Two Stories	134
	6	Comparison and Contrast (3) Compare and Comment	159
	7	Interpreting the Artwork	187

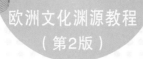
欧洲文化渊源教程
（第2版）

	Unit	Task/Topic	Page
Reading	1	Story One ǀ Creation of the Universe	4
		Story Two ǀ Rule of the Titans and Rise of Olympians	6
		Story Four ǀ Creation of Man and Prometheus' Gift	8
		Further Reading	24
	2	Story One ǀ Olympians	31
		Story Three ǀ Aphrodite and Adionis	36
		Story Five ǀ Apollo and Daphne	38
		Story Six ǀ Birth of Dionysus	39
		Story Seven ǀ Eros and Psyche	41
		Further Reading	53
	3	Story Two ǀ Gathering of Forces	59
		Story Three ǀ The Sack of the City	61
		Story Four ǀ Odysseus and Polyphemus	63
		Story Five ǀ Odysseus' Return and the Reunion	65
		Further Reading	82
	4	Story One ǀ Perseus	88
		Story Two ǀ Heracles and the Twelve Labours	90
		Story Four ǀ Jason and the Golden Fleece	93
		Story Five ǀ Theseus	96
		Story Six ǀ Oedipus	98
		Further Development ǀ III	110
		Further Reading	114
	5	Story One ǀ Creation	120
		Story Three ǀ Abraham and Isaac	124
		Story Four ǀ Jacob and Esau	126
		Story Five ǀ Joseph and His Brothers	128
		Further Reading	140

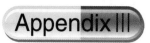

续表

Unit		Task/Topic	Page
Reading	6	Story Two | Moses	147
		Story Three | The Exodus and the Ten Commandments	149
		Story Four | King David	152
		Story Five | Solomon	154
		Further Reading	165
	7	Story Two | The Magi's visit and the Escape to Egypt	173
		Story Three | Jesus' Miracles and Parables	175
		Story Four | The Last Supper	177
		Story Five | The Death of Jesus	179
		Story Six | The Resurrection of Jesus	181
		Further Reading	198
Writing	1	Narrative Summary	16
	2	Assignment Summary (1) Paragraph Summary	48
	3	Assignment Summary (2) A Complete Essay	73
	4	Comparison and Contrast (1) Two People	107
	5	Comparison and Contrast (2) Two Subjects	135
	6	Critical Review (1)	160
	7	Critical Review (2)	191
Cultural Exploration	1	Great Flood	23
	2	Anthropomorphism	52
	3	Legend and History	81
	4	Heroism	112
	5	Human Nature	139
	6	Justice and Revenge	164
	7	Prejudice	197

235

Bibliography

李正栓.床头灯英语学习读本——圣经故事[M].北京:航空工业出版社,2005.

王泰栋.把历史、传说、戏说区分开来看——也谈徐福东渡[J].中共宁波市委党校学报,1998,05:45-47.

萨莫瓦尔,波特,麦克丹尼尔.跨文化交际(第7版)[M].董晓波编译.北京:北京大学出版社,2012.

SWALES J M, FEAK C B. Academic Writing for Graduate Students. Ann Arbor: the University of Michigan Press,2004.

http://www.academia.edu/11627364/SAMPLE_CRITICAL_REVIEW

http://www.angelfire.com/sc3/wedigmontana/Genesis.html

http://www.bbc.co.uk/history/ancient/greeks/jason_01.shtml

http://www.bible.ca/ef/expository-john-1-45-46.htm

http://www.biblegateway.com/

http://www.chinavoc.com

http://www.chinahistoryforum.com/index.php?/topic/6799-is-human-nature-good-or-evil/

http://www.christianbiblereference.org/story_AdmAndEve.htm

http://www.crystalinks.com

http://www.custom-essays.org/examples/Ilia_essay_Agamemnon_the_King.html

http://www.desy.de/gna/interpedia/greek_myth/creation.html

https://www.gotquestions.org/eye-for-an-eye.html accessed on Sept. 22, 2018

https://www.history.com/topics/ancient-history/trojan-war

http://www.lbcc.edu/wrsc/documents/summarizingparagraph.pdf

http://www.lc.unsw.edu.au/onlib/pdf/critical_review.pdf

http://www.mainlesson.com

https://www.philosophytalk.org/shows/eye-eye-morality-revenge-1 accessed on Nov. 28, 2018

http://www.prefixsuffix.com

http://www.tolearnenglish.com/exercises/exercise-english-2/exercise-english-12958.php

http://www.wikihow.com/Critique-Artwork

http://archaeology.about.com/od/ancientgreece/a/homericl.htm

https://becomingchristians.com/2017/02/09/what-does-an-eye-for-an-eye-and-a-tooth-for-a-tooth-really-mean/ accessed on Nov. 28, 2018

http://christianity.about.com/od/biblestorysummaries/p/creationstroy.htm

http://en.wikipedia.org/wiki/Book_of_Exodus

http://en.wikipedia.org/wiki/Perseus

http://en.wikipedia.org/wiki/theseus

http://hubpages.com/hub/How-to-Write-a-Summary-Analysis-and-Response-Essay

https://humanisticpaganism.com/2011/07/17/being-human-when-surrounded-by-greek-gods-by-m-j-lee/

http://library.thinkquest.org

http://teacherisites.schoolworld.com

https://wenku.baidu.com/view/4a921e272f60ddccda38a0cd.html, Nov. 28, 2018

https://writingexplained.org/idiom-dictionary/eye-for-an-eye accessed on January 2, 2019